Sisters of the Earth

Women's Prose and Poetry About Nature

Sisters of the Earth

Women's Prose and Poetry About Nature

EDITED AND WITH A PREFACE BY

Lorraine Anderson

Vintage Books
A Division of Random House, Inc.   *New York*

A VINTAGE ORIGINAL, APRIL 1991

FIRST EDITION

Compilation copyright © 1991 by Lorraine Anderson

All rights reserved under International and Pan-American Copyright Conventions. Published in the United States by Vintage Books, a division of Random House, Inc., New York, and simultaneously in Canada by Random House of Canada Limited, Toronto.

A portion of the editor's proceeds from the sale of this book will be donated to the Green Belt Movement founded by Wangari Maathai, empowering the women of Kenya to plant trees.

Pages 417–426 constitute an extension of this copyright page.

Library of Congress Cataloging-in-Publication Data
Sisters of the Earth : women's prose and poetry about nature /
    edited and with a preface by Lorraine Anderson.—
    1st ed.
       p.   cm.
    Includes bibliographical references and index.
    ISBN 0-679-73382-5
    1. Nature—Literary collections. 2. American
literature—Women authors.
    I. Anderson, Lorraine, 1952–   .
    PS509.N3S5 1991
    810.8'036—dc20   90-55686
                        CIP

Book design by Maura Fadden Rosenthal

This book has been printed on
recycled acid-free paper.

Manufactured in the United States of America
B98765432

To Gaia—fertile mother, wise sister

This earth is my sister;
I love her daily grace, her silent daring, and how
loved I am
how we admire this strength in each other,
all that we have lost, all that we have suffered, all that
we know:
we are stunned by this beauty,
and I do not forget: what she is to me, what I am
to her.

—Susan Griffin
Woman and Nature:
The Roaring Inside Her

Acknowledgments

Many people provided invaluable help to me as I compiled this book. I want especially to thank Wendy Smith, for opening her library to me; Elizabeth Weal, for research support, feedback, and enthusiasm; and Patria Brown, Chris Cragg, Maria Dammon, Dorian Gossy, Bruce Hodge, Matt Holdreith, Dottie Horn, Judith McKibben, Marta Rose, Jane Swigart, Jane Townsend, and Kathy Williams for perceptive and helpful comments on drafts. For material and moral support, I'm grateful to Kevin Anderson, Cheryl Bartley, Meg Beeler, Brad Bunnin, Liz Currie, Lauren Davis, Duane Elgin, Jim and Pauline Hoopes, Kevin Howat, Sharon LeBell, Edward Lueders, Patricia Michelin, Barbara Mor, Bonnie Nardi, Ann Niehaus, Mark Ouimet, and Apple Computer. Audrey and Edward Anderson exposed me early and often to nature and books; a heartfelt thanks, folks. Karen Schmidt and Louisa Morris gave me food for thought in their stimulating Stanford course "Women and Ecology."

My work was made easier by the valuable reference *American Women Writers,* ed. Lina Mainiero and Langdon Lynne Faust (Frederick Ungar, 1979). The following anthologists and authors called my attention to writers I might otherwise have missed: Vera Norwood and Janice Monk, eds., *The Desert Is No Lady* (Yale University Press, 1987); Kate H. Winter, ed., *The Woman in the Mountain* (SUNY Press, 1989); Deborah Strom, ed., *Birdwatching with Ameri-*

can Women (Norton, 1986); Theresa Corrigan and Stephanie Hoppe, eds., *With a Fly's Eye, Whale's Wit, and Woman's Heart: Animals and Women* (Cleis Press, 1989); Vicki Piekarski, ed., *Westward the Women* (Doubleday, 1984); Alicia Ostriker, *Stealing the Language* (Beacon Press, 1986); Robert C. Baron and Elizabeth Darby Junkin, eds., *Of Discovery and Destiny* (Fulcrum, 1986); William T. Anderson, ed., *A Little House Sampler* (University of Nebraska Press, 1988); Joseph Wood Krutch, ed., *Great American Nature Writing* (William Sloane, 1950); Paul Brooks, *Speaking for Nature* (Houghton Mifflin, 1980). I'm indebted to the libraries of Stanford University, to the Stanford Bookstore, and to the Palo Alto libraries, where most of my research was done.

Elizabeth Pomada, Marty Asher, Linda Rosenberg, George Donahue, Maura Fadden Rosenthal, and Brenda Woodward helped make my dream a reality. Rick Palkovic gets my warmest thanks for his love, companionship, humor, perceptive comments on the manuscript, and equitable sharing of housework; and Quinka, for keeping me in front of the computer while she warmed my lap. A special thanks to Joanna Hurley, whose caring involvement with the book has made all the difference; and to Terry Tempest Williams, for insightful and inspiring conversation and for recognizing the importance of women's collective voices.

Contents

Her Wildness: What Is Untamed in Nature and in Us

Her Solace: How Nature Heals Us

Her Creatures:
Animal, Vegetable, and Mineral Presences

Her Rape: How Nature Has Been Abused

Healing Her: Walking in Balance with Nature

Preface

Nature has been for me, for as long as I can remember, a source of solace, inspiration, adventure, and delight; a home, a teacher, a companion. Inevitably, I read *Walden,* and Thoreau became my passion. It was a revelatory moment for me when, in Boston on a college trip, I sat at a massive wooden table in Houghton Library at Harvard, opened a manila folder holding fragments of Thoreau's writing, and saw his words scrawled in black ink in an old-fashioned hand. His humanness struck me then, his crankiness, the courage of his principled life, his vision, his struggle against the odds.

I had another revelatory moment regarding nature writers and nature writing years later. I was leafing through a magazine when an ad for the Sierra Club caught my eye. "Wild Should Wild Remain" it proclaimed, and backed these fighting words with quotes from Aldo Leopold, Robinson Jeffers, Edward Abbey, and Wallace Stegner. These were all men whose writing I admired and whose defense of the earth's wild places I agreed with wholeheartedly. Nevertheless, in that moment a question took shape in my mind.

Where were the women's voices?

I dug up my notes from "Literature of the American Wilderness," a college class I had taken in the 1970s. I found we had read Hawthorne, Emerson, Irving, Whitman, Thoreau, Muir, Leopold, and Abbey.

I went to the library and thumbed through all the nature anthologies I could find. They consistently focused on work by male writers, overlooking altogether or giving short shrift to women writers.

And they referred often to the issue of "man and nature."

The canon of nature writing, like the literary canon in general, has been male-centered, both a reflection and a reinforcement of a culture that once defined only men's experience as important and only men's voices as authoritative. As China Galland notes in her book *Women in the Wilderness*, "Most of what we have now is a record of the world as experienced and perceived by men. It is valid. Yet there is something missing: the world as perceived by women, out of our own experience rather than as defined in opposition to masculine experience."

We live in a time of rebalancing. At this point in our journey as a species, we are opening to two ecological truths: that all of life is a circle within which everything has value and serves an indispensable purpose, and that strength and health derive from diversity. The important social and political movements of this century all have been concerned with extending our culturally defined circle of value to include those previously excluded: women, people of color, foreign "enemies," animals—even trees, water, mountains, soil. The time is ripe for bringing women's voices into the circle of nature literature valued by our culture. I began compiling this anthology as a step toward realizing that vision.

At the outset, I wondered if there was such a thing as a woman's view of nature. Traditional gender socialization in our society helps women relate well to nature by encouraging caring, nurturing, receptivity, empathy, emotional responsiveness, appreciation of beauty, and a feeling of kinship with animals; on the other hand, it hinders women's relationship to nature by assigning us to the indoor domestic sphere. Some writers have claimed that women as a group are innately closer to nature than men are, but this is a matter of some debate and isn't a claim for which I see much evidence. Women, like men, are individuals, each with a slightly different perspective conditioned by both innate sensibility and experience. It now seems to me that there are as many women's views of nature as there are women.

Indeed, in my quest to piece together a literary account of women's experiences with and responses to nature, I've deliberately cast my net wide to encompass writers of varied backgrounds and perspectives. Few of the writers included here can be classified strictly as literary naturalists; what I've looked for instead is an authentic, heartfelt response to nature. By weaving together different kinds of literary materials—poems, short stories, essays, novel excerpts, journal entries, autobiography, natural history—I've hoped to create a tapestry revealing the full range and strength of women's imaginative responses to nature.

To keep this volume to an approachable length, I've used writing only by women of the United States. My choices have been subjective, as any anthologist's must be, and I've no doubt missed writing that deserves to be included here. The bibliography points to additional authors and titles, but even this is not an exhaustive survey. Consider this anthology a starting point, not the final word. New literature is being created every day, and I hope this volume itself will inspire a new generation of women to write about nature.

Although I've concluded that there is no such thing as a woman's view of nature, I do think there is a feminine way of being in relationship to nature. This way is caring rather than controlling; it seeks harmony rather than mastery; it is characterized by humility rather than arrogance, by appreciation rather than acquisitiveness. It's available to both men and women, but it hasn't been exercised much in the history of Western civilization. The women's voices I've chosen to include here speak for this way of being.

I've adopted the metaphor of earth as female in naming the themes I've grouped the writing around. Some feminist writers, such as Elizabeth Dodson Gray and Carolyn Merchant, reject the practice of projecting female attributes upon nature, seeing this as an inadequate male symbolization of nature, and pointing out that to personify the earth as a woman is to invite treating it as the second-class citizen women have been. With that objection in mind, I've nevertheless used the metaphor because it has poetic beauty and historical import, having been used by varied cultures throughout the ages. My hope is that if we teach ourselves to revere what is feminine, the image of earth as mother will evoke the reverence that is earth's due.

To me, the story most worth telling in the last decade of the twentieth century has to do with the earth, and with the relationship to it of the one species that while utterly reliant on it has nonetheless seemed bent on, or perhaps just oblivious to, its destruction. If we're to give our endangered planet the time and space to heal, we must begin to see nature not just as a backdrop against which the human drama is enacted, but as an integral part of our lives, as something we must respond to, respect, actively care about. I hope the writing in this volume will encourage that attitude.

Lorraine Anderson
Palo Alto, CA

Sisters of the Earth

Women's Prose and Poetry
About Nature

Our Kinship with Her:
How We Are Embedded
in Nature

Whenever I hear someone boast of having conquered a mountain by climbing it or a wild river by paddling it, I am struck by the foolishness of this attitude. It seems to me a pitiful bravado in the face of a great and powerful mystery, like whistling in the dark to give oneself courage. Worse, it arrogantly pits the ego against the matrix of being, conveying the harmful illusion that one creature can dominate the creation of which it is a part and on which it depends for its very life. How vastly healthier and more functional is the attitude expressed by the women whose writing is included in this section! To them, we are kin with nature, not adversaries or dominators or conquerors, and our kinship is worthy of celebration.

Our kinship with nature can be realized in a number of different ways. Some of the writers in this section identify closely with a particular place, feeling its features to be part of their personal geography. Others write about a special attunement to the voices of nature. Still others experience kinship with nature in moments of mystical union with the larger fabric of life, including moments of birth and death, when our physical bond with the earth is perhaps most apparent.

JOY HARJO

FIRE

from *What Moon Drove Me to This?* (1978)

Joy Harjo (1951–   ) has written that a woman "has to go constantly outside of herself to find herself," and for Harjo, a Creek Indian, this often means turning to nature and the spirits that dwell there. Born in Oklahoma and educated at the University of New Mexico (B.A.) and the University of Iowa (M.F.A.), Harjo has published four volumes of poetry and one of prose. She is currently an associate professor of English at the University of Arizona in Tucson. Her poems have been influenced both by the oral tradition of her people, which imbues the world with spirits, and by feminist thought.

a woman can't survive
by her own breath
             alone
she must know
the voices of mountains
she must recognize
the foreverness of blue sky
she must flow
with the elusive
bodies
of night wind women
who will take her into
her own self

look at me
i am not a separate woman

i am a continuance
of blue sky
i am the throat
of the sandia mountains
a night wind woman
who burns
with every breath
she takes

SUSAN GRIFFIN

PROLOGUE

from *Woman and Nature* (1978)

Susan Griffin (1943–) writes in the preface to her uncon-
ventional book *Woman and Nature: The Roaring Inside Her*
that "in this matter of woman and nature, *we have cause to feel
deeply.*" Griffin, a radical feminist writer born in Los Angeles
and educated at San Francisco State University (B.A.,
M.A.), began writing *Woman and Nature* after she was asked
to give a lecture on women and ecology. In looking for links
between the feminist movement and the ecology move-
ment, she observed that although men are as capable of
merging with nature as women, in Western civilization
"man does not consider himself a part of nature, but indeed
considers himself superior to matter," an attitude she found
particularly significant "when placed against man's attitude
that woman is both inferior to him and closer to nature."
Woman and Nature is a dialogue between two voices, "one
the chorus of women and nature, an emotional, animal,

embodied voice, and the other a solo part, cool, professorial, pretending to objectivity, carrying the weight of cultural authority.''

He says that woman speaks with nature. That she hears voices from under the earth. That wind blows in her ears and trees whisper to her. That the dead sing through her mouth and the cries of infants are clear to her. But for him this dialogue is over. He says he is not part of this world, that he was set on this world as a stranger. He sets himself apart from woman and nature.

And so it is Goldilocks who goes to the home of the three bears, Little Red Riding Hood who converses with the wolf, Dorothy who befriends a lion, Snow White who talks to the birds, Cinderella with mice as her allies, the Mermaid who is half fish, Thumbelina courted by a mole. *(And when we hear in the Navaho chant of the mountain that a grown man sits and smokes with bears and follows directions given to him by squirrels, we are surprised. We had thought only little girls spoke with animals.)*

We are the bird's eggs. Bird's eggs, flowers, butterflies, rabbits, cows, sheep; we are caterpillars; we are leaves of ivy and sprigs of wallflower. We are women. We rise from the wave. We are gazelle and doe, elephant and whale, lilies and roses and peach, we are air, we are flame, we are oyster and pearl, we are girls. We are woman and nature. And he says he cannot hear us speak.

But we hear.

OPAL WHITELEY

THE JOY-SONG OF NATURE

from *The Singing Creek Where the Willows Grow* (1986)

Opal Whiteley (1897–) seems to manifest in her child-hood diary the kind of crystalline attunement to nature that our culture's mythology has led us to expect from little girls. Born in Colton, Washington, Opal moved with her family to an Oregon logging community when she was six. From then until she was nine, she kept a diary in which she confided, "I so do love trees. I have thinks I was once a tree, growing in the forest. Now all trees are my brothers." Opal grew up teaching other children about the forest and its ways. To earn money for college, she traveled throughout Oregon one summer giving lectures with such titles as "In the Woods," "In the Fields," "Music and Musicians of the Out-of-Doors" (perhaps influenced by Gene Stratton-Porter's 1910 book, *Music of the Wild*), and (her favorite) "Nearer to the Heart of Nature."

In 1918 Opal self-published a book for children about the natural world entitled *The Fairyland Around Us,* and went to the East Coast the following year to find a publisher for it there. Ellery Sedgwick of the *Atlantic Monthly* turned down this book but was interested in her diary. Opal's sister had torn it up when Opal was thirteen, but Opal had saved the fragments, and she spent the next nine months piecing them back together. When the diary was published in 1920 as *The Story of Opal: The Journal of an Understanding Heart,* it caused a sensation. Skeptics called it a hoax, saying that no little girl could have written it, and hounded it out of print. Opal's subsequent travels and eventual commitment to Napsbury Hospital in London are recounted in Benjamin Hoff's fine introduction to *The Singing Creek Where the Wil-*

lows Grow: The Rediscovered Diary of Opal Whiteley, in which Opal's diary is reprinted in its entirety and from which the following selection is taken.

Very early in the morning of today, I did get out of my bed and I did get dressed in a quick way. Then I climbed out the window of the house we live in. The sun was up, and the birds were singing. I went my way. As I did go, I did have hearing of many voices—they were the voices of earth, glad for the spring. They did say what they had to say in the growing grass, and in the leaves growing out from tips of branches. The birds did have knowing, and sang what the grasses and leaves did say of the gladness of living. I too did feel glad feels, from my toes to my curls.

I went down by the swamp. I went there to get reeds. There I saw a black bird with red upon his wings. He was going in among the rushes. I made a stop to watch him. I have thinks tomorrow I must be going in among the rushes, where he did go. I shall pull off my shoes and stockings first, for mud is there, and there is water. I like to go in among the rushes where the black birds with red upon their wings do go. I like to touch fingertips with the rushes. I like to listen to the voices that whisper in the swamp. And I do so like to feel the mud ooze up between my toes. Mud has so much of interest in it—slippery feels, and sometimes little seeds that someday will grow into plant-folk, if they do get the right chance. And some were so growing this morning, and more were making begins—I did have seeing of them while I was looking looks about for reeds.

With the reeds I did find there, I did go a-piping. I went adown the creek, and out across the field, and in along the lane. Every stump I did come to, I did climb upon. . . .

Most every day, I do dance. I dance with the leaves and the grass. I feel thrills from my toes to my curls. I feel like a bird, sometimes. Then I spread my arms for wings, and I go my way from stump to stump, and on adown the hill. Sometimes I am a demoiselle, flitting near unto the water.

Then I nod unto the willows, and they nod unto me. They wave their arms, and I wave mine. They wiggle their toes in the water a bit, and I do so, too. And every time we wiggle our toes, we do drink into our souls the song of the brook—the glad song it is always singing. And the joy-song does sing on in our hearts. So did it today.

LUCILLE CLIFTON

BREAKLIGHT

from *An Ordinary Woman* (1974)

> Lucille Clifton (1936–   ) is a poet whose simple but powerful verses in the black idiom express a sense of her roots in earth, family, and religious tradition. Clifton was born in Depew, New York, and attended Howard University and Fredonia State Teachers College. The mother of six children, she has written numerous books for children as well as several volumes of poetry, and has taught at a number of colleges and universities, most recently St. Mary's College of Maryland.

> light keeps on breaking.
> i keep knowing
> the language of other nations.
> i keep hearing
> tree talk
> water words

OPAL WHITELEY

and i keep knowing what they mean.
and light just keeps on breaking.
last night
the fears of my mother came
knocking and when i
opened the door
they tried to explain themselves
and i understood
everything they said.

LINDA HOGAN

WALKING

from *Parabola* magazine (Summer 1990)

Linda Hogan (1947–   ) is a mixed-blood Chickasaw whose voice as a poet, essayist, and novelist gently calls us home to an ancestral sense of time and place. Although she was born in Denver, her tribal homeland is Oklahoma, where most of her family remains. Still, she says she has sent down a long taproot in the mountain lands of Colorado and wants to stay there. "I've become familiar with the edible plants, with the seasons, the migrations of owls and geese, the deer herd, the position of stars and planets, when things grow, when the hills thaw and fall with rockslides, what goes on with the lives of the people." She was educated and now teaches at the University of Colorado. Her book *Seeing Through the Sun* (1985), one of several volumes of poetry she has written, won the American Book Award from the Before Columbus Foundation.

It began in dark and underground weather, a slow hunger moving toward light. It grew in a dry gully beside the road where I live, a place where entire hillsides are sometimes yellow, windblown tides of sunflower plants. But this one was different. It was alone, and larger than the countless others who had established their lives further up the hill. This one was a traveler, a settler, and like a dream beginning in conflict, it grew where the land had been disturbed.

I saw it first in early summer. It was a green and sleeping bud, raising itself toward the sun. Ants worked around the unopened bloom, gathering aphids and sap. A few days later, it was a tender young flower, soft and new, with a pale green center and a troop of silver gray insects climbing up and down the stalk.

Over the summer this sunflower grew into a plant of incredible beauty, turning its face daily toward the sun in the most subtle of ways, the black center of it dark and alive with a deep blue light, as if flint had sparked an elemental fire there, in community with rain, mineral, mountain air, and sand.

As summer changed from green to yellow there were new visitors daily: the lace-winged insects, the bees whose legs were fat with pollen, and grasshoppers with their clattering wings and desperate hunger. There were other lives I missed, lives too small or hidden to see. It was as if this plant with its host of lives was a society, one in which moment by moment, depending on light and moisture, there was great and diverse change.

There were changes in the next larger world around the plant as well. One day I rounded a bend in the road to find the disturbing sight of a dead horse, black and still against a hillside, eyes rolled back. Another day I was nearly lifted by a wind and sandstorm so fierce and hot that I had to wait for it to pass before I could return home. On this day the faded dry petals of the sunflower were swept across the land. That was when the birds arrived to carry the new seeds to another future.

In this one plant, in one summer season, a drama of need and survival took place. Hungers were filled. Insects coupled. There was escape, exhaustion, and death. Lives touched down a moment and were gone.

I was an outsider. I only watched. I never learned the sunflower's golden language or the tongues of its citizens. I had a small understanding, nothing more than a shallow observation of the flower, insects, and birds. But they knew what to do, how to live. An old voice from somewhere, gene or cell, told the plant how to evade the pull of gravity and find its way upward, how to open. It was instinct, intuition, necessity. A certain knowing directed the seedbearing birds on paths to ancestral homelands they had never seen. They believed it. They followed.

There are other summons and calls, some even more mysterious than those commandments to birds or those survival journeys of insects. In bamboo plants, for instance, with their thin green canopy of light and golden stalks that creak in the wind. Once a century, all of a certain kind of bamboo flower on the same day. Whether they are in Malaysia or in a greenhouse in Minnesota makes no difference, nor does the age or size of the plant. They flower. Some current of an inner language passes between them, through space and separation, in ways we cannot explain in our language. They are all, somehow, one plant, each with a share of communal knowledge.

John Hay, in *The Immortal Wilderness,* has written: "There are occasions when you can hear the mysterious language of the Earth, in water, or coming through the trees, emanating from the mosses, seeping through the undercurrents of the soil, but you have to be willing to wait and receive."

Sometimes I hear it talking. The light of the sunflower was one language, but there are others, more audible. Once, in the redwood forest, I heard a beat, something like a drum or heart coming from the ground and trees and wind. That underground current stirred a kind of knowing inside me, a kinship and longing, a dream barely remembered that disappeared back to the body.

Another time, there was the booming voice of an ocean storm thundering from far out at sea, telling about what lived in the distance, about the rough water that would arrive, wave after wave revealing the disturbance at center.

Tonight I walk. I am watching the sky. I think of the people who came before me and how they knew the placement of stars in the sky, watched the moving sun long and hard enough to witness how a certain angle of light touched a stone only once a year. Without written records, they knew the gods of every night, the small, fine details of the world around them and of immensity above them.

Walking, I can almost hear the redwoods beating. And the oceans are above me here, rolling clouds, heavy and dark, considering snow. On the dry, red road, I pass the place of the sunflower, that dark and secret location where creation took place. I wonder if it will return this summer, if it will multiply and move up to the other stand of flowers in a territorial struggle.

It's winter and there is smoke from the fires. The square, lighted windows of houses are fogging over. It is a world of elemental attention, of all things working together, listening to what speaks in the blood. Whichever road I follow, I walk in the land of many gods, and they love and eat one another.

Walking, I am listening to a deeper way. Suddenly all my ancestors are behind me. Be still, they say. Watch and listen. You are the result of the love of thousands.

SARAH ORNE JEWETT

A WHITE HERON

from *A White Heron and Other Stories* (1886)

Sarah Orne Jewett (1849–1909) was born, raised, and died in the same pre-Revolutionary house in South Berwick, Maine, and divided her time as an adult between Maine, Boston, and travels in Europe. Jewett's regional novels and short stories portray characters whose identification with the landscape of rural New England is as complete as was her own. As a young girl, she often accompanied her father, a country doctor, on house calls, learning from him a sensitive appreciation of nature and literature. Jewett was later a mentor to the young Willa Cather, who rated Jewett's *The Country of the Pointed Firs* (1896), a series of loosely connected sketches about life in a declining Maine seacoast town, as one of three enduring masterpieces of American literature. In dedicating *O Pioneers!* to Jewett, Cather wrote that in Jewett's "beautiful and delicate work there is the perfection that endures," praise that surely applies to the much-reprinted "A White Heron."

I

The woods were already filled with shadows one June evening, just before eight o'clock, though a bright sunset still glimmered faintly among the trunks of the trees. A little girl was driving home her cow, a plodding, dilatory, provoking creature in her behavior, but a valued companion for all that. They were going away from the western light, and striking deep into the dark woods, but their feet were familiar with the path, and it was no matter whether their eyes could see it or not.

There was hardly a night the summer through when the old cow could be found waiting at the pasture bars; on the contrary, it was her greatest pleasure to hide herself away among the high huckleberry bushes, and though she wore a loud bell she had made the discovery that if one stood perfectly still it would not ring. So Sylvia had to hunt for her until she found her, and call Co'! Co'! with never an answering Moo, until her childish patience was quite spent. If the creature had not given good milk and plenty of it, the case would have seemed very different to her owners. Besides, Sylvia had all the time there was, and very little use to make of it. Sometimes in pleasant weather it was a consolation to look upon the cow's pranks as an intelligent attempt to play hide and seek, and as the child had no playmates she lent herself to this amusement with a good deal of zest. Though this chase had been so long that the wary animal herself had given an unusual signal of her whereabouts, Sylvia had only laughed when she came upon Mistress Moolly at the swamp-side, and urged her affectionately homeward with a twig of birch leaves. The old cow was not inclined to wander farther, she even turned in the right direction for once as they left the pasture, and stepped along the road at a good pace. She was quite ready to be milked now, and seldom stopped to browse. Sylvia wondered what her grandmother would say because they were so late. It was a great while since she had left home at half past five o'clock, but everybody knew the difficulty of making this errand a short one. Mrs. Tilley had chased the hornéd torment too many summer evenings herself to blame any one else for lingering, and was only thankful as she waited that she had Sylvia, nowadays, to give such valuable assistance. The good woman suspected that Sylvia loitered occasionally on her own account; there never was such a child for straying out-of-doors since the world was made! Everybody said that it was a good change for a little maid who had tried to grow for eight years in a crowded manufacturing town, but, as for Sylvia herself, it seemed as if she never had been alive at all before she came to live at the farm. She thought often with wistful compassion of a wretched dry geranium that belonged to a town neighbor. " 'Afraid of folks,' " old Mrs. Tilley said to herself, with a smile, after she had made the unlikely choice of Sylvia from her daughter's houseful of children, and was returning to the farm. " 'Afraid of folks,' they said! I guess she won't be troubled no great with 'em up to the old place!" When they reached the door of the lonely house and stopped to unlock it, and the cat came to purr loudly, and rub against them, a deserted pussy, indeed, but fat with young robins, Sylvia whispered that this was a beautiful place to live in, and she never should wish to go home.

The companions followed the shady woodroad, the cow taking slow steps, and the child very fast ones. The cow stopped long at the brook to drink, as if the pasture were not half a swamp, and Sylvia stood still and waited, letting her bare feet cool themselves in the shoal water, while the great twilight moths struck softly against her. She waded on through the brook as the cow moved away, and listened to the thrushes with a heart that beat fast with pleasure. There was a stirring in the great boughs overheard. They were full of little birds and beasts that seemed to be wide-awake, and going about their world, or else saying good-night to each other in sleepy twitters. Sylvia herself felt sleepy as she walked along. However, it was not much farther to the house, and the air was soft and sweet. She was not often in the woods so late as this, and it made her feel as if she were a part of the gray shadows and the moving leaves. She was just thinking how long it seemed since she first came to the farm a year ago, and wondering if everything went on in the noisy town just the same as when she was there; the thought of the great red-faced boy who used to chase and frighten her made her hurry along the path to escape from the shadow of the trees.

Suddenly this little woods-girl is horror-stricken to hear a clear whistle not very far away. Not a bird's whistle, which would have a sort of friendliness, but a boy's whistle, determined, and somewhat aggressive. Sylvia left the cow to whatever sad fate might await her, and stepped discreetly aside into the bushes, but she was just too late. The enemy had discovered her, and called out in a very cheerful and persuasive tone, "Halloa, little girl, how far is it to the road?" and trembling Sylvia answered almost inaudibly, "A good ways."

She did not dare to look boldly at the tall young man, who carried a gun over his shoulder, but she came out of her bush and again followed the cow, while he walked alongside.

"I have been hunting for some birds," the stranger said kindly, "and I have lost my way, and need a friend very much. Don't be afraid," he added gallantly. "Speak up and tell me what your name is, and whether you think I can spend the night at your house, and go out gunning early in the morning."

Sylvia was more alarmed than before. Would not her grandmother consider her much to blame? But who could have foreseen such an accident as this? It did not appear to be her fault, and she hung her head as if the stem of it were broken, but managed to answer "Sylvy," with much effort when her companion again asked her name.

Mrs. Tilley was standing in the doorway when the trio came into view. The cow gave a loud moo by way of explanation.

"Yes, you'd better speak up for yourself, you old trial! Where'd she tuck herself away this time, Sylvy?" Sylvia kept an awed silence; she knew by instinct that her grandmother did not comprehend the gravity of the situation. She must be mistaking the stranger for one of the farmer-lads of the region.

The young man stood his gun beside the door, and dropped a heavy game-bag beside it; then he bade Mrs. Tilley good-evening, and repeated his wayfarer's story, and asked if he could have a night's lodging.

"Put me anywhere you like," he said. "I must be off early in the morning, before day; but I am very hungry, indeed. You can give me some milk at any rate, that's plain."

"Dear sakes, yes," responded the hostess, whose long slumbering hospitality seemed to be easily awakened. "You might fare better if you went out on the main road a mile or so, but you're welcome to what we've got. I'll milk right off, and you make yourself at home. You can sleep on husks or feathers," she proffered graciously. "I raised them all myself. There's good pasturing for geese just below here towards the ma'sh. Now step round and set a plate for the gentleman, Sylvy!" and Sylvia promptly stepped. She was glad to have something to do, and she was hungry herself.

It was a surprise to find so clean and comfortable a little dwelling in this New England wilderness. The young man had known the horrors of its most primitive housekeeping, and the dreary squalor of that level of society which does not rebel at the companionship of hens. This was the best thrift of an old-fashioned farmstead, though on such a small scale it seemed like a hermitage. He listened eagerly to the old woman's quaint talk, he watched Sylvia's pale face and shining gray eyes with ever growing enthusiasm, and insisted that this was the best supper he had eaten for a month; then, afterward, the new-made friends sat down in the doorway together while the moon came up.

Soon it would be berry-time, and Sylvia was a great help at picking. The cow was a good milker, though a plaguy thing to keep track of, the hostess gossiped frankly, adding presently that she had buried four children, so that Sylvia's mother, and a son (who might be dead) in California were all the children she had left. "Dan, my boy, was a great hand to go gunning," she explained sadly. "I never wanted for pa'tridges or gray squer'ls while he was to home. He's been a great wand'rer, I expect, and he's no hand to write letters. There, I don't blame him, I'd ha' seen the world myself if it had been so I could.

"Sylvia takes after him," the grandmother continued affectionately, after a minute's pause. "There ain't a foot o' ground she don't know her way over, and the wild creatur's

counts her one o' themselves. Squer'ls she'll tame to come
an' feed right out o' her hands, and all sorts o' birds. Last
winter she got the jay-birds to bangeing here, and I be-
lieve she'd 'a' scanted herself of her own meals to have
plenty to throw out amongst 'em, if I hadn't kep' watch.
Anything but crows, I tell her, I'm willin' to help sup-
port,—though Dan he went an' tamed one o' them that
did seem to have reason same as folks. It was round here
a good spell after he went away. Dan an' his father they
didn't hitch,—but he never held up his head ag'in after
Dan had dared him an' gone off."

The guest did not notice this hint of family sorrows in
his eager interest in something else.

"So Sylvy knows all about birds, does she?" he ex-
claimed, as he looked round at the little girl who sat, very
demure but increasingly sleepy, in the moonlight. "I am
making a collection of birds myself. I have been at it ever
since I was a boy." (Mrs. Tilley smiled.) "There are two or
three very rare ones I have been hunting for these five
years. I mean to get them on my own ground if they can be
found."

"Do you cage 'em up?" asked Mrs. Tilley doubtfully,
in response to this enthusiastic announcement.

"Oh, no, they're stuffed and preserved, dozens and
dozens of them," said the ornithologist, "and I have shot or
snared every one myself. I caught a glimpse of a white
heron three miles from here on Saturday, and I have fol-
lowed it in this direction. They have never been found in
this district at all. The little white heron, it is," and he
turned again to look at Sylvia with the hope of discovering
that the rare bird was one of her acquaintances.

But Sylvia was watching a hop-toad in the narrow foot-
path.

"You would know the heron if you saw it," the stranger
continued eagerly. "A queer tall white bird with soft feath-
ers and long thin legs. And it would have a nest perhaps in
the top of a high tree, made of sticks, something like a
hawk's nest."

Sylvia's heart gave a wild beat; she knew that strange white bird, and had once stolen softly near where it stood in some bright green swamp grass, away over at the other side of the woods. There was an open place where the sunshine always seemed strangely yellow and hot, where tall, nodding rushes grew, and her grandmother had warned her that she might sink in the soft black mud underneath and never be heard of more. Not far beyond were the salt marshes and beyond those was the sea, the sea which Sylvia wondered and dreamed about, but never had looked upon, though its great voice could often be heard above the noise of the woods on stormy nights.

"I can't think of anything I should like so much as to find that heron's nest," the handsome stranger was saying. "I would give ten dollars to anybody who could show it to me," he added desperately, "and I mean to spend my whole vacation hunting for it if need be. Perhaps it was only migrating, or had been chased out of its own region by some bird of prey."

Mrs. Tilley gave amazed attention to all this, but Sylvia still watched the toad, not divining, as she might have done at some calmer time, that the creature wished to get to its hole under the doorstep, and was much hindered by the unusual spectators at that hour of the evening. No amount of thought, that night, could decide how many wished-for treasures the ten dollars, so lightly spoken of, would buy.

The next day the young sportsman hovered about the woods, and Sylvia kept him company, having lost her first fear of the friendly lad, who proved to be most kind and sympathetic. He told her many things about the birds and what they knew and where they lived and what they did with themselves. And he gave her a jack-knife, which she thought as great a treasure as if she were a desert-islander. All day long he did not once make her troubled or afraid except when he brought down some unsuspecting singing creature from its bough. Sylvia would have liked him vastly better without his gun; she could not understand why he killed the very birds he seemed to like so much. But as the day waned, Sylvia still watched the young man with loving admiration. She had never seen anybody so charming and delightful; the woman's heart, asleep in the child, was vaguely thrilled by a dream of love. Some premonition of that great power stirred and swayed these young foresters who traversed the solemn woodlands with soft-footed silent care. They stopped to listen to a bird's song; they pressed forward again eagerly, parting the branches,—speaking to each other rarely and in whispers; the young man going first and Sylvia following, fascinated, a few steps behind, with her gray eyes dark with excitement.

She grieved because the longed-for white heron was elusive, but she did not lead the guest, she only followed, and there was no such thing as speaking first. The sound of her own unquestioned voice would have terrified her,—it was hard enough to answer yes or no when there was need of that. At last evening began to fall, and they drove the cow home together, and Sylvia smiled with pleasure when they came to the place where she heard the whistle and was afraid only the night before.

II

Half a mile from home, at the farther edge of the woods, where the land was highest, a great pine-tree stood, the last of its generation. Whether it was left for a boundary mark, or for what reason, no one could say; the woodchoppers who had felled its mates were dead and gone long ago, and a whole forest of sturdy trees, pines and oaks and maples, had grown again. But the stately head of this old pine towered above them all and made a landmark for sea and shore miles and miles away. Sylvia knew it well. She had always believed that whoever climbed to the top of it could see the ocean; and the little girl had often laid her hand on the great rough trunk and looked up wistfully at those dark boughs that the wind always stirred, no matter how hot and still the air might be below. Now she thought of the tree with a new excitement, for why, if one climbed it at break

SARAH ORNE JEWETT

of day, could not one see all the world, and easily discover whence the white heron flew, and mark the place, and find the hidden nest?

What a spirit of adventure, what wild ambition! What fancied triumph and delight and glory for the later morning when she could make known the secret! It was almost too real and too great for the childish heart to bear.

All night the door of the little house stood open, and the whippoorwills came and sang upon the very step. The young sportsman and his old hostess were sound asleep, but Sylvia's great design kept her broad awake and watching. She forgot to think of sleep. The short summer night seemed as long as the winter darkness, and at last when the whippoorwills ceased, and she was afraid the morning would after all come too soon, she stole out of the house and followed the pasture path through the woods, hastening toward the open ground beyond, listening with a sense of comfort and companionship to the drowsy twitter of a half-awakened bird, whose perch she had jarred in passing. Alas, if the great wave of human interest which flooded for the first time this dull little life should sweep away the satisfaction of an existence heart to heart with nature and the dumb life of the forest!

There was the huge tree asleep yet in the paling moonlight, and small and hopeful Sylvia began with utmost bravery to mount to the top of it, with tingling, eager blood coursing the channels of her whole frame, with her bare feet and fingers, that pinched and held like bird's claws to the monstrous ladder reaching up, up, almost to the sky itself. First she must mount the white oak tree that grew alongside, where she was almost lost among the dark branches and the green leaves heavy and wet with dew; a bird fluttered off its nest, and a red squirrel ran to and fro and scolded pettishly at the harmless housebreaker. Sylvia felt her way easily. She had often climbed there, and knew that higher still one of the oak's upper branches chafed against the pine trunk, just where its lower boughs were set close together. There, when she made the dangerous pass from one tree to the other, the great enterprise would really begin.

She crept out along the swaying oak limb at last, and took the daring step across into the old pine-tree. The way was harder than she thought; she must reach far and hold fast, the sharp dry twigs caught and held her and scratched her like angry talons, the pitch made her thin little fingers clumsy and stiff as she went round and round the tree's great stem, higher and higher upward. The sparrows and robins in the woods below were beginning to wake and twitter to the dawn, yet it seemed much lighter there aloft in the pine-tree, and the child knew that she must hurry if her project were to be of any use.

The tree seemed to lengthen itself out as she went up, and to reach farther and farther upward. It was like a great main-mast to the voyaging earth; it must truly have been amazed that morning through all its ponderous frame as it felt this determined spark of human spirit creeping and climbing from higher branch to branch. Who knows how steadily the least twigs held themselves to advantage this light, weak creature on her way! The old pine must have loved his new dependent. More than all the hawks, and bats, and moths, and even the sweet-voiced thrushes, was the brave, beating heart of the solitary gray-eyed child. And the tree stood still and held away the winds that June morning while the dawn grew bright in the east.

Sylvia's face was like a pale star, if one had seen it from the ground, when the last thorny bough was past, and she stood trembling and tired but wholly triumphant, high in the tree-top. Yes, there was the sea with the dawning sun making a golden dazzle over it, and toward that glorious east flew two hawks with slow-moving pinions. How low they looked in the air from that height when before one had only seen them far up, and dark against the blue sky. Their gay feathers were as soft as moths; they seemed only a little way from the tree, and Sylvia felt as if she too could go flying away among the clouds. Westward, the woodlands and farms reached miles and miles into the distance; here and there were church steeples, and white villages; truly it was a vast and awesome world.

The birds sang louder and louder. At last the sun came up bewilderingly bright. Sylvia could see the white sails of ships out at sea, and the clouds that were purple and rose-colored and yellow at first began to fade away. Where was the white heron's nest in the sea of green branches, and was this wonderful sight and pageant of the world the only reward for having climbed to such a giddy height? Now look down again, Sylvia, where the green marsh is set among the shining birches and dark hemlocks; there where you saw the white heron once you will see him again; look, look! a white spot of him like a single floating feather comes up from the dead hemlock and grows larger, and rises, and comes close at last, and goes by the landmark pine with steady sweep of wing and outstretched slender neck and crested head. And wait! wait! do not move a foot or a finger, little girl, do not send an arrow of light and consciousness from your two eager eyes, for the heron has perched on a pine bough not far beyond yours, and cries back to his mate on the nest, and plumes his feathers for the new day!

The child gives a long sigh a minute later when a company of shouting cat-birds comes also to the tree, and vexed by their fluttering and lawlessness the solemn heron goes away. She knows his secret now, the wild, light, slender bird that floats and wavers, and goes back like an arrow presently to his home in the green world beneath. Then Sylvia, well satisfied, makes her perilous way down again, not daring to look far below the branch she stands on, ready to cry sometimes because her fingers ache and her lamed feet slip. Wondering over and over again what the stranger would say to her, and what he would think when she told him how to find his way straight to the heron's nest.

"Sylvy, Sylvy!" called the busy old grandmother again and again, but nobody answered, and the small husk bed was empty, and Sylvia had disappeared.

The guest waked from a dream, and remembering his

day's pleasure hurried to dress himself that it might sooner begin. He was sure from the way the shy little girl looked once or twice yesterday that she had at least seen the white heron, and now she must really be persuaded to tell. Here she comes now, paler than ever, and her worn old frock is torn and tattered, and smeared with pine pitch. The grandmother and the sportsman stand in the door together and question her, and the splendid moment has come to speak of the dead hemlock-tree by the green marsh.

But Sylvia does not speak after all, though the old grandmother fretfully rebukes her, and the young man's kind appealing eyes are looking straight into her own. He can make them rich with money; he has promised it, and they are poor now. He is so well worth making happy, and he waits to hear the story she can tell.

No, she must keep silence! What is it that suddenly forbids her and makes her dumb? Has she been nine years growing, and now, when the great world for the first time puts out a hand to her, must she thrust it aside for a bird's sake? The murmur of the pine's green branches is in her ears, she remembers how the white heron came flying through the golden air and how they watched the sea and the morning together, and Sylvia cannot speak; she cannot tell the heron's secret and give its life away.

Dear loyalty, that suffered a sharp pang as the guest went away disappointed later in the day, that could have served and followed him and loved him as a dog loves! Many a night Sylvia heard the echo of his whistle haunting the pasture path as she came home with the loitering cow. She forgot even her sorrow at the sharp report of his gun and the piteous sight of thrushes and sparrows dropping silent to the ground, their songs hushed and their pretty feathers stained and wet with blood. Were the birds better friends than their hunter might have been,—who can tell? Whatever treasures were lost to her, woodlands and summertime, remember! Bring your gifts and graces and tell your secrets to this lonely country child!

MARGARET HASSE

BEING STILL

from *Stars Above, Stars Below* (1984)

> Margaret Hasse (1950–   ) draws on her midwestern roots
> in her collection of poems *Stars Above, Stars Below*. Born in
> South Dakota, Hasse received a B.A. from Stanford and an
> M.A. from the University of Minnesota. She lives in St.
> Paul, where she teaches creative writing courses at the col-
> lege level and in a local correctional facility. Her second
> book, *In a Sheep's Eye, Darling* (1988), won the Lakes and
> Prairies competition.

She's a quiet clapper in the bell of the prairie,
a girl who likes to be alone.
Today, she's hiked four miles down
ravines' low cool blueness.
Bending under a barbed wire, she's in grass fields.
She's at the edge of the great plains.
Wise to openness, she finds it a familiar place.
Her clothes swell like wheat bread.

When she returns to her parents' house,
the foxtails and burrs have come home, too.
The plants seem intent on living in new ground.
She's the carrier. "Carrier" is a precision
learned in summer's biology class.
She likes to think of ripening seeds,
a cargo inside the bellies of flying birds.
Birds like red-winged blackbirds who skim the air
and land, alert on their cattail stalks.

They allow her a silent manner.
They go about their red-winged business
of crying to each other, dipping their beaks
into the swampy stand of ditch water,
full of the phantom of green.
The stiller she is, the more everything moves
in the immense vocabulary of being.

SALLY CARRIGHAR

HOME TO THE WILDERNESS

from *Home to the Wilderness* (1973)

Sally Carrighar (c. 1905–1986) found her vocation in nature
writing only after trying and abandoning various other artis-
tic careers—pianist, dancer, film production assistant, fiction
writer. Born in Cleveland, and partially disfigured at birth
by a high-forceps delivery, she had a difficult childhood.
After finding encouragement in her years at Wellesley Col-
lege, she took a series of disillusioning commercial writing
jobs in Hollywood and San Francisco, which led her to the
brink of suicide and into psychoanalysis. In San Francisco,
convalescing from depression and heart disease, she devel-
oped a remarkable communication with the birds that came
to feed at her windowsill and a mouse living in her radio,
and in a flash she realized that she could write about birds
and animals.

Carrighar eventually wrote nature books about the crea-
tures of the Sierra (*One Day on Beetle Rock*, 1944), the Tetons
(*One Day at Teton Marsh*, 1947), and the Arctic (*Icebound*

Summer, 1953), as well as narratives of her adventures in Alaska. She also wrote a play, a historical novel, and an autobiography. Always the product of meticulous research, her nature writing has been compared favorably with Rachel Carson's for its scientific accuracy and poetic insight. The seeds of her intimate feeling for wildlife were perhaps planted by the experience of summering on a Canadian island that she describes in the following excerpt from her autobiography.

As amazing as miracles was a morning in June the year that I was fifteen and woke up in a tent on an island in Canada. We had arrived by lake steamer the previous night and, tired after the long trip from Kansas City, had gone straight to bed. Now it was daylight. I got up quickly, quietly and slipped out to see this new world.

The tent was a short way back from the shore with a path leading down to a little dock. I walked to the end of it. Ripples were gently rearranging the pebbles along the beach but the lake was smooth. Its wide and beautiful surface, delicate silver-blue, steamed with a mist that disappeared as I watched, for the light of the early sun, splintering on the tops of the mainland evergreen trees, was starting to fall on the mist and dissolve it. Curiously the lake's level surface seemed to be moving in alternate glassy streams, right and left, an effect that sometimes occurs on quiet water, I don't know why.

The bay in front of the dock was framed by the shores of the mainland, which curved together from both sides to meet in a point. At that vertex another island, rocky and tall, rose from the water. It looked uninhabited; and although a few cabins were scattered along the mainland, between and behind them was unbroken forest. It was my first sight of a natural wilderness. Behind our tent too, and several other tents here and a house in their midst, was the forest. Over everything, as pervasive as sunshine, was the fragrance of balsam firs. It was aromatic and sweet and I closed my eyes and breathed deeply to draw in more of it.

SALLY CARRIGHAR   27

Voices from some of the tents meant that others were stirring. At the house wood smoke rose from the chimney, another redolent fragrance mingling soon with the smell of bacon frying. It is a combination familiar to everyone who has known woodland mornings. There would be talk at breakfast, the meeting with strangers—a loss. The sunrise across the wild northern lake seemed a kind of holiness that human chatter was bound to destroy a little. The water, so still and lucent, beyond it the dark mystery of the forest, and the firs' fragrance: for this sacred experience, enjoyed alone, I would get up at dawn every day during that summer.

We would be here for three months with my father joining us for July. Neither of my parents had been here before but friends, the Wymans from Painesville, had written to say that they knew of this island in the Muskoka Lakes and suggested our spending some weeks there together. After three summers in Kansas City, where the temperature day and night can stay above ninety, we were going to get away somewhere, and since my father had not been back to his native Canada for some time, the Wymans' idea appealed to my parents.

On the island were five or six visiting families. Some had children, of whom only one was a girl near my age. She would turn out to be very lively, never happy unless she was engaged in some boisterous game. I thought of her as an enemy. The family who owned this tiny resort were named White. They had several grown sons and a daughter. One of the sons, Dalton, nineteen, was just back from Montreal where he had won the junior world championship in canoeing. He was dark-haired and tall, with a puckish smile, to me that year probably the most glamorous youth in the world. One could never, of course, hope to be friends with him.

At the back of the house were a large vegetable garden, two or three sheds and an old boat with grass growing up through its timbers. Past them one reached a thicket. I pushed through it that first afternoon, into the woods beyond.

The brush was thinner here but the trees grew densely. I wandered on, memorizing some landmarks: this boulder, this berry bush, this fallen log. I looked back. All had disappeared! It was a different grove when one turned around. The house was no longer in sight and my heart beat faster. I was lost! But one couldn't get lost on an island, although this one was large, three and a half miles long. It was only necessary to find the shore, mostly rocky and wild, and follow it back. But I still felt lost and curiously afraid.

The trees, vaguely and strangely, were menacing. Not in any park, cemetery or pasture had I ever been so entirely enclosed by trees. These were massive, like giants. One surrounded by them felt helpless. They spread above, forming together a cavelike dark. They were presences. *Which way had I come*—where was the shore!

Fear of trees is an old reaction, still a familiar emotion on primitive levels. Eskimos camping among trees, found along Northern rivers, dare not settle down beneath one for the night until they have stood off and thrown a knife into its trunk. Many other tribes have been awed by trees. If a branch has been broken off, if its bark has been damaged, or in the case of having to fell it, an apology would be made to a tree. The blood of a slaughtered animal was brushed onto it, or it was given a drink of water. In the Punjab, a former province of India, human sacrifices were made to a certain tree every year. Trees and groves in many parts of the world have been considered sacred.

In the Canadian woods I didn't believe consciously that a tree might be hostile. I was just strangely uneasy there in the eerie atmosphere of the grove. One can name this dread and call it claustrophobia, which probably is an ancient fear. A prehistoric man might have felt trapped in dense woods, and recently Sir Frank Fraser Darling, the eloquent conservationist, has said that many modern people are afraid of a wilderness, which is why they are so willing to see it destroyed. Anyway I was slightly alarmed by that island forest, and although I was rather eager to know what was there I couldn't force myself to continue farther.

My going and coming were noted, for I met Dalton on the way back and he said, "You didn't stay in the woods very long."

"I was getting lost." He smiled with amusement.

There were always three or four canoes pulled up on the beach. One day I got one of them out on the water and was floundering around in it when Dalton came down to the dock. He called, "Try to bring it back to the beach and I'll show you how to paddle." I sat in the bow facing him as with his strong, quick stroke he shot us out onto the lake. There he gave me the first lesson, demonstrating the right way to hold the paddle, how to turn it so smoothly in pulling it back that a canoe doesn't vary its course by an inch. "Line up the prow with some tree on the shore," he said, "and don't let it swing either side off the trunk." In shallow water again we changed places and awkwardly I tried to put into practice what he had demonstrated. A skill, a start in learning a new skill—inspiring prospect—from this young man who himself was dedicated to perfecting a skill: was it possible that we might have something in common?

The Whites had a piano. It was in the sitting room of the house and I could no more stay away from it than I could have gone without food. My frequent playing must have been a trial to some of the other guests, especially a violinist who practiced several hours a day in his tent (a situation I didn't remind him of when I met him years later in San Francisco where he was teaching the young Yehudi Menuhin). But Dalton enjoyed my music. He used to come and stand at one end of the piano with his elbow on top, listening and watching.

He gave me more paddling lessons and after a while I too could hold a canoe's prow on the trunk of a shoreline tree. In the afternoons I went out with him in his racing canoe, as ballast he said, while he kept up his training. His canoe was a little sliver of a thing with graphite all over the outside to make it slip through the water faster. In Montreal he had paddled a mile in four minutes and seven seconds, a record which probably has been beaten many times, but when he dipped in his paddle, his canoe leapt away like a dolphin.

He landed us on the mainland one day and said, "Let's take a little walk." With a companion one could enjoy a forest. Besides, the trees here were of varying heights, they didn't form caves. It was an intricate scene, everything was prolifically growing—and dying. The ground was a litter of brown leaves and fir needles and sticks. It was unkempt compared with a park but fascinating.

All around us was limber movement. The grasses and wildflowers bent quivering in the flow of the breeze and the trees above were a green ruffling commotion. Their leaves, as they tossed and swung, seemed to be cutting the sky into bits, to be scattered as scraps of sunlight along the ground.

Birds were lacing the air, in and out of the trees and bushes. One on the ground was jumping forward and scratching back through dead leaves and one, also searching for insects, was spiralling up a tree trunk, pressing its stiff, short tail on the bark as a prop. At that time, in June, most of the birds would be feeding young, Dalton said, and they had to work all day catching insects for them. Besides this bright movement of wings, then, there must be thousands of tinier creatures doing whatever insects do on a summer afternoon: a world everywhere *alive.*

Dalton seemed to have realized that I knew almost nothing about what was here and was showing me things: a porcupine's tracks, a bee tree, a fox's burrow. He knocked on a tree and a flying squirrel poked its little head out of a hole. It was all wonderful, even exciting, but strange.

We came out on a small elevation. Below was a meadow brimful of yellow-green sunlight. Perhaps this was the pleasantest way to enjoy a forest: with trees and brush at your back but a wide escape if anything should approach from behind. Unmentionable were wolves, bears. (They may have been there in fact. That forest is now built up but resorts not far away advertise that guests can hear wolves baying.) Dalton had brought his rifle. Was he just thinking of shooting something for fun, or was the gun for protection?

The thought of escape was still there. Compare a park: only a few, spaced-out trees were allowed to grow, their dead branches were pruned away, the flowers were all in neat beds, the grass was kept mowed, never allowed to become weeds or "grasses." All controlled, therefore safe.

Here the plants grew their own way and the animals went their own way—one might appear anywhere, any time. No one knew what might happen—did happen, for there were dead broken trees among the live ones. Everything was wild—naturally. That was the meaning of forests of course, that they were wild. Therefore unpredictable.

Yet the wilderness was a beautiful, even enchanting place with its graceful movement and active life. Even underfoot if one scratched away the brown leaves as the bird had done, one might come upon small, secret lives. But might there be things that would bite? I had heard of tarantulas. With a feeling of cowardice, shrinking back, I wanted to leave, to return to the wide placid lake. And then I did something which made it seem that, on nature's terms, I had no right to be here at all.

Dalton said, "Look!" Pointing: "There's a porcupine in the crotch of that tree over there." One of the wild inhabitants of this forest, only medium sized for an animal, sat on the branch, his back a high curve, with his quills raised and bristling. He might be lying like that to let the sunshine come into his fur, warm down to his skin. He looked sleepy. Dalton handed the rifle to me and said, "Let's see if you can hit it."

He showed the way the gun should be held, braced against my shoulder, how to sight the target along the barrel. "Now pull the trigger back with your right hand—slowly, just squeeze it." I pulled the trigger and with astonishment saw the porcupine fall to the ground.

Dalton was full of praise. "Very good! I didn't think you could do it." We went down along the side of the meadow. Beneath the tree lay the porcupine, limp and still.

Even his fur and quills were flat, lifeless now. Looking smaller, this was the little creature who, a few moments earlier, had been up on the bough wrapped in sunshine, enjoying life. I burst into tears.

Dalton went over alone the next day and drew out the quills and brought them to me to decorate the basket of scented sweet-grass that I, like all the women, was making. I gave them away.

I never returned to the mainland forest alone, but by midsummer I'd made my own a small peninsula on the island. Paddling along its shore one morning I had tied the canoe to a tree overhanging the lake and sat in its shade doing embroidery. The point—it was the southern tip of the island—was narrow, not more than fifty yards wide. Through its trees I could see across to the bay on the other side and the center was open, with a thin cover of grass and wildflowers among sun-warmed rocks. It looked perfectly safe and I went ashore to investigate.

There was no trail leading away from here, the point seemed private, peculiarly mine, and it pleased me very much. I came back the next day and then other days. Sometimes I walked about but more often sat under one of the trees, which were firs and quivering aspens, listening to the songs of the birds and watching them and a squirrel who was always there. I had a wonderful feeling—I had had it too with the chipmunk—that I was acceptable here, that I was liked, for they made little overtures even before I started feeding them bits of bread. Perhaps it helped that I talked to them.

Gradually, a few moments one day, more moments the next, being there in that small safe woodland began to seem almost the same experience as making music, as the way, when I played the piano, I *was* the music, my physical body feeling as if it dissolved in the sounds. I could say my dimensions then were those of the melodies and the harmony that spread out from the piano in all directions. I had no consciousness of my individual self.

Tenuously, imperfectly that Canadian summer, the

same thing happened when I would walk around the peninsula, unafraid. It was not a wide going out and out, as with music, but again of losing myself—this time by becoming identified with whatever I was especially aware of. It happened first with a flower. I held a blue flower in my hand, probably a wild aster, wondering what its name was, and then thought that human names for natural things are superfluous. Nature herself does not name them. The important thing is to *know* this flower, look at its color until the blueness becomes as real as a keynote of music. Look at the exquisite yellow flowerettes in the center, become very small with them. *Be* the flower, be the trees, the blowing grasses. Fly with the birds, jump with the squirrel!

Finally I spent every morning there. No one knew where I had gone.

MARJORIE KINNAN RAWLINGS

THE MAGNOLIA TREE

from *Cross Creek* (1942)

Marjorie Kinnan Rawlings (1896–1953) found her authentic literary voice only after she bought and began to farm an orange grove near Cross Creek, Florida. Born in Washington, D.C., and educated at the University of Wisconsin, Rawlings wrote for the *Louisville Courier-Journal* and the *Rochester Journal-American* before settling in Florida in 1928. There she found her main subject in the human bond to the earth, evident in her Pulitzer Prize–winning novel, *The*

Yearling (1938), as well as in her memoir, *Cross Creek*. In the following passage from her memoir, Rawlings describes the hammock (in Florida, a fertile area usually higher than its surroundings and characterized by hardwoods and humus-rich soil) on the shore of Orange Lake that she often used as a retreat in her early days there.

I do not understand how any one can live without some small place of enchantment to turn to. In the lakeside hammock there is a constant stirring in the tree-tops, as though on the stillest days the breathing of the earth is yet audible. The Spanish moss sways a little always. The heavy forest thins into occasional great trees, live oaks and palms and pines. In spring, the yellow jessamine is heavy on the air, in summer the red trumpet vine shouts from the gray trunks, and in autumn and winter the holly berries are small bright lamps in the half-light. The squirrels are unafraid, and here I saw my first fox-squirrel, a huge fellow made of black shining plush. Here a skunk prowled close to me, digging industrious small holes for grubs. I sat as still as a stump, and if he saw me, as I suspect, he was a gentleman and went on steadily with his business, then loped away with a graceful rocking motion. A covey of quail passed me often, so that I came to know their trail into the blackberry thicket where they gathered in a circle for the night, making small soft cries. It is impossible to be among the woods animals on their own ground without a feeling of expanding one's own world, as when any foreign country is visited.

To the west, the hammock becomes damp, the trees stand more sparsely. Beyond is a long stretch of marsh where the cattle feed lazily, belly-deep in water hyacinths and lily pads, then the wide lake itself. There is a clamor of water birds, long-legged herons and cranes, visiting sea-gulls from the coasts, wild ducks, coots, the shrill scream of fish-hawks, with now and then a bald-headed eagle loitering in the sky, ready to swirl down and take the fish-hawk's catch from him in midair. Across the lake, visible the four miles only on a clear day, is the tower of the old Samson manse, decaying in the middle of the still prosperous orange grove. From the tower itself, decrepit and dangerous, is a sight of a tropical world of dreams, made up of glossy trees and shining water and palm islands. When I am an old woman, so that too much queerness will seem a natural thing, I mean to build a tower like it on my own side of the lake, and I shall sit there on angry days and growl down at any one who disturbs me.

I dig leaf mould from this hammock to enrich my roses and camellias and gardenias. When I went with my basket one morning a breath of movement, an unwonted pattern of color, caught my eye under a tangle of wild grapevines. A wild sow lay nested at the base of a great magnolia. At a little distance, piled one on the other, lay her litter, clean and fresh as the sunshine, the birth-damp still upon them. Sow and litter were exhausted with the business of birthing. The one lay breathing profoundly, absorbed in the immensity of rest. The others lay like a mass of puppies, the lowest-layered tugging himself free to climb again on top of the pile and warm his tender belly. The mass shifted. The most adventuresome, a pied morsel of pig with a white band like a belt around his middle, wobbled over to the sow's side. He gave a delighted whimper and the whole litter ambled over to discover the miracle of the hairy breasts.

The jungle hammock breathed. Life went through the moss-hung forest, the swamp, the cypresses, through the wild sow and her young, through me, in its continuous chain. We were all one with the silent pulsing. This was the thing that was important, the cycle of life, with birth and death merging one into the other in an imperceptible twilight and an insubstantial dawn. The universe breathed, and the world inside it breathed the same breath. This was the cosmic life, with suns and moons to make it lovely. It was important only to keep close enough to the pulse to feel its rhythm, to be comforted by its steadiness, to know that Life is vital, and one's own minute living a torn fragment of the larger cloth.

LUCI TAPAHONSO

A BREEZE SWEPT THROUGH

from *A Breeze Swept Through* (1987)

Luci Tapahonso (1953–   ) explains that "the land is an integral part of my history, my life, and even my name," which identifies her as one of the "Beside the Big Water" people. She was born in Shiprock, New Mexico, and educated at the University of New Mexico (B.A., M.A.). The author of three published volumes of poetry, she is currently a professor of English at the University of New Mexico. The important role of landscape in her writing comes through clearly in the following poem about the births of her two daughters, Lori Tazbah and Misty Dawn, who are the earth's daughters as well.

The first born of dawn woman
slid out amid crimson fluid streaked with stratus clouds
    her body glistening August sunset pink
    light steam rising from her like rain on warm
      rocks
          (A sudden cool breeze swept through
          the kitchen and grandpa smiled then sang
          quietly knowing the moment.)
She came when the desert day cooled
and dusk began to move in
in that intricate changing of time
    she gasped and it flows from her now
    with every breath   with every breath
    she travels now
          sharing scarlet sunsets

        named for wild desert flowers
        her smile a blessing song.

And in mid-November
early morning darkness
after days of waiting pain
        the second one cried   wailing
        sucking first earth breath
        separating the heavy fog
        she cried and kicked   tiny brown limbs
        fierce movements as outside
        the mist lifted as
        the sun is born again.
(East of Acoma, a sandstone boulder
split in two—a sharp, clean crack.)
She is born of damp mist and early sun.
She is born again   woman of dawn.
She is born knowing the warm smoothness of rock.
She is born knowing her own morning strength.

BARBARA DEAN

THE MANY AND THE ONE

from *Wellspring* (1979)

> Barbara Dean (1946–), along with fifteen friends, went to
> live on a square mile of wilderness land in northern Califor-
> nia in 1971. She built a yurt with her own hands and settled
> into a life close to nature. Her book, *Wellspring: A Story from
> the Deep Country*, tells the story of this life; in it, she writes,
> "The land, for me, is a wellspring of pure delight. . . . This
> is where . . . the world without and the world within become
> one, and I am pulled resolutely toward God." Dean was
> born in Grand Rapids, Michigan, and earned a B.A. in
> French from Duke University and an M.A. in psychology
> from Sonoma State University. She has taught school and
> written articles; currently she is executive editor at Island
> Press and consulting editor for Sierra Club Books' Nature
> and Natural Philosophy Library. She still lives in the north-
> ern California wilderness and is at work on a sequel to
> *Wellspring* that "explores the healing potential in our rela-
> tionship with nature."

Spring is in the air. The breeze is gentle with the smell of
birthing, the earth radiates freshness, the birds sing with
more abandon than they have for months. The first wild-
flowers are in bloom in the deep forest: the hardy tooth-
wort, the delicate purple shooting star. The tender green
of new growth is everywhere. Grass has even sprouted
through some cracks in the concrete of my floor: what
better testament to life renewed?

I cannot stay inside. I gather up my quilt, pull back the
blanket door, and venture forth.

The breeze plays with my hair as I make my way after an invisible pull toward the creek. On the southern slope of the hill that falls steeply to the stream, not far from the yurt, but out of sight, there is a tiny natural shelf in the hillside. I spread my quilt on the earth, which is still damp from winter rains.

The day is cool, but the slope is sheltered from the wind, and its angle catches the full power of the sun. I lie down, arms outstretched, motionless against the earth.

The earth molds itself to my curves: we fit. The sun reaches deep, through skin to bone, through surface to center. I smell the rich damp warmth of almost spring, see through my fingers and pores, listen with my bones, forget to breathe.

My attention is drawn to a small oak tree, not far from where I lie. Outlined against the clear blue sky, little bits of newborn green are barely visible on the tips of the gray moss-covered branches. Strings of Spanish moss drip toward the earth, dancing now and then in the breeze. A jay lands on a branch near me, cocks his head, and flies away again. The wind rises slightly; the whole tree responds, limbs swaying. Though my little shelf is hidden from the wind, I seem to feel its push against me, too, as I watch the little oak.

I sense the branches moving, feel the creak of winter stiffness, feel new life begin to run through its body as the sun and wind pull and push. I feel the pull on kinky limbs, the sluggishness of parts still half asleep that respond only slowly to the call of the sun. I feel the breeze blow off the tree's winter coat and awaken something inside, deep within the core. And I sense the tree responding, branches swaying, bulky body moving slowly, sluggishly, as it can.

And then I *am* the tree. Another jay alights and I feel its touch as on a distant extremity. I am still here, still flat on the hillside hidden from the wind, but somehow I extend above and beyond and around myself to include the tree, the earth, the rocks, the breeze.

The earth, the rocks, the sky, and I interpenetrate. We are one. I feel a deep, beatific relaxation. The boundaries that I think of as "me" are suddenly no more than illusion. My body's limits are a product of the same surface tension that allows a water bug to skate on top of a pond. Now, as I lie here, the tension is released, the illusion suspended. The varied personalities and centers of energy that make up my place on the hillside merge, and all of life flows into and out of one another. And the many—the wonderful, entertaining, diverse manifestations of life—become gloriously One.

MAY SWENSON

I WILL LIE DOWN

from *To Mix with Time* (1963)

May Swenson (1919–1989) was a keen observer of natural phenomena who won numerous honors for her poetry. She was born and raised in Logan, Utah, by Swedish parents who became American citizens. Her father was a professor at what was then Utah State Agricultural College, from which she graduated. She worked as a reporter for the Salt Lake City *Deseret News* and later moved to New York City, where she worked as an editor for the avant-garde publisher New Directions before devoting herself full-time to writing, with interludes as poet-in-residence at several American and Canadian universities.

I will lie down in autumn
let birds be flying

Swept into a hollow
by the wind
I'll wait for dying

I will lie inert unseen
my hair same-colored
with grass and leaves

Gather me
for the autumn fires
with the withered sheaves

I will sleep face down
in the burnt meadow
not hearing the sound of water
over stones

Trail over me cloud
and shadow
Let snow
hide the whiteness of my bones

Her Pleasures:
The Delight We Take
in Nature

Nature offers us a thousand simple pleasures—
plays of light and color, fragrances in the air, the
sun's warmth on skin and muscle, the audible
rhythm of life's stir and push—for the price of merely pay-
ing attention. What joy! But how unwilling or unable many
of us are to pay this price in an age when manufactured
sources of stimulation and pleasure are everywhere at hand.
For me, enjoying nature's pleasures takes a conscious
choice, a choice to slow down to seed time or rock time, to
still the clamoring ego, to set aside plans and busyness, and
simply to be present in my body, to offer myself up.

The writing in this section sings the praises of nature's
simple pleasures. For many of the authors, the pleasures of
nature are sensory and aesthetic, while for others the plea-
sure assumes an added spiritual dimension. All show us the
possibility of finding happiness, delight, and joy in the natu-
ral world.

PATTIANN ROGERS

ROLLING NAKED IN THE MORNING DEW
from *Splitting and Binding* (1989)

Pattiann Rogers (1940–   ) paints a lush physical world in her poems, tapestries that stun us with the profusion and extravagance of nature while hinting at a divinity that encompasses all. Rogers was born in Joplin, Missouri, and graduated from the University of Missouri (B.A.) and the University of Houston (M.A.). She has taught at the university level and now lives in Castle Rock, Colorado. Her poetry, published in four volumes so far, has received a number of awards.

Out among the wet grasses and wild barley-covered
Meadows, backside, frontside, through the white clover
And feather peabush, over spongy tussocks
And shaggy-mane mushrooms, the abandoned nests
Of larks and bobolinks, face to face
With vole trails, snail niches, jelly
Slug eggs; or in a stone-walled garden, level
With the stemmed bulbs of orange and scarlet tulips,
Cricket carcasses, the bent blossoms of sweet william,
Shoulder over shoulder, leg over leg, clear
To the ferny edge of the goldfish pond—some people
Believe in the rejuvenating powers of this act—naked
As a toad in the forest, belly and hips, thighs
And ankles drenched in the dew-filled gulches
Of oak leaves, in the soft fall beneath yellow birches,
All of the skin exposed directly to the *killy* cry
Of the kingbird, the buzzing of grasshopper sparrows,

Those calls merging with the dawn-red mists
Of crimson steeplebush, entering the bare body then
Not merely through the ears but through the skin
Of every naked person willing every event and
    potentiality
Of a damp transforming dawn to enter.

Lillie Langtry practiced it, when weather permitted,
Lying down naked every morning in the dew,
With all of her beauty believing the single petal
Of her white skin could absorb and assume
That radiating purity of liquid and light.
And I admit to believing myself, without question,
In the magical powers of dew on the cheeks
And breasts of Lillie Langtry believing devotedly
In the magical powers of early morning dew on the skin
Of her body lolling in purple beds of bird's-foot violets,
Pink prairie mimosa. And I believe, without doubt,
In the mystery of the healing energy coming
From that wholehearted belief in the beneficent results
Of the good delights of the naked body rolling
And rolling through all the silked and sun-filled,
Dusky-winged, sheathed and sparkled, looped
And dizzied effluences of each dawn
Of the rolling earth.

Just consider how the mere idea of it alone
Has already caused me to sing and sing
This whole morning long.

ANN ZWINGER

A RINSE IN THE RIVER

from *Run, River, Run* (1975)

Ann Zwinger (1925–   ) has commented that the thread she
finds running through all her books of natural history is "an
expanding sense of home." Born in Muncie, Indiana, and
trained as an art historian at Wellesley (B.A.) and Indiana
University (M.A.), she wrote her first book, *Beyond the Aspen
Grove* (1970), about the natural world at 8,300 feet in the
mountains near her home in Colorado Springs. Her third
book, *Run, River, Run,* from which the following selection
is taken and which won the John Burroughs Medal for na-
ture writing in 1976, recounts her journey down the Green
River of Wyoming, Colorado, and Utah. Later books, illus-
trated like her first books with her own precise and detailed
drawings, have explored the canyonlands of southeastern
Utah, New England rivers, the southern end of Baja Califor-
nia, and the four deserts of the southwestern United States.
A reviewer once noted that Zwinger "derives as much scien-
tific and aesthetic pleasure as possible from whatever agree-
able things serendipity sets in her path."

One of the delights of a river evening, especially after chin-
ning up sandstone and shale ledges and poking around dry,
silty terraces, is a rinse in the river. There is a place below
Turks Head which, at high water, fulfills the requirements
of privacy and a safe place out of the current. The water
temperature in May is hardly tepid, at 62° F., but the air is
warm. There are two table rocks, firm sandstones, upon
which I can stand and safely submerge, letting the water
swirl around me. In water that is so opaque, it is a matter

of some faith to sit down. The current nudges but little in this back eddy, yet it is still easy to feel the erosive power of a big springtime river. The river sounds ear close. Seated eye level with the surface, I feel like an apprentice Lorelei, learning the siren sounds of the river.

The silt wells and fumes, voluminous and soft, just beneath the surface. It is fascinating to discover that by moving a hand just under water I can evoke all kinds of kaleidoscopic patterns. This silt settles out of a container of river water within twenty-four hours, but the remaining water looks like clam juice, colored by finer particles that do not precipitate as quickly in response to gravity. These extremely small particles are colloidal; since they have more surface compared to their volume, and so a specific gravity less than that of water, they remain in suspension almost indefinitely, settling out only if they cluster together to form larger particles. Gravels in a stream may fall out in less than a second when the velocity drops; colloidal particles may remain for decades.

The Green River, at this time of moderately heavy runoff, is probably carrying more than half its silt load for the year. The average load held in suspension by the river is estimated at 19 tons a year, plus 2.5 million tons dissolved. The silt content near the mouth of the Green, by volume, was once estimated at 0.5 percent; it seems a minute amount, but evenly distributed by the current it forms an effective screen, creating the year-round turbidity in the river from the Gates of Lodore south.

The sandpaper surface of the rock, unslicked by algae, provides a sense of stability in a flowing, swirling, moving world. How to explain the pure delight of being here— some of it no doubt stems from the fact that, after a day of unrelenting sunshine, almost any kind of ablution feels welcome. But there is an ineffable sybaritic pleasure beyond the necessity. The cool slide of water slips down the back of my neck, down my arm, drips off my elbow, picks patterns on the river's surface. The water that tugs around my ankles is pure hedonistic enticement, issuing a reminder of downriver delights in a branch that bobs by, on its way to other appointments.

After seeing ruins all day, I am extremely conscious of those who came here before me. So too, on a warm spring evening, a thousand years ago, someone must have stood like this, soothing calloused feet, cactus-scratched legs. I feel no time interval, no difference in flesh between who stood here then and who stands here now. The same need exists for the essentials of food and shelter, the same need to communicate and to put down symbols for someone else to see, and, so I cannot help but believe, the same response to cool water and warm sun and heated rock and sandstone on bare feet.

The last rays of the sun keep it warm enough to air dry. The sun hangs for a moment above the cliff. As it disappears behind the rim, the air cools. And yet it is not cold; maybe time to robe and leave, but not yet, not cold yet. As long as I can stand, ankle deep, without civilization, without defense, going back to self, as long as there is yet enough warmth in the air to respect needful body temperature, so long as possible I stand here, submerged physically only to the ankles, psychologically to the base of being.

CLARE LEIGHTON

THE MAGIC OF THE FLATS
from *Where Land Meets Sea* (1954)

Clare Leighton (1898–1989), an artist and writer of distinction, once wrote, "My true happiness lay always among the people of the earth." Born in London, the daughter of two writers, she came to the United States in 1939, living in the South for a short while and then moving to Cape Cod just before she became a citizen in 1945. In a prolific and multi-faceted career, she became known as one of America's finest wood engravers, with her work represented in the permanent collections of the British Museum, the Metropolitan Museum of Art, and Boston's Museum of Fine Arts, among others; in addition, her stained glass windows grace several New England churches. She also wrote and illustrated fourteen books, ranging from juvenile and art technique books to essays, garden and travel writing, and a biography of her mother; and she illustrated numerous books by others. *Where Land Meets Sea: The Tide Line of Cape Cod* is her much-praised book of personal impressions of her deeply beloved Cape Cod home. Just how deep is her response to the beauty of Cape Cod can be felt in the following excerpt.

The best time to learn the world of the flats comes at the full of the moon. Then, for a few days in the Bay of Cape Cod, the big tides run high—nearly twelve feet at their peak—and, with the correspondingly extreme low, the water retreats far into the bay, exposing land that is never seen over the rest of the month.

This dramatically low tide occurs early in the day, when

the morning light is clean and clear, giving a pearly beauty to the world.

The mud flats are forsaken and desolate, frequented only by a scattering of quahog rakers. During the summer, when the Cape is filled with vacationists, you seldom find any of the visitors out there. To them the sea is something in which to swim. When it withdraws from them at low tide, they wait until the water returns. And this is fortunate, for some of the special quality of the flats lies in the eerie solitude.

The flats hold a subtle, rather than an obvious, beauty. It is the beauty of uncountable gradations of tone and hue, of the sheen and polish of exposed wet sand at low water. It is a world of reflections upon the wet sand from the slanted light of the morning sky.

There is a sense of vastness on such a morning. This stretch of mud and sand, merging imperceptibly in the far distance into remote water, seems to extend into eternity. In such a light, time and space become intermingled; we can no longer distinguish one from the other.

But it is not only the muted, opalescent coloring of the wet sand, shimmering and glinting upon the bed of the withdrawn ocean, that holds such magic. There are uncountable variations of form here, too. For this is the whole earth in microcosm, with Lilliputian valleys and hills, gorges and plateaux. It might be said to be a child's world, everything within the grasp of the hand, the range of the eye. To the right, past Otto the Finn's stranded dory, sucked deep into the sand and half-filled with water, the rope of its anchor lying curved and loose, over there the ocean bed must be definitely deeper, for always, I notice, however low the tide, a tiny river flows swiftly around the cliffs of the sand. Against the diminutive setting it might be a Ganges or a Mississippi. Wade in this miniature river and the water is cool and clear, in contrast to the warm mud of the flats.

The flats are threaded with these tiny rivulets following the course of the channels they have eroded. They are evident only at the moment of low tide. As I wade in them, though, I am reminded of the sudden, abruptly cool currents in the water of the bay when I swim at high tide; they must surely be caused by these same cold channels. The rivulets flow in narrow streams, twisting around the raised sand. Suddenly they broaden into mighty lakes, full fifteen feet wide.

And then we walk out on these flats, so muddy that the feet sink deep beneath the surface, into soft black ooze. Seen from a distance they appear devoid of all life, and all interest. But what do we discover? This is no dead world of mud. It is a living, agitated world, filled with pulsating rhythm and movement. Scarcely anything here lies motionless, except the long-vacated, sharp-edged shells of oysters and clams, clumped upright in the wet sand and looking as prehistoric as Stonehenge.

Stand still in your path across this mud. The flats appear to move. They heave. They vibrate. And then you hear a strange sound against the silence around. It is a sucking sound, and for a moment I wonder what it is that I am reminded of. Suddenly I am removed from this watery world. I am tossed backwards in time, far inland, upon the chalk downs of southern England in the spring of the year. I am watching with the bearded old shepherd as the newborn lambs nuzzle their dams. Further back in time and I am a child, crouching in the kennels in the back garden as the latest litter of puppies suckles the mother dog. It is a warm sound, and strange that it should come from this cold, watery setting. Suck, suck, suck, goes the sound. Suck, suck, suck.

Puzzled, I raise my eyes to the flats. Thin jets of water spout before me, like tiny fountains. The air sparkles as the sun catches them, tossing into them the colors of the rainbow. Sometimes they are flung far, and this spectrum-tinted water, bewitched by the early morning sun, describes great arcs across the mud.

What is it that causes this crazy happening?

It is the scallops. They lie here, countless in their numbers.

At this moment, when I am confused, still, by sight and sound and strange recollections from the past, the shellfish warden approaches me across the flats.

"A good scallop year," he informs me blandly, not knowing how he has smashed my fantasies. "Never seen so many scallops—not for years I haven't. Looks to me as if we'll have a real bumper season, come October and they've grown."

And then I see what is happening. It is a world of *Alice in Wonderland,* with the Walrus and the Carpenter and the Oysters. The uncountable scallops assume a fairy-tale quality, till you would feel little surprise were they suddenly to develop legs and feet and should walk and talk. They open and shut their shells, like a multitude of castanets, like a gigantic audience applauding the beauty of this earth on such a morning in late June.

But, too, they have a rude aspect to their behavior; they spit, as they open, in the manner of vulgar old men. They yawn, exposing that mighty muscle which is the part that we eat. Along the rim of each beautiful fluted shell they boast a row of brilliant turquoise-blue, green-edged, jewel-like eyes. Give them the slightest kick as they lie here in the mud at low tide, and they will retaliate by spitting you in the face. They imagine they are beneath the water, still, opening and shutting to breathe and propel themselves along the bay.

The scallop is never static. It is far more active and flexible than the heavy, uncouth quahog that noses its way downward into the mud and sand of the water bed. It has an adventurous spirit. The entire bay is its universe. And it is as beautiful of shape as it is mobile of movement, a delicate, graceful creature, the fluted shells subtly varied in color. And with this beauty it carries, too, the sense of history in its background; for did not the pilgrims of the Middle Ages adopt it as their symbol of pilgrimage?

Sometimes this sucking sound changes to a wheezing, squeezing noise, as the scallops force out the water before them, the better to propel themselves along. They do not even await disturbance, as does the razor fish, but act independently of all outside happenings.

Nothing is still here upon the flats, except the discarded clam and oyster shells; and even these ancient creatures are peopled with tiny sea snails perching on top of them, like Kings of the Castle in the game of a child. Over the floor of the sea swarm the hermit crabs, so minute and so active, trotting around on nervous little feet, or retiring into their shells to get sucked down deep into the bed of the wet sand. They creep among the colorless slabs of jellyfish, and the stranded shells, dull of hue against the rich scarlet of the frilly edged sponge that encrusts the oysters and clams.

And then, in a sudden little dip of sand, I see two crabs. They face each other caressingly. The larger one is deep dark brown, with yellow markings; he has beautiful sage-green legs. He faces the smaller, softer-toned crab, and, as I look at them, casting aside any scientific explanation, I like to feel they must be lovers, for they lie so close and so happily entwined. Mischievously I touch the big one with my foot, and he stirs and stretches. But then, within a short moment, he beds down once more, easing himself into the soft cushion of the sand, like a dog settling to sleep. I leave them in their embrace, upon a cold wet nuptial couch.

This morning the shallow water of the channels seems filled with crabs. Never have I come across so many. They wander around my feet, giving me occasional vicious little nips; there are big drab-colored fellows, a few prehistoric-looking horseshoe crabs, dwarfing the others by their enormous size, but chiefly the smaller, gayer-colored creatures, cavorting along upon the bed of the water with tremendous speed. . . .

The world of the flats has a seasonal element, every bit as much as though it were the vegetable world of dry land, with the blooming and ripening of fruit or grain. The "set" of the oyster takes place in the spring or the early summer, and the little scallops in the bay reach maturity only in October. June and July pass, and I wander over the flats at the end of August. The morning is foggy. I seem to move in space like a figure in an early Chinese landscape. I have lost all sense of dimension or element. It is already daylight, but the fog makes me recollect a walk I took many years before, at dusk, when the fog rolled in with the suddenness of the dropping of the curtain at the end of a play. That evening, as I stood there upon the flats, well out into the bay, I felt myself to be living upon an uninhabited planet. It was as I would imagine it to be were I to wander upon the surface of the moon. My feet sank deep into mud, plunging to the calves of my legs. My mind knew that this was black mud, though my eyes could see little of the color. I waded into channels of water, to the knees, water filled with unperceived crabs. And suddenly, as I stood there, knee-deep in water and mud, I felt panic. It was an unashamed, animal panic, the terror of complete loss of direction, and aloneness in space, with the tide turning and the sea advancing, and my not knowing exactly where to walk. In this eerie, scarifying world, formless and lightless, extending into fog, blurred by fog and darkening dusk, I stood still. I searched the sky, but above me was nothing but fog.

"Stupid," I found myself saying. "Nobody in their senses would have done such an idiotic thing. Why, perhaps I'll have to stay here till the incoming tide, with the water lapping higher and higher up my legs and thighs. That will show me where I am. Then I can walk away from it. . . . But suppose I go in circles, as people are supposed to do when they are lost?"

In a queer way I found something exciting in the sense of utter loneliness. I knew that if I were to manage to reach land, I would have experienced something that was worth this panic and fear.

But things always seem to turn out right in the end. At the moment when panic was beginning to envelop me, I stood completely still and very slowly turned myself around. There must have been a sudden break in the thickening fog, for I saw a light in the distance before me. I walked towards it, my eyes fixed upon it, regardless of whether I trod upon crab or sharp-edged oyster shell, or sank deep to my knees in mud. I shall never know how long it took me to reach shore, for I had forsaken the habitual world of dry land, with its sense of time. But I fastened my eyes to that solitary light, till finally I found my feet were treading safely on sand.

All this has come back to me, as I wander across the flats on a foggy morning in late August. But it is a thin fog today, simplifying the curves of Egg Island, dark gray against the silver water. At any moment it will lift, disclosing the form of the flats and the patterning of the cool, swift-running channels. I cross Egg Island, to the far edge, past the green-tinged part that is covered with tattered sea lettuce, and the desolate, lifeless mud gives way to the strangest accumulation of razor fish shells. My feet crunch upon them, in their thousands, mud-obscured, lying there at all angles. And I wonder why it should be that they are here at this particular spot, and nowhere else.

Then, as I look across at this flatness of mud, still infused with a sense of mystery in the silver and opal light, I see larger objects, humped upon the flatness. I go nearer to them to find out what they are. They are something I have never seen before. Each of the humped shapes, looking so large against the absolute flatness around, is a conch, or big winkle or whelk. In themselves they are nothing new; often have I collected the discarded shells along the shore, and know and love the rich whorled shapes and the delicate coloring. But these, here today, are no discarded conchs. They are alive and functioning at this moment in the laying of their eggs.

It is a beautiful, very moving sight, the conch as it spins its necklace of egg discs, fully fifteen inches in length. In some inexplicable fashion it holds a timeless, ageless quality of tender maternity. Against the cold, dead color of mud it glows with a warm pink; the egg discs are flesh color as they emerge from the obtruded mantle of the conch, and before they turn to pale biscuit by exposure to the air they are like the deep pink cream of a baby's skin.

The dignified, majestic mounds of conch shell litter the flats. I tug at one of the egg necklaces, but it is rooted deep into the mud like an umbilical cord. The chain of egg discs is secured along one side as with a strong spun tape, like the binding edge of a ruffle. The necklace twists and curls, from its anchorage in the mud, to the great ugly mass of fleshy folds of the mantle obtruding from the pearly lilac and pinks of the beautiful shell. Upon the back of the ugly flesh, and ready to clamp down when the soft mantle has fulfilled its purpose and shrinks back into its shell, the conch carries the hard, flat lid of its operculum.

The scene before me, here in the cold dark mud, holds all the ambivalent ugliness and beauty of procreation. Out from those clammy-looking folds of flesh emerge the beautiful, lengthy chains of egg discs. Over to the right, beyond the scarlet sponges, I see some necklaces that have been expelled by the conch. They will float here, on the incoming tide, secured into the mud, until the eggs have matured.

Transported by the beauty of what I have seen, I return home from the flats. At my feet I see a tiny baby sturgeon, a mere six inches long, its pointed snout already well defined. But my mind is too full just now. I can scarcely notice the beauty of the gulls, circling the mud, shrieking and mewing in their flight. Before my feet, as I walk across the sand by the fringe of the eel grass, regiments of minute fiddler crabs hurry into the grasses, crackling as they go. The muddy sand is punctured with the holes into which they disappear. And there, further along, close up against these grasses, stand the packed armies of mussels, fastened to the mud and grass by their dark threads.

Later on, when the impact of this morning's discoveries has lessened, I shall remember other flats I have known at low tide, each one holding its own especial character. I shall think of the stretching beach of Thumpertown, in Eastham, where the sand is clean and the water clear, and there is none of the mud of my own Wellfleet bay. The tide recedes at Thumpertown in parallel layers, so that, looking from the level of the dunes above the beach, there is a pattern of horizontal bands of pale, warm fawn and deep lilac where the drying sand meets the shallow water. You must wade over a quarter of a mile across these alternating bands of water and sand before you can reach the solid water of the bay. Standing in the rippling stretches of water, with the shifting shapes of the bright gold of sun-glint on its surface, you look down upon red-brown seaweed, waving beneath the wind-stirred sea like swaying ferns.

It is rich, varied, and beautiful, this world of the flats, this low-tide country of sand and mud. It may lack the dramatic violence of the Atlantic, but if you look closely at it, and stand still and listen, it will disclose immeasurable magic.

THEODORA STANWELL-FLETCHER

CHRISTMAS IN DRIFTWOOD VALLEY

from *Driftwood Valley* (1946)

Theodora Stanwell-Fletcher (1906–   ) and her husband, John, both had "a taste for the loneliness and realism of out-of-the-way places and peoples." With her naturalist father and fellow college students, she had studied natural science in such locations as New Zealand, the East Indies, Asia, the British Isles, and sub-Arctic Canada. From August 1937 to January 1939 and again from February to September 1941, she and her husband lived in Driftwood Valley, an unexplored wilderness in north-central British Columbia, many miles from neighbors, towns, or roads, and without communication with the outside world, collecting flora and fauna for the British Columbia Provincial Museum at Victoria. Theodora's journal of their wilderness experiences, from which the following selection is taken, won the John Burroughs Medal for nature writing in 1947.

Theodora was born in Pennsylvania and earned degrees in literature and animal ecology from Mount Holyoke (B.A.) and Cornell University (M.S. and Ph.D.). Besides *Driftwood Valley,* she wrote *The Tundra World* (1952) and *Clear Lands and Icy Seas* (1958), as well as numerous scientific and natural history articles. She now lives in the old family home in rural Pennsylvania and continues her association with conservation and humanitarian enterprises.

Christmas Day

Last night when we went to bed the windows on the inside were covered with frost an inch thick; the logs in the walls, and the shakes in the roof, cracked like gunshots, as they were split by the cold; and out on the lake the ice kept up an almost steady booming, interspersed with the horrid ripping and tearing that always makes my spine tingle. During the night I was waked repeatedly by such terrific cracks in the logs that I thought the cabin was coming down on our heads. When the temperature is falling, we expect a drop of 15 or 25 degrees during the night, beginning at sunset, but last night it broke all records.

This morning I was the first one out of bed. These days I can hardly wait to get up. Whether this is because I'm always hungry, or because the night is so long, I don't know, but it is refreshing to be able to jeer at J. as he lies lazily in bed with his morning smoke. Although when we went to bed last night we piled up the stove with slow-burning green wood, this morning the fire was practically out. It was still dark outside; dawn had not yet begun although it was long past eight. The windows were so densely frosted that it seemed as if daylight, even if it were there, could never penetrate the cabin. I lit the lamp, then carefully laid the pile of shavings, as always unfailingly prepared by J. the evening before, in the front of the stove and applied a match. After which I delicately laid on more shavings and then larger and larger sticks. Everything was ice cold and I was careful not touch any metal with bare hands, having learned from bitter experience that skin, especially moist skin, freezes fast and is sometimes peeled right off at the slightest contact with very cold metal. Still clad in bathrobe and slippers, I went to scrape away the frost and read the thermometer outside. I realized then that, although I didn't feel chilled, I could hardly move my arms.

"I'll just see what the temperature is *inside* first," I thought, and went to peer at the thermometer hanging above our dining table. It read 25 below. Gosh! That couldn't be right! How could we sleep like that, how could I be wandering around with only a wrapper on? I *must* see what it was outside!

I couldn't even find the mercury. It dawned on me, after a time, that it had gone its limit and jammed at 50 below. My exclamations roused J. and we were so busy arguing over the thermometer that we forgot to say "Merry Christmas." I was convinced that if the mercury could have gone beyond 50 it would have read at least 60 below. J. said it was not much colder than 50; that he could tell from past experience in the Arctic just how many degrees the temperature drops when it gets beyond 45 below. For one thing, if it is 55 or more below, when hot water is poured out of a window, it freezes solid before it reaches the snow level. I could hardly wait until we had hot water to try this experiment. Sure enough—when, later, I poured a stream from the teakettle onto the snow outside, the water steamed and twisted into threads, but did not turn actually solid till it reached the ground. We must put out our unused thermometer whose scale goes to 60 below.

By the time dawn was coming we had scraped two peepholes in the frost on the panes; and we stood quiet to watch the winter sunrise. The radiant peaks of the Drift-woods, cut like white icing into pinnacles and rims against the apple-green sky, were brushed with pink, that, even as we watched, spread down and down and turned to gold. Rays of the rising sun, coming between the pointed firs of the east shore, stretched straight across the white lake, and as they touched it huge crystals, formed by the intense cold, burst into sparkling, scintillating light. The snow-bowed trees of the south and west shores were hung with diamonds; and finally the willows, around our cabin, were decked with jewels as large as robins' eggs that flashed red and green and blue. No Christmas trees decorated by human hands were ever so exquisite as the frosted trees of this northern forest. The sky turned to deep, deep blue, and the white world burst into dazzling, dancing colors as the sun topped the forest. The dippers, undismayed by a cold that froze dumb all other living things, broke into their joyous tinkling melody by the open water patch below the bank. And our first Christmas Day in the wilderness was upon us.

After a breakfast of canned grapefruit which we had been saving especially, and pancakes with the last of our syrup, also preserved scrupulously for Christmas, we did our usual chores. I cleaned the cabin and began a round of baking. In addition to bannock, which I bake daily either in the drum oven or in an open frypan on top of the stove, I made tarts of strawberry jam and a chocolate cake. As these favorite articles of diet make inroads on a meager supply of Crisco, jam, and sugar we have them only for very special celebrations.

When I went outside to scatter crumbs for our furred and feathered friends, the jays were almost too stiff to move. Instead of flying down to snatch the food before it left my hand, they sat on the spruce branches, their feathers so fluffed up that I could hardly distinguish head from tail. Sometimes they moved near the smoke from our stovepipe, which was giving forth some warmth. The chickadees, tiny as they are, though also tremendously puffed out, were slightly more active than the jays.

Why are some animals in this country so much better equipped for cold than others? There are the dippers, for example, whose nerves and organs are, seemingly, completely unaffected by an almost arctic temperature. Twice, during this month, we've watched a pair performing the act of coition on a snowbank.

Toward noon the temperature moderated enough for us to enjoy a tramp. That is, it had gone up from 50, or whatever below it was, to 36 below. Our snowshoes tossed up clouds of crystals. Young trees which, in autumn, had reached above our heads had been completely covered with fresh snow, so that they were transformed into great mounds and small hills. Wherever we looked our eyes were dimmed by the twinkling brilliants scattered before us. The azure of the sky above, the unsullied whiteness below, the mountains and the woods, the intense pureness of the air, were exhilarating beyond imagining. And there was not a sound or a motion, anywhere, to distract our senses of sight and feeling.

Soon after noon the temperature began dropping again, fast. Our faces, which we rubbed constantly with wool mitts, began to show a tendency toward frostbite, and J.'s right big toe, once badly frozen in arctic tundras, was starting to pain severely. So we turned homeward.

As daylight faded, the rays of the sinking sun tinted the snow with red and lavender. The mountains grew purple and then came that period which, if I could make a choice of the wonders of all the twenty-four hours of a winter's day, seems the most wonderful of all. It is that moment of white twilight which comes on a particularly clear afternoon, after the last colors of sunset fade and just before the first stars shine out. I don't suppose its like can be seen anywhere except in the snowbound, ice-cold arctic places. Everything in the universe becomes a luminous white. Even the dark trees of the forest, and the sky overhead, are completely colorless. It is the ultimate perfection of purity and peace. But even as one looks and wonders, the white sky takes on a faint pale green, there are the stars, and then the great winter's night is upon one.

We had our Christmas dinner at five: dehydrated potatoes and onions and a bit of moose steak, especially saved and tendered, baked in a pan with stuffing. For dessert there were the jam tarts and chocolate cake. With these vanished the last vestiges of Christmas, the things which made it a little different from our other days.

Have we greatly missed the things that make Christmas Day in civilization? Other loved human beings, Christmas carols, wonderful food? I suppose so, but I think that this lack is more than made up for by the deep contentment of our healthy minds and bodies, by our closeness to and awareness of the earth, and of each other.

DIANE ACKERMAN

VISUAL OPIUM

from *A Natural History of the Senses* (1990)

Diane Ackerman (1948–   ) describes herself as "an earth-ecstatic and a poet." This enormously energetic woman has made expeditions from her home in Ithaca, New York, to the far reaches of the earth to write articles about penguins, bats, whales, and crocodilians for *The New Yorker;* to a New Mexico cattle ranch to learn to cowboy, an adventure chronicled in her book *Twilight of the Tenderfoot* (1980); and to various airports to learn to fly a small plane, as recounted in her book *On Extended Wings* (1985). Born in Waukegan, Illinois, Ackerman was educated at Pennsylvania State University (B.A.) and Cornell (M.F.A., M.A., Ph.D.). In addition to prose, she has written three collections of poetry and a play. Her latest book, *A Natural History of the Senses,* is an exploration of the origin and evolution of the senses, and of their uses in knowing this amazing world of ours.

Some years ago, when I had taken a job directing a writing program in St. Louis, Missouri, I often used color as a tonic. Regardless of the oasis-eyed student in my office, or the last itchlike whim of the secretary, or the fumings of the hysterically anxious chairman, I tried to arrive home at around the same time every evening, to watch the sunset from the large picture window in my living room, which overlooked Forest Park. Each night the sunset surged with purple pampas-grass plumes, and shot fuchsia rockets into the pink sky, then deepened through folded layers of peacock green to all the blues of India and a black across which clouds sometimes churned like alabaster dolls. The visual opium of the sunset was what I craved. Once, while eating a shrimp-and-avocado salad at the self-consciously stately faculty club, I found myself restless for the day to be over and all such tomblike encounters to pale, so I could drag my dinette-set chair up to the window and purge my senses with the pure color and visual tumult of the sunset. This happened again the next day in the coffee room, where I stood chatting with one of the literary historians, who always wore the drabbest camouflage colors and continued talking long after a point had been made. I set my facial muscles at "listening raptly," as she chuntered on about her specialty, the Caroline poets, but in my mind the sun was just beginning to set, a green glow was giving way to streaks of sulfur yellow, and a purple cloud train had begun staggering across the horizon. I was paying too much rent for my apartment, she explained. True, the apartment overlooked the park's changing seasons, had a picture window that captured the sunset every night, and was only a block away from a charming cobblestone area full of art galleries, antique stores, and ethnic restaurants. But this was all an ex*pense,* as she put it, with heavy emphasis on the second syllable, not just financial expense, but a too-extravagant experience of life. That evening, as I watched the sunset's pinwheels of apricot and mauve slowly explode into red ribbons, I thought: *The sensory misers will inherit the earth, but first they will make it not worth living on.*

When you consider something like death, after which (there being no news flash to the contrary) we may well go out like a candle flame, then it probably doesn't matter if we try too hard, are awkward sometimes, care for one another too deeply, are excessively curious about nature, are too open to experience, enjoy a nonstop expense of the senses in an effort to know life intimately and lovingly. It probably doesn't matter if, while trying to be modest and eager watchers of life's many spectacles, we sometimes look clumsy or get dirty or ask stupid questions or reveal our ignorance or say the wrong thing or light up with wonder like the children we all are. It probably doesn't matter if a passerby sees us dipping a finger into the moist pouches of dozens of lady's slippers to find out what bugs tend to fall into them, and thinks us a bit eccentric. Or a neighbor, fetching her mail, sees us standing in the cold with our own letters in one hand and a seismically red autumn leaf in the other, its color hitting our senses like a blow from a stun gun, as we stand with a huge grin, too paralyzed by the intricately veined gaudiness of the leaf to move.

EMILY DICKINSON

WHY?

from *Poems by Emily Dickinson* (1890)

Emily Dickinson (1830–1886) proclaimed her intoxication
with nature's pleasures in a poem containing the well-known
lines "Inebriate of air am I, / And debauchee of dew."
Although she spent most of her fifty-five years within the
confines of her family's house and garden in Amherst, Mas-
sachusetts, her poems make it clear that what her life lacked
in breadth it made up for in depth. Her nature poems range
from the ecstatic to the whimsical but clearly show a deep
and abiding pleasure in nature. Moreover, this eccentric
poet who refused to become a Christian seemed to find a key
element of her personal theology in nature's wonders, as
indicated in her slight poem "Why?"

The murmur of a bee
A witchcraft yieldeth me.
If any ask me why,
'T were easier to die
Than tell.

The red upon the hill
Taketh away my will;
If anybody sneer,
Take care, for God is here,
That's all.

The breaking of the day
Addeth to my degree;

If any ask me how,
Artist, who drew me so,
Must tell!

SUSAN FENIMORE COOPER

AFTERNOON IN THE WOODS

from *Rural Hours* (1887)

Susan Fenimore Cooper (1813–1894), an older contempo-
rary of Dickinson's, also saw the work of God (albeit a
conventional Christian one) in nature's beauty. She lived
most of her life in Cooperstown, New York, which was
founded by her grandfather. Never married, she devoted
her energies to humanitarian concerns in her community, to
serving as copyist for her father (the novelist James Feni-
more Cooper), and to producing a modest literary output,
including a journal of the natural events of the four seasons
in the countryside around her home (*Rural Hours,* dedicated
to her father), fiction (a novel, *Elinor Wyllys; or, The Young
Folk at Longbridge,* 1846, published under the pseudonym
Anabel Penfeather), articles, biographical sketches (*Worthy
Women of Our First Century,* 1877), and prefaces for her
father's works.

Rural Hours was first published in 1850, a year after
Thoreau's *A Week on the Concord and Merrimack Rivers* (four
years before *Walden*), and enjoyed much greater success at
the time. It was in print for nearly four decades, with Cooper
producing a revised version in 1887. Thoreau knew
Cooper's book, or at least had read parts of it, for in his

journal entry of October 8, 1852, he records a fact about loons gleaned from a newspaper and notes that "Miss Cooper has said the same." Her detailed and lengthy recounting of events and observations in the vicinity of Otsego Lake shows that Cooper was a great walker, undaunted by stormy or cold weather, knew her flora and fauna, and was a careful student of natural history. Her belief in the infinite endurance of the forests seems quaint now that we can foresee the clear-cutting of the last old-growth forest in the United States.

Saturday, [July] 28th. —Passed the afternoon in the woods. What a noble gift to man are the forests! What a debt of gratitude and admiration we owe for their utility and their beauty!

How pleasantly the shadows of the wood fall upon our heads, when we turn from the glitter and turmoil of the world of man! The winds of heaven seem to linger amid these balmy branches, and the sunshine falls like a blessing upon the green leaves; the wild breath of the forest, fragrant with bark and berry, fans the brow with grateful freshness; and the beautiful wood-light, neither garish nor gloomy, full of calm and peaceful influences, sheds repose over the spirit. The view is limited, and the objects about us are uniform in character; yet within the bosom of the woods the mind readily lays aside its daily littleness, and opens to higher thoughts, in silent consciousness that it stands alone with the works of God. The humble moss beneath our feet, the sweet flowers, the varied shrubs, the great trees, and the sky gleaming above in sacred blue, are each the handiwork of God. They were all called into being by the will of the Creator, as we now behold them, full of wisdom and goodness. Every object here has a deeper merit than our wonder can fathom; each has a beauty beyond our full perception; the dullest insect crawling about these roots lives by the power of the Almighty; and the discolored shreds of last year's leaves wither away upon the lowly herbs in a blessing of fertility. But it is the great trees, stretching their arms above us in a thousand forms of grace and strength, it is more especially the trees which fill the mind with wonder and praise.

Of the infinite variety of fruits which spring from the bosom of the earth, the trees of the wood are the greatest in dignity. Of all the works of the creation which know the changes of life and death, the trees of the forest have the longest existence. Of all the objects which crown the gray earth, the woods preserve unchanged, throughout the greatest reach of time, their native character: the works of man are ever varying their aspect; his towns and his fields alike reflect the unstable opinions, the fickle wills and fancies of each passing generation; but the forests on his borders remain to-day the same [as] they were ages of years since. Old as the everlasting hills, during thousands of seasons they have put forth and laid down their verdure in calm obedience to the decree which first bade them cover the ruins of the Deluge.

But, although the forests are great and old, yet the ancient trees within their bounds must each bend individually beneath the doom of every earthly existence; they have their allotted period when the mosses of Time gather upon their branches; when, touched by decay, they break and crumble to dust. Like man, they are decked in living beauty; like man, they fall a prey to death; and while we admire their duration, so far beyond our own brief years, we also acknowledge that especial interest which can only belong to the graces of life and to the desolation of death. We raise our eyes, and we see collected in one company vigorous trunks, the oak, the ash, the pine, firm in the strength of maturity; by their side stand a young group, elm, and birch, and maple, their supple branches playing in the breezes, gay and fresh as youth itself; and yonder, rising in unheeded gloom, we behold a skeleton trunk, an old fir, every branch broken, every leaf fallen,—dull, still, sad, like the finger of Death.

It is the peculiar nature of the forest, that life and death may ever be found within its bounds, in immediate presence of each other; both with ceaseless, noiseless, advances, aiming at the mastery; and if the influences of the first be most general, those of the last are the most striking. Spring, with all her wealth of life and joy, finds within the forest many a tree unconscious of her approach; a thousand young plants springing up about the fallen trunk, the shaggy roots, seek to soften the gloomy wreck with a semblance of the verdure it bore of old; but ere they have thrown their fresh and graceful wreaths over the mouldering wood, half their own tribe wither and die with the year. We owe to this perpetual presence of death an impression, calm, solemn, almost religious in character, a chastening influence, beyond what we find in the open fields. But this subdued spirit is far from gloomy or oppressive, since it never fails to be relieved by the cheerful animation of living beauty. Sweet flowers grow beside the fallen trees, among the shattered branches, the season through; and the freedom of the woods, the unchecked growth, the careless position of every tree, are favorable to a thousand wild beauties, and fantastic forms, opening to the mind a play of fancy which is in itself cheering and enlivening, like the bright sunbeams which checker with golden light the shadowy groves. That character of rich variety also, stamped on all the works of the creation, is developed in the forest in clear and noble forms; we are told that in the field we shall not find two blades of grass exactly alike, that in the garden we shall not gather two flowers precisely similar, but in those cases the lines are minute, and we do not seize the truth at once; in the woods, however, the same fact stands recorded in bolder lines; we cannot fail to mark this great variety of detail among the trees; we see it in their trunks, their branches, their foliage; in the rude knots, the gnarled roots; in the mosses and lichens which feed upon their bark; in their forms, their coloring, their shadows. And within all this luxuriance of varied beauty, there dwells a sweet quiet, a noble harmony, a calm repose, which we seek in vain elsewhere, in so full a measure.

CELIA LAIGHTON THAXTER

CHILDHOOD ON WHITE ISLAND

from *Among the Isles of Shoals* (1873)

Celia Laighton Thaxter (1835–1894), another contemporary of Cooper's and Dickinson's, was well known for her serious poetry in nineteenth-century literary circles but is chiefly remembered today for her gem of gardening writing, *An Island Garden* (1894). She was born in Portsmouth, New Hampshire, and grew up on the Isles of Shoals, a group of rocky islands nine miles off the New Hampshire coast. Her father became the lighthouse keeper on tiny White Island when she was five, and for many years Celia, her two brothers, and her mother and father were the only human inhabitants of the island. "To the heart of Nature one must needs be drawn in such a life; and very soon I learned how richly she repays in deep refreshment the reverent love of her worshipper," wrote Celia in the selection reprinted here from *Among the Isles of Shoals,* an engaging collection of essays describing the geography, natural history, and flora and fauna of her island home.

In 1848 the family moved to Appledore, the largest of the Isles of Shoals, where Thomas Laighton built a summer resort that began attracting writers and artists like Nathaniel Hawthorne, Henry Thoreau, Ralph Waldo Emerson, Sarah Orne Jewett, and Childe Hassam. At sixteen, Celia married her tutor. She bore three sons, and settled with her husband and children in Newtonville, Massachusetts, but she returned to Appledore every summer to help run the hotel, and she and her husband eventually began to live more and more apart. In the 1860s Celia established a literary salon at the resort. Finally she lived alone in a cottage there, and cultivated a small but colorful and richly imaginative garden, the topic of her gardening book. She was also involved in bird conservation: in the first issue of the original *Audubon Magazine* (1887), she published an influential essay entitled "Woman's Heartlessness," an impassioned attack on women who wore bird plumage on their hats, later reprinted as a pamphlet by the Pennsylvania Audubon Society. After her death, her cottage burned and her island garden went to weeds, but Cornell University now has an outpost on Appledore and has restored the garden and opened it to the public.

I well remember my first sight of White Island, where we took up our abode on leaving the mainland. I was scarcely five years old; but from the upper windows of our dwelling in Portsmouth, I had been shown the clustered masts of ships lying at the wharves along the Piscataqua River, faintly outlined against the sky, and, baby as I was, even then I was drawn, with a vague longing, seaward. How delightful was that long, first sail to the Isles of Shoals! How pleasant the unaccustomed sound of the incessant ripple against the boat-side, the sight of the wide water and limitless sky, the warmth of the broad sunshine that made us blink like young sandpipers as we sat in triumph, perched among the household goods with which the little craft was laden! It was at sunset in autumn that we were set ashore on that loneliest, lovely rock, where the lighthouse looked down on us like some tall, black-capped giant, and filled me with awe and wonder. At its base a few goats were grouped on the rock, standing out dark against the red sky as I looked up at them. The stars were beginning to twinkle; the wind blew cold, charged with the sea's sweetness; the sound of many waters half bewildered me. Some one began to light the lamps in the tower. Rich red and golden, they swung round in mid-air; everything was strange and fascinating and new.

We entered the quaint little old stone cottage that was for six years our home. How curious it seemed, with its low, whitewashed ceiling and deep window-seats, showing the great thickness of the walls made to withstand the breakers, with whose force we soon grew acquainted! A blissful home the little house became to the children who entered it that quiet evening and slept for the first time lulled by the murmur of the encircling sea. I do not think a happier triad ever existed than we were, living in that profound isolation. It takes so little to make a healthy child happy; and we never wearied of our few resources. True, the winters seemed as long as a whole year to our little minds, but they were pleasant, nevertheless. Into the deep window-seats we climbed, and with pennies (for which we had no other use) made round holes in the thick frost, breathing on them till they were warm, and peeped out at the bright, fierce, windy weather, watching the vessels scudding over the intensely dark blue sea, all "feather-white" where the short waves broke hissing in the cold, and the sea-fowl soaring aloft or tossing on the water. . . .

We waited for the spring with an eager longing; the advent of the growing grass, the birds and flowers and insect life, the soft skies and softer winds, the everlasting beauty of the thousand tender tints that clothed the world,—these things brought us unspeakable bliss. To the heart of Nature one must needs be drawn in such a life; and very soon I learned how richly she repays in deep refreshment the reverent love of her worshipper. With the first warm days we built our little mountains of wet gravel on the beach, and danced after the sandpipers at the edge of the foam, shouted to the gossiping kittiwakes that fluttered above, or watched the pranks of the burgomaster gull, or cried to the crying loons. The gannet's long, white wings stretched overhead, perhaps, or the dusky shag made a sudden shadow in mid-air, or we startled on some lonely ledge the great blue heron that flew off, trailing legs and wings, stork-like, against the clouds. Or, in the sunshine on the bare rocks, we cut from the broad, brown leaves of the slippery, varnished kelps, grotesque shapes of man and bird and beast that withered in the wind and blew away; or we fashioned rude boats from bits of driftwood, manned them with a weird crew of kelpies, and set them adrift on the great deep, to float we cared not whither. . . .

Few flowers bloomed for me upon the lonesome rock; but I made the most of all I had, and neither knew of nor desired more. Ah, how beautiful they were! Tiny stars of crimson sorrel threaded on their long brown stems; the blackberry blossoms in bridal white; the surprise of the blue-eyed grass; the crowfoot flowers, like drops of yellow gold spilt about among the short grass and over the moss; the rich, blue-purple beach-pea, the sweet, spiked germander, and the homely, delightful yarrow that grows thickly on all the islands. Sometimes its broad clusters of dull white bloom are stained a lovely reddish-purple, as if with the light of sunset. I never saw it colored so elsewhere. Quantities of slender, wide-spreading mustard-bushes grew about the house; their delicate flowers were like fragrant golden clouds. Dandelions, buttercups, and clover were not denied to us; though we had no daisies nor violets nor wild roses, no asters, but gorgeous spikes of golden-rod, and wonderful wild morning-glories, whose long, pale, ivory buds I used to find in the twilight, glimmering among the dark leaves, waiting for the touch of dawn to unfold and become each an exquisite incarnate blush,—the perfect color of a South Sea shell. They ran wild, knotting and twisting about the rocks, and smothering the loose boulders in the gorges with lush green leaves and pink blossoms.

Many a summer morning have I crept out of the still house before any one was awake, and, wrapping myself closely from the chill wind of dawn, climbed to the top of the high cliff called the Head to watch the sunrise. Pale grew the lighthouse flame before the broadening day as, nestled in a crevice at the cliff's edge, I watched the shadows draw away and morning break. Facing the east and south, with all the Atlantic before me, what happiness was mine as the deepening rose-color flushed the delicate cloudflocks that dappled the sky, where the gulls soared, rosy too, while the calm sea blushed beneath. Or perhaps it was a cloudless sunrise with a sky of orange-red, and the sea-line silver-blue against it, peaceful as heaven. Infinite variety of beauty always awaited me, and filled me with an absorbing, unreasoning joy such as makes the song-sparrow sing,—a sense of perfect bliss. Coming back in the sunshine, the morning-glories would lift up their faces, all awake, to my adoring gaze. Like countless rosy trumpets sometimes I thought they were, tossed everywhere about the rocks, turned up to the sky, or drooping toward the ground, or looking east, west, north, south, in silent loveliness. It seemed as if they had gathered the peace of the golden morning in their still depths even as my heart had gathered it.

KATHARINE S. WHITE

GREEN THOUGHTS IN A GREEN SHADE

from *Onward and Upward in the Garden* (1979)

Katharine Sergeant Angell White (1892–1977) was a highly influential editor at *The New Yorker* from its founding in 1925 until 1959. It was only upon her retirement that she began writing about "a field that had endless allure for her—the green world of growing things," as her husband, the writer E. B. White, explains in the preface to *Onward and Upward in the Garden,* a posthumously published collection of fourteen pieces she wrote for *The New Yorker* over a period of twelve years. Born in Winchester, Massachusetts, and educated at Bryn Mawr, Katharine "revered the beauty of flower form and the spiritual impact of the natural world as it was manifested in flowers," notes E. B. Her reviews of gardening and flower arranging books and seed and nursery stock catalogs are intensely personal, embellished with anecdote and charged with emotion, as the following introduction to a piece on flower catalogs attests.

I have read somewhere that no Japanese child will instinctively pick a flower, not even a very young child attracted by its bright color, because the sacredness of flowers is so deeply imbued in the culture of Japan that its children understand the blossoms are there to look at, not to pluck. Be that as it may, my observation is that Occidental children do have this instinctive desire, and I feel certain that almost every American must have a favorite childhood memory of picking flowers—dandelions on a lawn, perhaps, or daisies and buttercups in a meadow, trailing arbutus on a cold New England hillside in spring, a bunch of sweet peas in a hot July garden after admonishments from an adult to cut the stems *long,* or, when one had reached the age of discretion and could be trusted to choose the right rose and cut its stem correctly, a rosebud for the breakfast table. All these examples come from my own recollections of the simple pleasure of gathering flowers, but none of them quite equals my memories of the pure happiness of picking water lilies on a New Hampshire lake. The lake was Chocorua, and picking water lilies was not an unusual event for my next-older sister and me. We spent the best summers of our girlhood on, or in, this lake, and we picked the lilies in the early morning, paddling to the head of the lake, where the water was calm at the foot of the mountain and the sun had just begun to open the white stars of the lilies. The stern paddle had to know precisely how to approach a lily, stem first, getting near enough so the girl in the bow could plunge her arm straight down into the cool water and break off the rubbery stem, at least a foot under the surface, without leaning too far overboard. It took judgment to select the three or four freshest flowers and the shapeliest lily pad to go with them, and it took skill not to upset the canoe. Once the dripping blossoms were gathered and placed in the shade of the bow seat, we paddled home while their heavenly fragrance mounted all around us.

LAURA INGALLS WILDER

A BOUQUET OF WILD FLOWERS

from the *Missouri Ruralist* (20 July 1917)

Laura Ingalls Wilder (1867–1957) is remembered for her seven Little House books, but she wrote newspaper articles and columns about the life of a farm woman for decades before she began her famous books at age sixty-three. Born in a cabin in the Wisconsin woods, Laura Ingalls moved with her homesteading family to Missouri, Kansas, Iowa, Minnesota, and finally South Dakota, where she met and married Almanzo Wilder. After Laura bore a son, who died in infancy, and a daughter, the couple bought Rocky Ridge Farm near Mansfield, Missouri, where they lived the rest of their lives.

Laura wrote the Little House stories at the urging of her daughter, the writer Rose Wilder Lane, and in the belief that her childhood was "much richer and more interesting than that of children today, even with all the modern inventions and improvements." Some of that richness is conveyed in the following essay written for the *Missouri Ruralist,* lately collected along with other pieces by Laura and her daughter in *A Little House Sampler* (1988).

The Man of the Place brought me a bouquet of wild flowers this morning. It has been a habit of his for years. He never brings me cultivated flowers but always the wild blossoms of field and woodland and I think them much more beautiful.

In my bouquet this morning was a purple flag. Do you remember gathering them down on the flats and in the creek bottoms when you were a barefoot child? There was one marshy corner of the pasture down by the creek, where the grass grew lush and green; where the cows loved to feed and could always be found when it was time to drive them up at night. All thru the tall grass were scattered purple and white flag blossoms and I have stood in that peaceful grassland corner, with the red cow and the spotted cow and the roan taking their goodnight mouthfuls of the sweet grass, and watched the sun setting behind the hilltop and loved the purple flags and the rippling brook and wondered at the beauty of the world, while I wriggled my bare toes down into the soft grass.

The wild Sweet Williams in my bouquet brought a far different picture to my mind. A window had been broken in the schoolhouse at the country crossroads and the pieces of glass lay scattered where they had fallen. Several little girls going to school for their first term had picked handfuls of Sweet Williams and were gathered near the window. Someone discovered that the blossoms could be pulled from the stem and, by wetting their faces, could be stuck to the pieces of glass in whatever fashion they were arranged. They dried on the glass and would stay that way for hours and, looked at thru the glass, were very pretty. I was one of those little girls and tho I have forgotten what it was that I tried to learn out of a book that summer, I never have forgotten the beautiful wreaths and stars and other figures we made on the glass with the Sweet Williams. The delicate fragrance of their blossoms this morning made me feel like a little girl again.

The little white daisies with their hearts of gold grew

thickly along the path where we walked to Sunday school. Father and sister and I used to walk the 2½ miles every Sunday morning. The horses had worked hard all the week and must rest this one day, and Mother would rather stay at home with baby brother, so with Father and Sister Mary I walked to the church thru the beauties of the sunny spring Sundays. I have forgotten what I was taught on those days also. I was only a little girl, you know. But I can still plainly see the grass and the trees and the path winding ahead, flecked with sunshine and shadow and the beautiful golden-hearted daisies scattered all along the way.

Ah well! That was years ago and there have been so many changes since then that it would seem such simple things should be forgotten, but at the long last, I am beginning to learn that it is the sweet, simple things of life which are the real ones after all.

We heap up around us things that we do not need as the crow makes piles of glittering pebbles. We gabble words like parrots until we lose the sense of their meaning; we chase after this new idea and that; we take an old thought and dress it out in so many words that the thought itself is lost in its clothing like a slim woman in a barrel skirt and then we exclaim, "Lo, the wonderful new thought I have found!"

"There is nothing new under the sun," says the proverb. I think the meaning is that there are just so many truths or laws of life and no matter how far we may think we have advanced we cannot get beyond those laws. However complex a structure we build of living we must come back to those truths and so we find we have traveled in a circle.

The Russian revolution has only taken the Russian people back to the democratic form of government they had at the beginning of history in medieval times and so a republic is nothing new. I believe we would be happier to have a personal revolution in our individual lives and go back to simpler living and more direct thinking. It is the simple things of life that make living worth while, the sweet fundamental things such as love and duty, work and rest and living close to nature. There are no hothouse blossoms that can compare in beauty and fragrance with my bouquet of wild flowers.

ELIZABETH COATSWORTH

ON THE HILLS

from *Atlas and Beyond* (1924)

Elizabeth Coatsworth (1893–1986) began her writing career as a poet but achieved recognition as a writer of children's books, many of them set in rural New England and reflecting her love of nature. Born in Buffalo, New York, Coatsworth received a B.A. from Vassar and an M.A. from Columbia University and married writer Henry Beston (author of the nature classic *The Outermost House*). She traveled widely for many years in the Orient, North Africa, and Europe, but finally alighted happily in Nobleboro, Maine. "On the Hills" was later collected in *Down Half the World* (1968), which is, as Coatsworth wrote in the preface, "essentially a short record of my delight in the world and in living."

Today I walked on lion-colored hills
with only cypresses for company,
until the sunset caught me, turned the brush
to copper,
set the clouds

to one great roof of flame
above the earth,
so that I walked through fire, beneath fire,
and all in beauty.
Being alone
I could not be alone, but felt
(closer than flesh) the presences of those
who once had burned in such transfigurations.
My happiness ran through the centuries
and linked itself to other happiness
in one continual brightness. Looking down,
I saw the earth beneath me like a rose
petaled with mountains,
fragrant with deep peace.

HANNAH HINCHMAN

IN NAMELESS PLACES

from *Sierra* magazine (1990)

Hannah Hinchman (1953–   ) began keeping a field journal
during a summer internship at a nature center in the early
1970s. Since then, she has filled more than forty volumes
with her observations of the world around and inside her.
"I try to see it all as natural history, and have become a
naturalist on the trail of my own life," she writes. Born and
raised in suburban Ohio, she attended Earlham College in
Indiana before moving west to work as a graphic artist and
columnist for *High Country News* in Lander, Wyoming. She

moved east again briefly to complete a B.F.A. degree in Portland, Maine, and then returned to Wyoming, where she now works as an artist, graphic designer, and illustrator. She also teaches natural history journal-keeping at the Teton Science School and the Yellowstone Institute, and has recently published a book on that topic. Her essay "In Nameless Places" won the Neltje Blanchan Award for nature writing and the Frank Nelson Doubleday Award for women's writing in 1989.

There's a raven's wing in the wash. Angled sleekly, it reveals a blue sheen, the color of space through thin atmosphere. I picture it in a coyote pup's mouth. He drops it to follow his mother through one of the animal-mapped paths out of the canyon, routes I can never find. Raven's Wing Draw.

Twenty miles upriver, where the spruces throng, it was snowing a mean spring pellet snow when I left the house. Knowing a little about Wyoming microclimates, I decided to rummage for something better in the badlands. Until recently, before four-wheelers, only cows foraged dismally here each spring before being sent to the mountains. A few hunters, a few walkers. It's just more Bureau of Land Management land, little attention paid to it.

In the badlands it's not only the colors that capture me—layers of red, pink, pearl-gray, and buff—but the substances. Scramble along steep terra-cotta flutings and break off a piece. Out pours red sand so fine it must have been sifted by crickets. Thunderstorm sheet-floods are responsible, mixing up a muck that then settles into a clay outer shell with sand inside. But vertically? These columns always look just poured, or melting.

Then there are walls of conglomerate: granite cobbles smoothed by some ancient river, entombed here way back in the Eocene. I like to spring a few, let 'em rejoin the dance after sitting out for 55 million years. There's also a harder layer of pale sandstone that forms lips, brinks, falls, and traps, and is responsible for many a thwarted route.

I'm following the wash, the least efficient path, admiring the braidings in the steambed and the crisp mud curls that look good enough to eat. This little canyon, offered up to the southern sun arc, is now warm enough to make me stop and look for a sandy bank away from anthills where I can lie down. To the north the pellet-spitting cloud is still closed over the spruces, but I'm sweating, and a hover fly is looking me over. Two bends of the draw block any sound from Route 287, a mile away. Now I hear only the spring air molding itself into notes of a mountain bluebird. Time for a snooze, full length, given over, cowboy hat on face, the ground fairly twanging with working roots and ready shoots.

Later, when the shadows start breathing coolness out of the side canyons, I cross the color threshold. After an hour outside walking, colors begin to appear much more brilliant, more saturated. Oxygen to the brain? Rods and cones sufficiently steeped? I get out the paints and brushes and pour canteen water into a cup. How many times have I felt this urge, almost desperate, to paint the badlands? It's the repeated lines here, a regular pattern, like the designs on African bark-cloth painting. Cascades of intersecting Vs. Yet if you get too seduced by the flat pattern, you miss the sensuousness—a creamy expanse of sandstone curved and chiaroscuroed just so, a Botticelli forehead of pink clay, siltstone in languorous poses.

Sometimes I imagine that if I get the arrangement and proportions exactly right—a massive columned wall above a ribbon of wash, the precise slant of an alluvial fan—I will be able to conjure up the particular emptiness of this place. When people accustomed to cities, those people who avoid being alone, encounter this almost obstinate stillness, they run, sure they'll be crazy in a matter of hours. The mind does at first rebel, churning out a steady flow of thoughts, then core-memory debris, and sometimes, when the disturbance deepens, gibberish.

As you leave the car and start into the canyon, the place is just another setting. A little while later you look up and realize it might swallow you. Whenever I approach the canyon in that frame of mind, I know I must stop at the first bend and sift through a gravel bar, or go to sleep on the ground, or just sit. By the time I get out the paints I've reached an accord with the emptiness, knowing it to be the original expression of the world. "Stillness becoming alive, yet still," Theodore Roethke described it.

Next time I look up from my paper, the horizon has changed, sprouting big Vs of ears: a dozen mule deer.

Another dozen deer look up, startled, as I emerge from a juniper grove farther down the canyon. I try the grazing method to put them at ease: look at the ground and paw it with my boot, turn my back on them idly. Unthreatening gestures. They remove to the next bench, turn their backs on me, and browse on new growth of a wiry grass. Lofty Doe Draw.

I remember seeing a dead fawn in one of the narrow arms of this canyon. There was no sign of how it died, no dismantling by ravens or coyotes. Dead in a cave-painting position, ribs like a Tang dynasty ivory birdcage, a little haystack where its rumen had been.

What about death, its evidence and presence everywhere? Briefly, occasionally, I think I glimpse how life and death embrace. Of course I know the story of their mutual dependence, and keep reciting it to myself for reassurance, but it reads more like a legal document or economics paper. Sadness from witnessing pain has left me with a permanent wince. The vulnerability of all creatures to pain often seems like the most vicious of jokes, and the best I can do is to envision a tangled web of empathy: If the worm isn't stuffed alive down the nestling's throat, the nestling may starve. If the fox doesn't bring the nestling to her kit, the kit may die. We cling to life; the transition is rough.

Many days I'm not content to stay in the draws, but feel a need to get up onto the plateaus, the high mesas, the remnants of an ancient plain. The geometric change from vertical wall to horizontal plateau is itself satisfyingly precise—no halfway about it. My favorite of these I've named for its giddy aerial wreaths of horned larks. Lark Lyric Plateau. To be accurate, it's a peninsula linked to a long, ascending ridge that becomes a foothill of the Absaroka Range. Except for a few sections, this is all BLM land too.

About a mile long and equally wide, Lark Lyric is napped with low grasses and fragrant white phlox. Oddly, it supports no sagebrush, and there are no badger holes. Rising gently, ringed by mountains, it's cowgirl heaven.

My pony Scout carries me up. We carefully open and shut gates, following trails that avoid the steepest badland walls. This is the time to slouch comfortably, to sing whatever best fits our pace: "Blue Shadows on the Trail" or "Riding Down the Canyon." We top the last rise and suddenly there it is, spread out before us, perfectly smooth and empty. For a while there are just wind-streaming eyes and thundering pony hooves. Then we pull up and the plateau, its sky and larks, its level swell, resolve into a particular music, a pealing air, a welling carol.

All this open western space, unattended! I always get out the maps when I come home and trace my route, amazed at how little ground I've covered, and at how unremarkable the places look on paper. My Lofty Doe Draw, my incomparably lovely canyon filled with bluebirds and echoing swifts, is nameless to the U.S. Geological Survey. Lark Lyric Plateau, an island of heaven, is not considered worth naming either. So I get out my smallest pen, bend over the topo, and carefully write the names the places gave me.

MARY AUSTIN

THE STREETS OF THE MOUNTAINS

from *The Land of Little Rain* (1903)

Mary Hunter Austin (1868–1934) was a literary maverick who did her best writing about the "Country of Lost Borders," the high California desert to the east of the Sierra peak that today bears her name. Born in Carlinville, Illinois, Mary Hunter graduated from Blackburn College and journeyed to California with her widowed mother at age twenty, to join her brother in a homesteading project near Bakersfield. She taught school before marrying and following Stafford Austin to the Owens Valley, the landscape that was to be the most important influence on her writing. After the birth of a severely retarded daughter in 1892, she began writing and selling essays to the *Overland Review,* a regional journal based in Los Angeles. In 1903 she published her first and most celebrated book, *The Land of Little Rain,* a collection of fourteen essays about the California desert and adjoining mountains. The only one of her thirty-two published books to remain continuously in print, it was also a financial success, enabling her to flee a bad marriage and an Owens Valley doomed by the pumping of its water to Los Angeles, a venture she actively opposed. She settled in Carmel with her daughter and devoted herself to writing, becoming part of a literary circle that included Jack London and others.

In 1914 her daughter died and the Austins were divorced, closing an anguished chapter in her life. Over the ensuing years, she traveled to Rome, London, and New York, writing and lecturing, ardently advocating unpopular causes from women's suffrage and birth control to Indian and Mexican-American rights. In 1924 she moved to Santa Fe, New Mexico, where she continued her mystical love affair with nature and her association with noted writers and artists. She provided a place for Willa Cather to stay while completing *Death Comes for the Archbishop* (1927) and collaborated with an unknown photographer named Ansel Adams on a book about Taos Pueblo (1930). By the time of her death she had written novels, poetry, tales for children, plays, short stories, more than two hundred essays, an autobiography, and many works of nonfiction, all documenting her penetrating intellect, her strong feminist beliefs, and her emotional and spiritual commitment to the life of the land and its native peoples. The following essay about the Sierra Nevada range west of the Owens Valley shows the vitality and intensity of her response to wild country, her sensitivity to its human history, and her capacity for taking in the fullness of nature and seeing God in it.

All streets of the mountains lead to the citadel; steep or slow they go up to the core of the hills. Any trail that goes otherwise must dip and cross, sidle and take chances. Rifts of the hills open into each other, and the high meadows are often wide enough to be called valleys by courtesy; but one keeps this distinction in mind,—valleys are the sunken places of the earth, cañons are scored out by the glacier ploughs of God. They have a better name in the Rockies for these hill-fenced open glades of pleasantness; they call them parks. Here and there in the hill country one comes upon blind gullies fronted by high stony barriers. These head also for the heart of the mountains; their distinction is that they never get anywhere.

All mountain streets have streams to thread them, or deep grooves where a stream might run. You would do well to avoid that range uncomforted by singing floods. You will find it forsaken of most things but beauty and madness and death and God. Many such lie east and north away from the mid Sierras, and quicken the imagination with the sense of purposes not revealed, but the ordinary traveler brings nothing away from them but an intolerable thirst.

MARY AUSTIN   87

The river cañons of the Sierras of the Snows are better worth while than most Broadways, though the choice of them is like the choice of streets, not very well determined by their names. There is always an amount of local history to be read in the names of mountain highways where one touches the successive waves of occupation or discovery, as in the old villages where the neighborhoods are not built but grow. Here you have the Spanish Californian in *Cero Gordo* and piñon; Symmes and Shepherd, pioneers both; Tunawai, probably Shoshone; Oak Creek, Kearsarge,— easy to fix the date of that christening,—Tinpah, Paiute that; Mist Cañon and Paddy Jack's. The streets of the west Sierras sloping toward the San Joaquin are long and winding, but from the east, my country, a day's ride carries one to the lake regions. The next day reaches the passes of the high divide, but whether one gets passage depends a little on how many have gone that road before, and much on one's own powers. The passes are steep and windy ridges, though not the highest. By two and three thousand feet the snow-caps overtop them. It is even possible to wind through the Sierras without having passed above timber-line, but one misses a great exhilaration.

The shape of a new mountain is roughly pyramidal, running out into long shark-finned ridges that interfere and merge into other thunder-splintered sierras. You get the saw-tooth effect from a distance, but the near-by granite bulk glitters with the terrible keen polish of old glacial ages. I say terrible; so it seems. When those glossy domes swim into the alpenglow, wet after rain, you conceive how long and imperturbable are the purposes of God.

Never believe what you are told, that midsummer is the best time to go up the streets of the mountain—well— perhaps for the merely idle or sportsmanly or scientific; but for seeing and understanding, the best time is when you have the longest leave to stay. And here is a hint if you would attempt the stateliest approaches; travel light, and as much as possible live off the land. Mulligatawny soup and tinned lobster will not bring you the favor of the wood-landers.

Every cañon commends itself for some particular pleas-antness; this for pines, another for trout, one for pure bleak beauty of granite buttresses, one for its far-flung irised falls; and as I say, though some are easier going, leads each to the cloud shouldering citadel. First, near the cañon mouth you get the low-heading full-branched, one-leaf pines. That is the sort of tree to know at sight, for the globose, resin-dripping cones have palatable, nourishing kernels, the main harvest of the Paiutes. That perhaps accounts for their growing accommodatingly below the limit of deep snows, grouped sombrely on the valleyward slopes. The real pro-cession of the pines begins in the rifts with the long-leafed *Pinus jeffreyi,* sighing its soul away upon the wind. And it ought not to sigh in such good company. Here begins the manzanita, adjusting its tortuous stiff stems to the sharp waste of boulders, its pale olive leaves twisting edgewise to the sleek, ruddy, chestnut stems; begins also the meadow-sweet, burnished laurel, and the million unregarded trum-pets of the coral-red pentstemon. Wild life is likely to be busiest about the lower pine borders. One looks in hollow trees and hiving rocks for wild honey. The drone of bees, the chatter of jays, the hurry and stir of squirrels, is inces-sant; the air is odorous and hot. The roar of the stream fills up the morning and evening intervals, and at night the deer feed in the buckthorn thickets. It is worth watching the year round in the purlieus of the long-leafed pines. One month or another you get sight or trail of most roving mountain dwellers as they follow the limit of forbidding snows, and more bloom than you can properly appreciate.

Whatever goes up or comes down the streets of the mountains, water has the right of way; it takes the lowest ground and the shortest passage. Where the rifts are nar-row, and some of the Sierra cañons are not a stone's throw from wall to wall, the best trail for foot or horse winds considerably about the watercourses; but in a country of cone-bearers there is usually a good strip of swardy sod along the cañon floor. Pine woods, the short-leafed Balfour and Murryana of the high Sierras, are sombre, rooted in the litter of a thousand years, hushed, and corrective to the spirit. The trail passes insensibly into them from the black pines and a thin belt of firs. You look back as you rise, and strain for glimpses of the tawny valley, blue glints of the Bitter Lake, and tender cloud films on the farther ranges. For such pictures the pine branches make a noble frame. Presently they close in wholly; they draw mysteriously near, covering your tracks, giving up the trail indifferently, or with a secret grudge. You get a kind of impatience with their locked ranks, until you come out lastly on some high, windy dome and see what they are about. They troop thickly up the open ways, river banks, and brook borders; up open swales of dribbling springs; swarm over old moraines; circle the peaty swamps and part and meet about clean still lakes; scale the stony gullies; tormented, bowed, persisting to the door of the storm chambers, tall priests to pray for rain. The spring winds lift clouds of pollen dust, finer than frankincense, and trail it out over high altars, staining the snow. No doubt they understand this work better than we; in fact they know no other. "Come," say the churches of the valleys, after a season of dry years, "let us pray for rain." They would do better to plant more trees.

It is a pity we have let the gift of lyric improvisation die out. Sitting islanded on some gray peak above the encompassing wood, the soul is lifted up to sing the Iliad of the pines. They have no voice but the wind, and no sound of them rises up to the high places. But the waters, the evidences of their power, that go down the steep and stony ways, the outlets of ice-bordered pools, the young rivers swaying with the force of their running, they sing and shout and trumpet at the falls, and the noise of it far outreaches the forest spires. You see from these conning towers how they call and find each other in the slender gorges; how they fumble in the meadows, needing the sheer nearing walls to give them countenance and show the way; and how the pine woods are made glad by them.

Nothing else in the streets of the mountains gives such a sense of pageantry as the conifers; other trees, if there are any, are home dwellers, like the tender-fluttered sisterhood of quaking asp. They grow in clumps by spring borders, and all their stems have a permanent curve toward the down slope, as you may also see in hillside pines, where they have borne the weight of sagging drifts.

Well up from the valley, at the confluence of cañons, are delectable summer meadows. Fireweed flames about them against the gray boulders; streams are open, go smoothly about the glacier slips and make deep bluish pools for trout. Pines raise statelier shafts and give themselves room to grow,—gentians, shinleaf, and little grass of Parnassus in their golden checkered shadows; the meadow is white with violets and all outdoors keeps the clock. For example, when the ripples at the ford of the creek raise a clear half tone,— sign that the snow water has come down from the heated high ridges,—it is time to light the evening fire. When it drops off a note—but you will not know it except the Douglas squirrel tells you with his high, fluty chirrup from the pines' aerial gloom—sign that some star watcher has caught the first far glint of the nearing sun. Whitney cries it from his vantage tower; it flashes from Oppapago to the front of Williamson; LeConte speeds it to the westering peaks. The high rills wake and run, the birds begin. But down three thousand feet in the cañon, where you stir the fire under the cooking pot, it will not be day for an hour. It goes on, the play of light across the high places, rosy, purpling, tender, glint and glow, thunder and windy flood, like the grave, exulting talk of elders above a merry game.

Who shall say what another will find most to his liking in the streets of the mountains. As for me, once set above the country of the silver firs, I must go on until I find white columbine. Around the amphitheatres of the lake regions and above them to the limit of perennial drifts they gather flock-wise in splintered rock wastes. The crowds of them, the airy spread of sepals, the pale purity of the petal spurs, the quivering swing of bloom, obsesses the sense. One must learn to spare a little of the pang of inexpressible beauty, not to spend all one's purse in one shop. There is always another year, and another.

MABEL DODGE LUHAN

TREK TO BLUE LAKE

from *Winter in Taos* (1935)

Mabel Dodge Luhan (1879–1962), born into a conservative Buffalo banking family, was for years patroness of the avant-garde in Greenwich Village, writing undistinguished poems, book reviews, essays, biographies, and social criticism, and seeking an identity through the famous artists and activists with whom she surrounded herself. It was not until she moved to Taos, New Mexico, in December 1917 that she found her true literary voice, home, and identity. "My life broke in two right then, and I entered into the second half, a new world . . . more strange and terrible and sweet than any I had ever been able to imagine," she wrote in *Edge of Taos Desert: An Escape to Reality* (1937), one of four volumes of her *Intimate Memories*. What she found in Taos were the simple pleasures of daily life in tune with the changing seasons, the rhythm of planting and harvesting, the beauty of flowers, the smell of sage after rain, the antics of her cats, dogs, and horses, the play of light over the mountains.

In Taos, Mabel married her fourth husband, a Pueblo Indian named Tony Luhan, and together they built a seventeen-room adobe hacienda on the edge of the Pueblo reservation, to which they welcomed writers and artists including D. H. Lawrence, Dorothy Brett, Robinson Jeffers, and Willa Cather. In this atmosphere, Mabel wrote her masterpiece of regional literature, *Winter in Taos,* a lyrical narrative that marries details of the southwestern landscape with the author's emotional life. The excerpt reprinted here expresses her revitalized relationship with the land and her admiration for the way of life of the Pueblo Indians. Her account of Blue Lake and of its sacred significance to the Indians is made more interesting by the fact that since the early 1970s, access to the lake has been restricted. Only Taos Pueblo Indians are allowed there today.

One of the nicest things we do in the summer in the short period when it has grown warm and dry on the ground, and before the cold weather comes at the end of August, is to go up to Blue Lake for a night and a day and we leave early in the morning when there is a dew sparkling on everything and cobwebs stretching all in one direction across the grasses and trees. We take the long trail behind the Pueblo Mountain for twenty-five miles; we plod, with our camping things on pack horses behind us, and it is a slow ride, for we can rarely go beyond a walk, and only occasionally into the jog trot.

We leave behind us everything that we love in houses and gardens and all we have is what the Indians say God gave them: "Just what grows on the mountain." But the richness of it! The mountainsides are covered with patches of mauve-blue columbine and the "little scarlet rain" and all the other flowers. The forests are deep in vivid green moss and dozens of varieties of birds sing on all sides. The vividness of all this growing life is startling when one leaves furniture and curtains, silk and cloth and made things behind one.

The little river is beside us until we climb above it, and

we hear it below in the crevices of the giant hills. After a while, as we go higher and higher, the color fades out of the sunshine so it is as though everything is drawn in black and white! The trail leads up into the very high mountains that tumble and billow, roll on roll beyond us. We never see anyone except an occasional Indian wrapped in his white sheet riding over the slopes.

Sometimes across a deep abyss an Indian, so far away over on the opposite mountainside I cannot even see him, will accost us with a call like a bird, and Tony and Trinidad will answer him with their hands cupping their mouths.

Sound grows strange up on these heights. It seems squeezed and solid. Our voices are unfamiliar to us and we do not talk much.

By noon we reach the halfway place where the tribe stops on the first halt when it makes the journey up to Blue Lake for its great August Ceremony.

Here there is a spring so we can drink and water our horses, and we like to lie on the ground a while to rest our tired backs, and then we eat our dinner.

Tony is a fine camp cook and makes good grilled steaks, fried potatoes and onions and coffee, and soon we are rested and ready to go on.

Our little string of horses are like ants crawling over these enormous spaces. The trail winds around mountain after mountain and in some places it is cut into the steep sides until there is just a narrow shelf to ride on with the earth rising perpendicular and straight up above one on one hand and on the other falling away so abruptly one looks down past the horse into miles of green bottomless darkness. This part of the ride is always a little frightening, and one leans as far as possible towards the mountain; one can reach out and touch it with one's hand! Looking back, one sees the bulging packs on the pack horses are hanging right out over the abyss.

We took Brett up there once and she prepared herself for her customary vertigo in high places by carrying a long rope and a policeman's whistle. When we reached the first steep mountain where we had to crawl around the ledge, she roped herself to Trinidad who rode ahead of her. She tied her rope around her waist and gave him the other end which he carried in his hand. Then, she shut her eyes and sat.

However, she made the mistake of opening them too soon and caught a sudden glimpse down into those depths! We heard the shrill whistle blasting the terrible summits and Trinidad singing against it. Looking back, we saw him laughing and Brett blowing for all she was worth to hearten herself and show us how she felt.

Upon one of these mountainsides the osha plant grows. It has stalks and leaves like celery and the root is wonderful to burn in the house, for it has a sweet, heavy, oriental perfume, like an incense, and it obliterates all other stale smells of cigarettes or cooking. The Indians use it for colds and sore throats, chewing it and swallowing the juice, which is very spicy and sharp and stings one's mouth. It is considered a very powerful medicine, for snakes, witches and other harmful entities cannot endure it. When Autumn comes we get an Indian boy to go up and dig a sackful of roots for us that we burn on winter evenings and we never have known anyone who did not love its lovely fragrance.

The afternoon passes, the light fades, and evening is coming when we are upon the cold, treeless ridges in austerity and awe, utterly removed from everyday life and everything we are used to in light and sound. As we top the last bleak, shale-covered edge we see below us Blue Lake. Bottomless, peacock blue, smooth as glass, it lies there like an uncut, shining jewel. Symmetrical pine trees, in thick succession, slope down to its shores in a rapid descent on three sides.

This Blue Lake is the most mysterious thing I have ever seen in nature, having an unknowable, impenetrable life of its own, and a definite emanation that rises from it. Here is the source of most of the valley life. From this unending water supply that flows out of the east end of the lake and down the miles and miles of the rocky bed of the stream to the Pueblo, the Indian fields are irrigated. It is turned into the *acequia madre,* that winds on down through the Indian land until it reaches the town and feeds all our fields and orchards that lie on the eastern side of the valley. The west portion of the valley is watered from Bear Lake, another deep pool with a perpetual spring feeding it.

The Indians call this one Star Water, it is so light and clear. Near the opening of the canyon there is a little, sheltered glade where the Indian sweet grass grows and of it they make bundles to perfume their clothes.

It has never been surprising to me that the Indians call Blue Lake a sacred lake, and worship it. Indeed, at first I felt we should not camp upon its shore, but after I found out how they conduct the camp there I knew it was all right and fitting that one should sleep beside it and try to draw what one could for oneself from its strong being.

The evening fire is soon burning and the food ready; the Indians are speaking in low voices that yet are very distinct at that altitude of nearly fourteen thousand feet, and the horses are hobbled and we hear them crunching their oats over in the trees. When the dishes are washed and all the scraps are burned and we are sitting in a circle around the fire, the Indians begin to chant, at first in faint, humming tones, that gradually grow strong and full. They look over to the lake and sing to it. Their faces show they are deep in communion with the place they are in. They experience it and adore it as we do not know how to do.

The dark night is soon full of the repeated mantric song. The sound of it goes back and forth between the singers and the mountains, the lake and the fire. They go on singing for hours, long after I have gone into the pine shelter and wrapped myself in blankets to go to sleep. It isn't easy to sleep as high as that, but to lie awake in the marvelous air and feel the potency of the place has a kind of active repose in it and one is always refreshed by the night up there.

Riding back to the valley late the next day has the same surprise in it every time. The fields of corn and wheat that we ride through seem terribly rich and luxurious and there is a thickness of living in the downy, sumptuous, golden valley. When we reach our house in the dusk, the living room seems crowded with comforts, the bright colors and glints of metal and glass startle one whose eyes, just in those few hours, grew used to the holy look of natural life. Most of us are used only to the awesome holiness of churches and lofty arches, cathedrals where, with stained glass and brooding silences, priests try to emulate the religious atmosphere that is to be found in the living earth in some of her secret places.

GENE STRATTON-PORTER

THE SONG OF THE LIMBERLOST

from *Music of the Wild* (1910)

Gene Stratton-Porter (1863–1924) once wrote, "I am a creature so saturated with earth, water, and air that if I do not periodically work some of it out of my system in ink, my nearest and dearest cannot live with me." Work it out of her system in ink she did, in the enormously popular novels (usually vehicles for nature lore) that the publisher Frank Doubleday persuaded her to alternate with her nonfiction nature books, and in magazine articles, short stories, and poetry. In all her writing, and in her production of more than twenty films based on the novels, her aim was to teach love of nature, God, and fellow humans. This aim is apparent in her shallow romantic novel *A Girl of the Limberlost* (1909), which reached a vast audience with nature lore and whose Bird Woman character is modeled after herself.

Stratton-Porter was born on an Indiana farm, the last of twelve children, and from her earliest recollection was "the friend and devoted champion of every bird that nested in the garden, on the fences, on the ground, in the bushes, in the dooryard, or in the orchard trees." With her husband, a druggist, she designed and built a cabin on the edge of Indiana's Limberlost Swamp in 1887, and began to explore and photograph this preserve of wild birds, plants, and moths. Largely self-educated as a naturalist and photographer, she relied wholly on her own observations of nature as the basis of her work, and often risked life and limb to obtain accurate photographs without unduly disturbing the wildlife. She had a strong conservationist leaning and foresaw the climatic effects of cutting down forests, declaring in *Music of the Wild*, "Pity of pities it is; but man can change and is changing the forces of nature. I never told a sadder truth, but it is truth that man can 'cut down the clouds.' In utter disregard or ignorance of what he will do to himself, his children, and his country he persists in doing it wherever he can see a few cents in the sacrifice."

The roads run systematically across the face of earth, singing the song of travel and commerce. Then there is a far sweeter song, sung by little streams of water, wandering as they will, in beneficent course, quenching the thirst of the earth, enhancing its beauty, and lulling us with their melody. Any one of these little streams is typical of all, but each nature-lover has his own particular brook that to him is most beautiful.

"I come from haunts of coot and hern,"

sang Tennyson of his. My Limberlost comes from the same haunts, and nothing can convince me that any running water on the face of earth is more interesting or more beautiful. I have read of the streams that flow over India's golden sands, down Italy's mountains, through England's meadows; but none of them can sing sweeter songs or have more interest to the inch than the Limberlost.

It is born in the heart of swampy wood and thicket, flows over a bed of muck or gravel, the banks are grass and flower-lined, its water cooled and shaded by sycamore, maple, and willow. June drapes it in misty white, and November spreads a blanket of scarlet and gold. In the water fish, turtle, crab, muskrat, and water puppy disport themselves. Along the shores the sandpiper, plover, coot, bittern, heron, and crane take their pleasure and seek their food. Above it the hawk and vulture wheel, soar, and sail in high heaven, and the kingfisher dashes in merry rattling flight between the trees, his reflection trailing after him across sunlit pools. The quail leads her chickens from the thicket to drink, and the wild ducks converse among the rushes. In it the coon carefully washes the unwary frog caught among the reeds, and the muskrat furrows deeper ripples than the stones.

The lambs play on the pebbly banks and drink eagerly, the cattle roll grateful eyes as they quench their thirst and stand belly-deep for hours lazily switching their tails to drive away flies. Little children come shouting to wade in the cool waters, and larger ones solemnly sit on the banks with apple-sucker rods, wrapping twine lines and bent pin hooks, supporting their families by their industry, if the gravity of their faces be token of the importance of their work. Sweethearts linger beside the stream and surprise themselves with a new wonder they have discovered—their secret; but the Limberlost knows, and promises never to tell.

Perhaps that is what it chuckles about while slipping around stones, over fallen trees, and whispering across beds of black ooze. The Limberlost is a wonderful musician, singing the song of running water throughout its course. Singing that low, somber, sweet little song that you must get very close to earth to hear, because the creek has such mighty responsibility it hesitates to sing loudly lest it appear to boast. All these creatures to feed and water; all these trees and plants to nourish! The creek is so happy that it can do all this, and if it runs swiftly other woods, thickets, fields, and meadows can be watered. Then the river must be reached as soon as possible, for there are factory wheels to be turned, boats to be carried, and the creek has heard that some day it is to be part of the great ocean. When the Limberlost thinks of that its song grows a little more exultant and proud, bends are swept with swifter measure, louder notes are sung, and every bird, bee, insect, man, and child along the banks joins in the accompaniment. All the trees rustle and whisper, shaking their branches to shower it with a baptism of gold in pollen time. The rushes and blue flags murmur together, and the creek and every sound belonging to it all combine in the song of the Limberlost.

LESLIE MARMON SILKO

LOVE POEM

from *Voices of the Rainbow: Contemporary Poetry by American Indians,* edited by Kenneth Rosen (1975)

Leslie Marmon Silko (1948–) is a writer steeped in the folklore of the Laguna Pueblo people. She was born of mixed ancestry—Laguna Pueblo, Mexican, and white—in Albuquerque, New Mexico, and grew up at Laguna Pueblo listening to her great-grandmother and great-aunts tell stories. She explains that "the ancient people perceived the world and themselves within that world as part of an ancient continuous story composed of innumerable bundles of other stories." In Silko's work as a poet, novelist (*Ceremony*, 1977), and writer of short stories and film scripts, the stories continue. In the following poem, the story uniting Silko with her ancestral past deepens and intensifies for her the beauty of rain coming to a dry land.

Rain smell comes with the wind
                                    out of the southwest.

Smell of sand dunes
                    tall grass glistening
                                    in the rain.

Warm raindrops that fall easy
                              (this woman)

The summer is born.
Smell of her breathing new life
                              small gray toads on
        damp sand.

(this woman)
                whispering to dark wide leaves
                white moon blossoms dripping
                                    tracks in the
        sand.

Rain smell
        I am full of hunger
        deep and longing to touch
wet tall grass, green and strong beneath.

This woman loved a man
and she breathed to him
                    her damp earth song.

I am haunted by this story
I remember it in cottonwood leaves

                                       their fragrance in
   the shade.

I remember it in the wide blue sky
when the rain smell comes with the wind.

Her Wildness:
What Is Untamed in
Nature and in Us

One warm October afternoon in 1989 as I sat at my desk working on this book, the earth beneath me and millions of other northern Californians suddenly rumbled, jerked, and shuddered like boxcars coupling, like continents coupling and giving birth to mountains. In that instant the sharp edge of reality cut through the comfortable trance we habitually dwell in. The pounding of our hearts woke us up and the force of an immense power under the thin veneer of our life support systems ripped away our illusions of safety and control. While there was something terrifying about the violence of that message from the wild heart of earth, there was also something bracing and thrilling in it, something illuminating, a deep remembering of who we really are and where we really live.

Short of a natural disaster, what chance do we have in modern life to make contact with the raw power of nature and the corresponding wildness in ourselves? Some of the writers in this section have won through to a keener, sharper sense of life in encounters with wild creatures or expeditions to wild places. Simply going out-of-doors has helped others shed socially assigned roles and discover an untamed, authentic self. And one author included here focuses on the fact that, as women, we are drawn closer to the wild heart of nature in pregnancy, when we can feel the primal force of life pushing through us.

JUDITH MINTY

WHY DO YOU KEEP THOSE CATS?

from *Lake Songs and Other Fears* (1974)

Judith Minty (1937–   ) is concerned with articulating "the
unity between two worlds: the human, and what we call 'the
natural world.'" She explains, "I'm convinced that there is
something we once knew which has been lost to us in the
evolutionary process. Sometimes we get glimpses of it; I'm
particularly interested in those moments." Born in Detroit,
Michigan, she was educated at Ithaca College (B.S.) and
Western Michigan University (M.A.) and became poet-in-
residence at Humboldt State University in Arcata, Califor-
nia, in 1982. She is part Mohawk and returns to the Great
Lakes every summer, feeling that "I've belonged to these
places for longer than my lifetime." She has had five books
of poems published and has contributed short stories, arti-
cles, and poems to many magazines.

All winter, those cats of mine
doze like old women in front of the fire,
curl their fur around saucers of sunlight
they have trapped on my rug. Sometimes
they bury themselves in the wool of blankets
to sniff dreams I left there.

Awake, their eyes reflect deeper sleeps.
Delicate tongues yawn, hide needles of teeth.
I listen for their soft paws,
for their purrs to rattle in slow circles
near my bed. They want to capture
warmth from my body. "Why do you

keep those cats?" my neighbors ask.
Why? It is for summer that I wait
for their claws to unsheath, for their eyes
to blaze orange in dark hallways.
Soon they will tear at my door, howl
to walk with lions along the fence.

It is not for winter. It is instead
for the flame of yellow moons.
Then I run wild with them,
hide in trees, sleep again in leaves;
in August I will sink my teeth,
as they do, into the warm necks of mice.

ANNIE DILLARD

LIVING LIKE WEASELS

from *Teaching a Stone to Talk* (1982)

Annie Dillard (1945–   ) says that her books are about
"what it feels like to be alive." She was born in Pittsburgh
and educated at Hollins College in Virginia. The Blue
Ridge Mountains near the college were the setting for the
quest she describes in *Pilgrim at Tinker Creek* (1974), her
first published book of prose, which won the Pulitzer Prize
in 1975. Since then, she has lived on an island in Puget
Sound, Washington, become writer-in-residence at Wes-
leyan University in Connecticut, and written volumes of
narrative and criticism, as well as a memoir.

A weasel is wild. Who knows what he thinks? He sleeps in his underground den, his tail draped over his nose. Sometimes he lives in his den for two days without leaving. Outside, he stalks rabbits, mice, muskrats, and birds, killing more bodies than he can eat warm, and often dragging the carcasses home. Obedient to instinct, he bites his prey at the neck, either splitting the jugular vein at the throat or crunching the brain at the base of the skull, and he does not let go. One naturalist refused to kill a weasel who was socketed into his hand deeply as a rattlesnake. The man could in no way pry the tiny weasel off, and he had to walk half a mile to water, the weasel dangling from his palm, and soak him off like a stubborn label.

And once, says Ernest Thompson Seton—once, a man shot an eagle out of the sky. He examined the eagle and found the dry skull of a weasel fixed by the jaws to his throat. The supposition is that the eagle had pounced on the weasel and the weasel swiveled and bit as instinct taught him, tooth to neck, and nearly won. I would like to have seen that eagle from the air a few weeks or months before he was shot: was the whole weasel still attached to his feathered throat, a fur pendant? Or did the eagle eat what he could reach, gutting the living weasel with his talons before his breast, bending his beak, cleaning the beautiful airborne bones?

I have been reading about weasels because I saw one last week. I startled a weasel who startled me, and we exchanged a long glance.

Twenty minutes from my house, through the woods by the quarry and across the highway, is Hollins Pond, a remarkable piece of shallowness, where I like to go at sunset and sit on a tree trunk. Hollins Pond is also called Murray's Pond; it covers two acres of bottomland near Tinker Creek with six inches of water and six thousand lily pads. In winter, brown-and-white steers stand in the middle of it, merely dampening their hooves; from the distant shore they look like miracle itself, complete with miracle's nonchalance.

Now, in summer, the steers are gone. The water lilies have blossomed and spread to a green horizontal plane that is terra firma to plodding blackbirds, and tremulous ceiling to black leeches, crayfish, and carp.

This is, mind you, suburbia. It is a five-minute walk in three directions to rows of houses, though none is visible here. There's a 55 mph highway at one end of the pond, and a nesting pair of wood ducks at the other. Under every bush is a muskrat hole or a beer can. The far end is an alternating series of fields and woods, fields and woods, threaded everywhere with motorcycle tracks—in whose bare clay wild turtles lay eggs.

So. I had crossed the highway, stepped over two low barbed-wire fences, and traced the motorcycle path in all gratitude through the wild rose and poison ivy of the pond's shoreline up into high grassy fields. Then I cut down through the woods to the mossy fallen tree where I sit. This tree is excellent. It makes a dry, upholstered bench at the upper, marshy end of the pond, a plush jetty raised from the thorny shore between a shallow blue body of water and a deep blue body of sky.

The sun had just set. I was relaxed on the tree trunk, ensconced in the lap of lichen, watching the lily pads at my feet tremble and part dreamily over the thrusting path of a carp. A yellow bird appeared to my right and flew behind me. It caught my eye; I swiveled around—and the next instant, inexplicably, I was looking down at a weasel, who was looking up at me.

Weasel! I'd never seen one wild before. He was ten inches long, thin as a curve, a muscled ribbon, brown as fruitwood, soft-furred, alert. His face was fierce, small and pointed as a lizard's; he would have made a good arrow-head. There was just a dot of chin, maybe two brown hairs' worth, and then the pure white fur began that spread down his underside. He had two black eyes I didn't see, any more than you see a window.

The weasel was stunned into stillness as he was emerging from beneath an enormous shaggy wild rose bush four feet away. I was stunned into stillness twisted backward on the tree trunk. Our eyes locked, and someone threw away the key.

Our look was as if two lovers, or deadly enemies, met unexpectedly on an overgrown path when each had been thinking of something else: a clearing blow to the gut. It was also a bright blow to the brain, or a sudden beating of brains, with all the charge and intimate grate of rubbed balloons. It emptied our lungs. It felled the forest, moved the fields, and drained the pond; the world dismantled and tumbled into that black hole of eyes. If you and I looked at each other that way, our skulls would split and drop to our shoulders. But we don't. We keep our skulls. So.

He disappeared. This was only last week, and already I don't remember what shattered the enchantment. I think I blinked, I think I retrieved my brain from the weasel's brain, and tried to memorize what I was seeing, and the weasel felt the yank of separation, the careening splash-down into real life and the urgent current of instinct. He vanished under the wild rose. I waited motionless, my mind suddenly full of data and my spirit with pleadings, but he didn't return.

Please do not tell me about "approach-avoidance conflicts." I tell you I've been in that weasel's brain for sixty seconds, and he was in mine. Brains are private places, muttering through unique and secret tapes—but the weasel and I both plugged into another tape simultaneously, for a sweet and shocking time. Can I help it if it was a blank?

What goes on in his brain the rest of the time? What does a weasel think about? He won't say. His journal is tracks in clay, a spray of feathers, mouse blood and bone: uncollected, unconnected, loose-leaf, and blown.

I would like to learn, or remember, how to live. I come to Hollins Pond not so much to learn how to live as, frankly, to forget about it. That is, I don't think I can learn from a wild animal how to live in particular—shall I suck warm blood, hold my tail high, walk with my footprints precisely over the prints of my hands?—but I might learn something of mindlessness, something of the purity of living in the physical senses and the dignity of living without bias or motive. The weasel lives in necessity and we live in choice, hating necessity and dying at the last ignobly in its talons. I would like to live as I should, as the weasel lives as he should. And I suspect that for me the way is like the weasel's: open to time and death painlessly, noticing everything, remembering nothing, choosing the given with a fierce and pointed will.

I missed my chance. I should have gone for the throat. I should have lunged for that streak of white under the weasel's chin and held on, held on through mud and into the wild rose, held on for a dearer life. We could live under the wild rose wild as weasels, mute and uncomprehending. I could very calmly go wild. I could live two days in the den, curled, leaning on mouse fur, sniffing bird bones, blinking, licking, breathing musk, my hair tangled in the roots of grasses. Down is a good place to go, where the mind is single. Down is out, out of your ever-loving mind and back to your careless senses. I remember muteness as a prolonged and giddy fast, where every moment is a feast of utterance received. Time and events are merely poured, unremarked, and ingested directly, like blood pulsed into my gut through a jugular vein. Could two live that way? Could two live under the wild rose, and explore by the pond, so that the smooth mind of each is as everywhere present to the other, and as received and as unchallenged, as falling snow?

We could, you know. We can live any way we want. People take vows of poverty, chastity, and obedience— even of silence—by choice. The thing is to stalk your calling in a certain skilled and supple way, to locate the most tender and live spot and plug into that pulse. This is yielding, not fighting. A weasel doesn't "attack" anything; a weasel lives as he's meant to, yielding at every moment to the perfect freedom of single necessity.

I think it would be well, and proper, and obedient, and pure, to grasp your one necessity and not let it go, to dangle from it limp wherever it takes you. Then even death, where you're going no matter how you live, cannot you part. Seize it and let it seize you up aloft even, till your eyes burn out and drop; let your musky flesh fall off in shreds, and let your very bones unhinge and scatter, loosened over fields, over fields and woods, lightly, thoughtless, from any height at all, from as high as eagles.

ROBERTA HILL WHITEMAN

THE RECOGNITION

from *Star Quilt* (1984)

Roberta Hill Whiteman (1947–) is a member of the Oneida Tribe of Wisconsin. Her poetry, published so far in one collection and in many magazines and anthologies, is rich with nature imagery and awareness of the spiritual reality of our relation to the earth. Born in Wisconsin, she earned a B.A. from the University of Wisconsin and an M.F.A. from the University of Montana, and is an associate professor of English at the University of Wisconsin, Eau Claire.

We learn too late the useless way light leaves
footprints of its own. We traveled miles to Kilgore
in the submarine closeness of a car. Sand hills
recalling the sea. A coyote slipped across the road
before we knew. Night, the first skin around him.
He was coming from the river
where laughter calls out fish. Quietly a heavy wind
breaks against cedar. He doubled back,
curious, to meet the humming moons we rode
in this gully, without grass or stars. Our footprints
were foreign to him. He understood the light
and paused before the right front wheel, a shadow
of the mineral earth, pine air in his fur.
Such dogs avoid our eyes, yet he recognized and held
my gaze. A being both so terrible and shy
it made my blood desperate
for the space he lived in:
broad water cutting terraced canyons,
and ice gleaming under hawthorne like a floor of scales.
Thick river, remember we were light thanking light,
slow music rising. Trees perhaps, or my own voice
out of tune. I danced a human claim for him
in this gully. No stars. He slipped
by us, old as breath, moving in the rushing dark
like moonlight through tamarack,
wave on wave of unknown country.
Crazed, I can't get close enough
to this tumble wild and tangled miracle.
Night is the first skin around me.

GRETEL EHRLICH

RIVER HISTORY

from *Montana Spaces,* edited by William Kittredge (1988)

Gretel Ehrlich (1946–   ) first went to Wyoming to make a
film while her partner in the project—a man she loved—was
dying. After the rough beauty of Wyoming saw her through
the tragedy, as recounted in her book *The Solace of Open
Spaces* (1985), she lost her appetite for the life she had left.
She worked on ranches and became a full-time writer. Born
and raised in California and educated at Bennington Col-
lege, UCLA, and the New School for Social Research, Ehr-
lich has published prose pieces, poetry, stories, and a novel.
She lives with her husband on a ranch near Shell, Wyoming.
The following essay was first published as an introduction to
the 1989 Sierra Club Wilderness Calendar, and then col-
lected in the anthology *Montana Spaces.*

It's morning in the Absaroka Mountains. The word *absaroka*
means "raven" in the Crow language, though I've seen no
ravens in three days. Last night I slept with my head butted
against an Engelmann spruce and on waking the limbs
looked like hundreds of arms swinging in a circle. The
trunk is bigger than an elephant's leg, bigger than my torso.
I stick my nose against the bark. Tiny opals of sap stick to
my cheeks and the bark breaks up, textured: red and gray,
coarse and smooth, wet and flaked.

A tree is an aerial garden, a botanical migration from
the sea, from those earliest plants, the seaweeds; it is a
purchase on crumbled rock, on ground. The human, stand-
ing, is only a different upsweep and articulation of cells.
How treelike we are, how human the tree.

But I've come here to seek out the source of a river and as we make the daylong ascent from a verdant valley, I think about walking and wilderness. We use the word "wilderness," but perhaps we mean wildness. Isn't that why I've come here? In wilderness, I seek the wildness in myself—and in so doing, come on the wildness everywhere around me because, after all, being part of nature, I'm cut from the same cloth.

Following the coastline of a lake, I watch how wind picks up water in dark blasts and drops it again. Ducks glide in Vs away from me, out onto the fractured, darkening mirror. I stop. A hatch of mayflies powders the air and the archaic, straight-winged dragonflies hang, blunt-nosed, above me. A friend talks about aquatic bugs: water beetles, spinners, assassin bugs, and one that hatches, mates, and dies in a total lifespan of two hours. At the end of the meadow the lake drains into a fast-moving creek. I quicken my pace and trudge upward. Walking is also an ambulation of mind. The human armour of bones rattles, fat rolls, and inside this durable, fleshy prison of mine, I make a beeline toward otherness, lightness, or, maybe like a moth, toward flame.

Somewhere along the trail I laugh out loud. How shell-like the body seems suddenly—not fleshy at all, but inhuman and hard. And farther up, I step out of my body though I'm still held fast by something, but what? I don't know.

How foolish the preparations for wilderness trips seem now. We pore over our maps, chart our expeditions. We "gear up" at trailheads with pitons and crampons, horsepacks and backpacks, fly rods and cameras, forgetting the meaning of simply going, of lifting thought-covers, of disburdenment. I look up from these thoughts. A blue heron rises from a gravel bar and glides behind a gray screen of dead trees, appears in an opening where an avalanche downed pines, and lands again on water.

I stop to eat lunch. Ralph Waldo Emerson wrote, "The Gautama said that the first men ate the earth and found it sweet." I eat baloney and cheese and think about eating the earth. It's another way of framing our wonder in which the width of the mouth stands for the generous palate of consciousness. I cleanse my palate with miner's lettuce and streamwater and try to imagine what kinds of sweetness the earth provides: the taste of glacial flour, or the mineral taste of basalt, the fresh and foul bouquets of rivers, the dessicated, stinging flavor of a snowstorm—like eating red ants, my friend says.

As I begin to walk again it occurs to me that this notion of "eating the earth" is not about gluttony, hedonism, or sin, but, rather, unconditional love. Everywhere I look I see the possibility of love. To find wildness, I must first offer myself up, accept all that comes before me: a bullfrog breathing hard on a rock; moose tracks under elk scats; a cloud that looks like a clothespin; a seep of water from a high cirque, black on brown rock, draining down from the brain of the world.

At treeline, birdsong stops. I'm lifted into another movement of music, one with no particular notes, only windsounds becoming watersounds, becoming windsounds. Above, a cornice crowns a ridge and melts into a teal and turquoise lake, like a bladder, leaking its wine.

On top of Marston Pass I'm in a ruck of steep valleys and gray, treeless peaks. The alpine carpet, studded with red paintbrush and alpine buttercups, gives way to rock. Now all the way across a vertiginous valley, I see where water oozes from moss and mud, how, at its source, it quickly becomes something else.

Emerson also said: "Every natural fact is an emanation, and that from which it emanates is an emanation also, and from every emanation is a new emanation." The ooze, the source of a great river, is now a white chute tumbling over soft folds of conglomerate rock. Wind tears at it, throwing sheets of water to another part of the mountainside: soft earth gives way under my feet, clouds spill upward and spit rain. Isn't everything redolent with loss, with momentary radiance, a coming to different ground? Stone basins catch the waterfall, spill it again, like thoughts strung together, laddered down.

I see where meltwater is split by a rock—half going west to the Pacific, the other going east to the Atlantic, for this is the Continental Divide. Down the other side the air I gulp feels softer. Ice spans and tunnels the creek, then, when night comes but before the full moon, falling stars have the same look as that white chute of water, falling against the rock of night.

To rise above treeline is to go above thought, and after, the descent back into birdsong, bog orchids, willows, and firs is to sink into the preliterate parts of ourselves. It is to forget discontent, undisciplined needs. Here the world is only space, raw loneliness, green valleys hung vertically. Losing myself to it—if I can—I do not fall . . . or, if I do, I'm only another cataract of water.

Wildness has no conditions, no sure routes, no peaks or goals, no source that is not instantly becoming something more than itself, then letting go of that, always becoming. It cannot be stripped to its complexity by cat scan or telescope. Rather, it is a many-pointed truth, almost a bluntness, a sudden essence like the wild strawberries strung along the ground on scarlet runners under my feet. Wildness is source and fruition at once, as if every river circled round, the mouth eating the tail—and the tail, the source.

Now I am camped among trees again. Four yearling moose, their chestnut coats shiny from a summer's diet of willow shoots, tramp past my bedroll and drink from a spring that issues sulphurous water. The ooze, the white chute, the narrow stream—now almost a river—joins this small spring and slows into skinny oxbows and deep pools before breaking again on rock, a stepladder of sequined riffles.

To trace the history of a river, or a raindrop, as John Muir would have done, is also to trace the history of the soul, the history of the mind descending and arising in the body. In both, we constantly seek and stumble on divinity, which, like the cornice feeding the lake and the spring becoming a waterfall, feeds, spills, falls, and feeds itself over and over again.

MERIDEL LE SUEUR

ANNUNCIATION

from *Salute to Spring* (1940)

Meridel Le Sueur (1900–   ) has had a long and prolific career as a scribe for the oppressed and exploited—farm laborers, factory workers, native peoples, women. "I am a woman speaking for us all," she writes. Her work—including novels, short stories, poetry, children's books, history, journalism, and essays—is rooted in the prairie, influenced by her association with radical leftists, Marxists, and prairie populists, and often luminous with an earth-based wisdom. One of her central themes, apparent in her early and perhaps finest short story, "Annunciation," is celebration of the unrestrainable fecundity of earth and woman.

Of her origins, she writes that she was "conceived in the riotous summer and fattened on light and stars that fell on my underground roots, and every herb, corn plant, cricket, beaver, red fox leaped in me in the old Indian dark." Born in Iowa to socialist parents, she dropped out of high school and lived in a New York anarchist commune with Emma Goldman, acted in early movies like *The Last of the Mohicans* and *The Perils of Pauline,* married a labor organizer and had two daughters, and began writing of the lives and struggles of women before such was popular. Though she was highly regarded as a novelist and short story writer in the 1930s, her books fell into a long period of obscurity when she was branded subversive for her political views and activities by Senator Joseph McCarthy in the 1950s. Now she is an aged matriarch, and her work is once again gaining the appreciation it deserves.

Ever since I have known I was going to have a child I have kept writing things down on these little scraps of paper. There is something I want to say, something I want to make clear for myself and others. One lives all one's life in a sort of way, one is alive and that is about all that there is to say about it. Then something happens.

There is the pear tree I can see in the afternoons as I sit on this porch writing these notes. It stands for something. It has had something to do with what has happened to me. I sit here all afternoon in the autumn sun and then I begin to write something on this yellow paper; something seems to be going on like a buzzing, a flying and circling within me, and then I want to write it down in some way. I have never felt this way before, except when I was a girl and was first in love and wanted then to set things down on paper so that they would not be lost. It is something perhaps like a farmer who hears the swarming of a host of bees and goes out to catch them so that he will have honey. If he does not go out right away, they will go, and he will hear the buzzing growing more distant in the afternoon.

My sweater pocket is full of scraps of paper on which I have written. I sit here many afternoons while Karl is out looking for work, writing on pieces of paper, unfolding, reading what I have already written.

We have been here two weeks at Mrs. Mason's boarding house. The leaves are falling and there is a golden haze over everything. This is the fourth month for me and it is fall. A rich powerful haze comes down from the mountains over the city. In the afternoon I go out for a walk. There is a park just two blocks from here. Old men and tramps lie on the grass all day. It is hard to get work. Many people besides Karl are out of work. People are hungry just as I am hungry. People are ready to flower and they cannot. In the evenings we go there with a sack of old fruit we can get at the stand across the way quite cheap, bunches of grapes and old pears. At noon there is a hush in the air and at evening there are stirrings of wind coming from the sky, blowing in the fallen leaves, or perhaps there is a light rain, falling quickly on the walk. Early in the mornings the sun comes up hot in the sky and shines all day through the mist. It is strange, I notice all these things, the sun, the rain falling, the blowing of the wind. It is as if they had a meaning for me as the pear tree has come to have.

In front of Mrs. Mason's house there is a large magnolia tree with its blossoms yellow, hanging over the steps almost within reach. Its giant leaves are motionless and shining in the heat, occasionally as I am going down the steps towards the park one falls heavily on the walk.

This house is an old wooden one, that once was quite a mansion I imagine. There are glass chandeliers in the hall and fancy tile in the bathrooms. It was owned by the rich once and now the dispossessed live in it with the rats. We have a room three flights up. You go into the dark hallway and up the stairs. Broken settees and couches sit in the halls. About one o'clock the girls come down stairs to get their mail and sit on the front porch. The blinds go up in the old wooden house across the street. It is always quite hot at noon.

Next to our room lies a sick woman in what is really a kind of closet with no windows. As you pass you see her face on the pillow and a nauseating odor of sickness comes out the door. I haven't asked her what is the matter with her but everyone knows she is waiting for death. Somehow it is not easy to speak to her. No one comes to see her. She has been a housemaid all her life tending other people's children; now no one comes to see her. She gets up sometimes and drinks a little from the bottle of milk that is always sitting by her bed covered with flies.

Mrs. Mason, the landlady, is letting us stay although we have only paid a week's rent and have been here over a week without paying. But it is a bad season and we may be able to pay later. It is better perhaps for her than having an empty room. But I hate to go out and have to pass her door and I am always fearful of meeting her on the stairs. I go down as quietly as I can but it isn't easy, for the stairs creak frightfully.

The room we have on the top floor is a back room, opening out onto an old porch which seems to be actually tied to the wall of the house with bits of wire and rope. The floor of it slants downward to a rickety railing. There is a box perched on the railing that has geraniums in it. They are large, tough California geraniums. I guess nothing can kill them. I water them since I have been here and a terribly red flower has come. It is on this porch I am sitting. Just over the banisters stand the top branches of a pear tree.

Many afternoons I sit here. It has become a kind of alive place to me. The room is dark behind me, with only the huge walnut tree scraping against the one window over the kitchenette. If I go to the railing and look down I can see far below the backyard which has been made into a garden with two fruit trees and I can see where a path has gone in the summer between a small bed of flowers, now only dead stalks. The ground is bare under the walnut tree where little sun penetrates. There is a dog kennel by the round trunk but there doesn't ever seem to be a dog. An old wicker chair sits outdoors in rain or shine. A woman in an old wrapper comes out and sits there almost every afternoon. I don't know who she is, for I don't know anybody in this house, having to sneak downstairs as I do.

Karl says I am foolish to be afraid of the landlady. He comes home drunk and makes a lot of noise. He says she's lucky in these times to have anybody in her house, but I notice in the mornings he goes down the stairs quietly and often goes out the back way.

I'm alone all day so I sit on this rickety porch. Straight out from the rail so that I can almost touch it is the radiating frail top of the pear tree that has opened a door for me. If the pears were still hanging on it each would be alone and separate with a kind of bloom upon it. Such a bloom is upon me at this moment. Is it possible that everyone, Mrs. Mason who runs this boarding house, the woman next door, the girls downstairs, all in this dead wooden house have hung at one time, each separate in a mist and bloom upon some invisible tree? I wonder if it is so.

I am in luck to have this high porch to sit on and this tree swaying before me through the long afternoons and the long nights. Before we came here, after the show broke up in S.F. we were in an old hotel, a foul smelling place with a dirty chambermaid and an old cat in the halls, and night and day we could hear the radio going in the office. We had a room with a window looking across a narrow way into another room where a lean man stood in the mornings looking across, shaving his evil face. By leaning out and looking up I could see straight up the sides of the tall building and above the smoky sky.

Most of the time I was sick from the bad food we ate. Karl and I walked the streets looking for work. Sometimes I was too sick to go. Karl would come in and there would be no money at all. He would go out again to perhaps borrow something. I know many times he begged although we never spoke of it, but I could tell by the way he looked when he came back with a begged quarter. He went in with a man selling Mexican beans but he didn't make much. I lay on the bed bad days feeling sick and hungry, sick too with the stale odor of the foul walls. I would lie there a long time listening to the clang of the city outside. I would feel thick with this child. For some reason I remember that I would sing to myself and often became happy as if mesmerised there in the foul room. It must have been because of this child. Karl would come back perhaps with a little money and we would go out to a dairy lunch and there have food I could not relish. The first alleyway I must give it up with the people all looking at me.

Karl would be angry. He would walk on down the

street so people wouldn't think he was with me. Once we walked until evening down by the docks. "Why don't you take something?" he kept saying. "Then you wouldn't throw up your food like that. Get rid of it. That's what everybody does nowadays. This isn't the time to have a child. Everything is rotten. We must change it." He kept on saying, "Get rid of it. Take something why don't you?" And he got angry when I didn't say anything but just walked along beside him. He shouted so loud at me that some stevedores loading a boat for L.A. laughed at us and began kidding us, thinking perhaps we were lovers having a quarrel.

Some time later, I don't know how long it was, for I hadn't any time except the nine months I was counting off, but one evening Karl sold enough Mexican jumping beans at a carnival to pay our fare, so we got on a river boat and went up the river to a delta town. There might be a better chance of a job. On this boat you can sit up all night if you have no money to buy a berth. We walked all evening along the deck and then when it got cold we went into the saloon because we had pawned our coats. Already at that time I had got the habit of carrying slips of paper around with me and writing on them, as I am doing now. I had a feeling then that something was happening to me of some kind of loveliness I would want to preserve in some way. Perhaps that was it. At any rate I was writing things down. Perhaps it had something to do with Karl wanting me all the time to take something. "Everybody does it," he kept telling me. "It's nothing, then it's all over." I stopped talking to him much. Everything I said only made him angry. So writing was a kind of conversation I carried on with myself and with the child.

Well, on the river boat that night after we had gone into the saloon to get out of the cold, Karl went to sleep right away in a chair. But I couldn't sleep. I sat watching him. The only sound was the churning of the paddle wheel and the lap of the water. I had on then this sweater and the notes

I wrote are still in the breast pocket. I would look up from writing and see Karl sleeping like a young boy.

"Tonight, the world into which you are coming"—then I was speaking to the invisible child—"is very strange and beautiful. That is, the natural world is beautiful. I don't know what you will think of man, but the dark glisten of vegetation and the blowing of the fertile land wind and the delicate strong step of the sea wind, these things are familiar to me and will be familiar to you. I hope you will be like these things. I hope you will glisten with the glisten of ancient life, the same beauty that is in a leaf or a wild rabbit, wild sweet beauty of limb and eye. I am going on a boat between dark shores, and the river and the sky are so quiet that I can hear the scurryings of tiny animals on the shores and their little breathings seem to be all around. I think of them, wild, carrying their young now, crouched in the dark underbrush with the fruit-scented land wind in their delicate nostrils, and they are looking out at the moon and the fast clouds. Silent, alive, they sit in the dark shadow of the greedy world. There is something wild about us too, something tender and wild about my having you as a child, about your crouching so secretly here. There is something very tender and wild about it. We, too, are at the mercy of many hunters. On this boat I act like the other human beings, for I do not show that I have you, but really I know we are as helpless, as wild, as at bay as some tender wild animals who might be on the ship.

"I put my hand where you lie so silently. I hope you will come glistening with life power, with it shining upon you as upon the feathers of birds. I hope you will be a warrior and fierce for change, so all can live."

Karl woke at dawn and was angry with me for sitting there looking at him. Just to look at me makes him angry now. He took me out and made me walk along the deck although it was hardly light yet. I gave him the "willies" he said, looking at him like that. We walked round and round the decks and he kept talking to me in a low voice, trying to persuade me. It was hard for me to listen. My teeth were chattering with cold, but anyway I found it hard to listen to anyone talking, especially Karl. I remember I kept thinking to myself that a child should be made by machinery now, then there would be no fuss. I kept thinking of all the places I had been with this new child, traveling with the show from Tia Juana to S.F. In trains, over mountains, through deserts, in hotels and rooming houses, and myself in a trance of wonder. There wasn't a person I could have told it to, that I was going to have a child. I didn't want to be pitied. Night after night we played in the tent and the faces were all dust to me, but traveling, through the window the many vistas of the earth meant something—the bony skeleton of the mountains, like the skeleton of the world jutting through its flowery flesh. My child too would be made of bone. There were the fields of summer, the orchards fruiting, the berry fields and the pickers stooping, the oranges and the grapes. Then the city again in September and the many streets I walk looking for work, stopping secretly in doorways to feel beneath my coat.

It is better in this small town with the windy fall days and the sudden rain falling out of a sunny sky. I can't look for work anymore. Karl gets a little work washing dishes at a wienie place. I sit here on the porch as if in a deep sleep waiting for this unknown child. I keep hearing this far flight of strange birds going on in the mysterious air about me. This time has come without warning. How can it be explained? Everything is dead and closed, the world a stone, and then suddenly everything comes alive as it has for me, like an anemone on a rock, opening itself, disclosing itself, and the very stones themselves break open like bread. It has all got something to do with the pear tree too. It has come about some way as I have sat here with this child so many afternoons, with the pear tree murmuring in the air.

The pears are all gone from the tree but I imagine them hanging there, ripe curves within the many scimitar leaves, and within them many pears of the coming season. I feel like a pear. I hang secret within the curling leaves, just as the pear would be hanging on its tree. It seems possible to me that perhaps all people at some time feel this, round and full. You can tell by looking at most people that the world remains a stone to them and a closed door. I'm afraid it will become like that to me again. Perhaps after this child is born, then everything will harden and become small and mean again as it was before. Perhaps I would even have a hard time remembering this time at all and it wouldn't seem wonderful. That is why I would like to write it down.

How can it be explained? Suddenly many movements are going on within me, many things are happening, there is an almost unbearable sense of sprouting, of bursting encasements, of moving kernels, expanding flesh. Perhaps it is such an activity that makes a field come alive with millions of sprouting shoots of corn or wheat. Perhaps it is something like that that makes a new world.

I have been sitting here and it seems as if the wooden houses around me had become husks that suddenly as I watched began to swarm with livening seed. The house across becomes a fermenting seed alive with its own movements. Everything seems to be moving along a curve of creation. The alley below and all the houses are to me like an orchard abloom, shaking and trembling, moving outward with shouting. The people coming and going seem to hang on the tree of life, each blossoming from himself. I am standing here looking at the blind windows of the house next door and suddenly the walls fall away, the doors open, and within I see a young girl making a bed from which she had just risen having dreamed of a young man who became her lover . . . she stands before her looking-glass in love with herself.

I see in another room a young man sleeping, his bare arm thrown over his head. I see a woman lying on a bed after her husband has left her. There is a child looking at me. An old woman sits rocking. A boy leans over a table reading a book. A woman who has been nursing a child comes out and hangs clothes on the line, her dress in front wet with milk. A young woman comes to an open door looking up and down the street waiting for her young husband. I get up early to see this young woman come to the door in a pink wrapper and wave to her husband. They have only been married a short time, she stands waving until he is out of sight and even then she stands smiling to herself, her hand upraised.

Why should I be excited? Why should I feel this excitement, seeing a woman waving to her young husband, or a woman who has been nursing a child, or a young man sleeping? Yet I am excited. The many houses have become like an orchard blooming soundlessly. The many people have become like fruits to me, the young girl in the room alone before her mirror, the young man sleeping, the mother, all are shaking with their inward blossoming, shaken by the windy blooming, moving along a future curve.

I do not want it all to go away from me. Now many doors are opening and shutting, light is falling upon darkness, closed places are opening, still things are now moving. But there will come a time when the doors will close again, the shouting will be gone, the sprouting and the movement and the wonderous opening out of everything will be gone. I will be only myself. I will come to look like the women in this house. I try to write it down on little slips of paper, trying to preserve this time for myself so that afterwards when everything is the same again I can remember what all must have.

This is the spring there should be in the world, so I say to myself, "Lie in the sun with the child in your flesh shining like a jewel. Dream and sing, pagan, wise in your vitals. Stand still like a fat budding tree, like a stalk of corn athrob and aglisten in the heat. Lie like a mare panting with the dancing feet of colts against her sides. Sleep at night as the spring earth. Walk heavily as a wheat stalk at its full time bending towards the earth waiting for the reaper. Let your life swell downward so you become like a vase, a vessel. Let the unknown child knock and knock against you and rise like a dolphin within."

I look at myself in the mirror. My legs and head hardly make a difference, just a stem my legs. My hips are full and tight in back as if bracing themselves. I look like a pale and shining pomegranate, hard and tight, and my skin shines like crystal with the veins showing beneath blue and distended. Children are playing outside and girls are walking with young men along the walk. All that seems over for me. I am a pomegranate hanging from an invisible tree with the juice and movement of seed within my hard skin. I dress slowly. I hate the smell of clothes. I want to leave them off and just hang in the sun ripening . . . ripening.

It is hard to write it down so that it will mean anything. I've never heard anything about how a woman feels who is going to have a child, or about how a pear tree feels bearing its fruit. I would like to read these things many years from now, when I am barren and no longer trembling like this, when I get like the women in this house, or like the woman in the closed room, I can hear her breathing through the afternoon.

When Karl has no money he does not come back at night. I go out on the street walking to forget how hungry I am. This is an old town and along the streets are many old strong trees. Night leaves hang from them ready to fall, dark and swollen with their coming death. Trees, dark, separate, heavy with their down hanging leaves, cool surfaces hanging on the dark. I put my hand among the leaf sheaves. They strike with a cool surface, their glossy surfaces surprising me in the dark. I feel like a tree swirling upwards too, muscular sap alive, with rich surfaces hanging from me, flaring outward rocket-like and falling to my roots, a rich strong power in me to break through into a new life. And dark in me as I walk the streets of this decayed town are the buds of my child. I walk alone under the dark flaring trees. There are many houses with the lights shining out but you and I walk on the skirts of the lawns amidst the downpouring darkness. Houses are not for us. For us many kinds of hunger, for us a deep rebellion.

Trees come from a far seed walking the wind, my child

too from a far seed blowing from last year's rich and revolutionary dead. My child budding secretly from far walking seed, budding secretly and dangerously in the night.

The woman has come out and sits in the rocker, reading, her fat legs crossed. She scratches herself, cleans her nails, picks her teeth. Across the alley lying flat on the ground is a garage. People are driving in and out. But up here it is very quiet and the movement of the pear tree is the only movement and I seem to hear its delicate sound of living as it moves upon itself silently, and outward and upward.

The leaves twirl and twirl all over the tree, the delicately curving tinkling leaves. They twirl and twirl on the tree and the tree moves far inward upon its stem, moves in an invisible wind, gently swaying. Far below straight down the vertical stem like a stream, black and strong into the ground, runs the trunk; and invisible, spiraling downward and outwards in powerful radiation, lie the roots. I can see it spiraling upwards from below, its stem straight, and from it, spiraling the branches season by season, and from the spiraling branches moving out in quick motion, the forked stems, and from the stems twirling fragilely the tinier stems holding outward until they fall, the half curled pear leaves.

Far below lies the yard, lying flat and black beneath the body of the upshooting tree, for the pear tree from above looks as if it had been shot instantaneously from the ground, shot upward like a rocket to break in showers of leaves and fruits twirling and falling. Its movement looks quick, sudden and rocketing. My child when grown can be looked at in this way as if it suddenly existed . . . but I know the slow time of making. The pear tree knows.

Far inside the vertical stem there must be a movement, a river of sap rising from below and radiating outward in many directions clear to the tips of the leaves. The leaves are the lips of the tree speaking in the wind or they move like many tongues. The fruit of the tree you can see has been a round speech, speaking in full tongue on the tree, hanging in ripe body, the fat curves hung within the small curves of the leaves. I imagine them there. The tree has shot up like a rocket, then stops in midair and its leaves flow out gently and its fruit curves roundly and gently in a long slow curve. All is gentle on the pear tree after its strong upward shooting movement.

I sit here all the afternoon as if in its branches, midst the gentle and curving body of the tree. I have looked at it until it has become more familiar to me than Karl. It seems a strange thing that a tree might come to mean more to one than one's husband. It seems a shameful thing even. I am ashamed to think of it but it is so. I have sat here in the pale sun and the tree has spoken to me with its many tongued leaves, speaking through the afternoon of how to round a fruit. And I listen through the slow hours. I listen to the whisperings of the pear tree, speaking to me, speaking to me. How can I describe what is said by a pear tree? Karl did not speak to me so. No one spoke to me in any good speech.

There is a woman coming up the stairs, slowly. I can hear her breathing. I can hear her behind me at the screen door.

She came out and spoke to me. I know why she was looking at me so closely. "I hear you're going to have a child," she said. "It's too bad." She is the same color as the dead leaves in the park. Was she once alive too?

I am writing on a piece of wrapping paper now. It is about ten o'clock. Karl didn't come home and I had no supper. I walked through the streets with their heavy, heavy trees bending over the walks and the lights shining from the houses and over the river the mist rising.

Before I came into this room I went out and saw the pear tree standing motionless, its leaves curled in the dark, its radiating body falling darkly, like a stream far below into the earth.

MARY DONAHOE

WILD

from *You Are Mountain* (1984)

Mary Donahoe (1941–   ) has Native American roots, lives
in the mountain forests of Oregon, has raised children, and
writes poetry that reflects her deep acquaintance with the
earth. She was born in Hot Springs, Arkansas, and is earning
her Ph.D. in theater arts at the University of Oregon, while
writing and performing theater pieces on the lives of women
artists. "Wild" is from *You Are Mountain,* selected poems
from a longer collection to be called *Coming to the Country.*

Most late summer evenings
my dog sits about the door and howls,
I toss under a full moon,
admire the hair on my legs, under my arms.
By day geese eat our grain
and tolerate our trespassing.
They look to the sky

                    far into light
                    a V of honkers
                    follow their hearts
                    to the northland

When it rains,
we strip and run through trees
our bodies free to dance,
and in the night

I'll make a song that satisfies
like no other lover,
and when sleep comes, I dream
of shuffling through a forest,
licking bark and stones,
floor wet with leaf and pine,
growling over a bed of boughs,
breasts hanging to my cubs' mouths,
I,
the woman who wakes in my house
to make morning coffee,
to butter toast,
I look to the sky

                        far into light
                        a V of honkers
                        follow their hearts
                        to the northland

MARTHA REBEN

NIGHT SONG

from *A Sharing of Joy* (1963)

Martha Reben (1911–1964), though city bred, spent most
of her life in the Adirondack wilderness. Born Martha
Rebentisch in Manhattan, she discovered at sixteen that she
had an advanced case of tuberculosis, of which her mother
had died ten years earlier. She was sent to various sanitori-
ums and finally to Saranac Lake in the Adirondacks, a popu-
lar resort for those afflicted with TB. After three bedridden
years and three operations, Martha decided she had to get
out of the hospital environment to recover. At that time
Fred Rice, a woodsman who advocated the outdoors as a
cure for TB, was seeking a patient on whom to test his
theory. Martha responded to his ad in the local paper, and
he took her twelve miles into the woods to the shore of
Weller Pond to camp.

  With the guidance of Rice, Martha slept out in the open
and learned to hunt (although she soon gave this up, having
"no heart for killing"), fish, and find her way through the
forest with a compass. She spent many subsequent summer
seasons alone there, coming to terms with freedom and
loneliness, developing her inner life, and forming deep
bonds with animal companions. Each winter she returned to
a small cabin on the outskirts of the village. Her recovery
was remarkable; ten years later, the doctors pronounced her
free of TB. In the wilderness, Martha found not only a cure
but also a growing spirit of independence and self-reliance,
chronicled in the three books she wrote under the name
Martha Reben: *The Healing Woods* (1952), *The Way of the
Wilderness* (1955), and *A Sharing of Joy*.

I sat alone before my campfire one evening, watching as the sunset colors deepened to purple, the sky slowly darkened, and the stars came out. A deep peace lay over the woods and waters.

Gradually the wilderness around me merged into the blue of night. There was no sound save the crackle of my fire as the flames blazed around the birch and cedar logs.

The moon came up behind the black trees to the east, and the wilderness stood forth, vast, mysterious, still. All at once the silence and the solitude were touched by wild music, thin as air, the faraway gabbling of geese flying at night.

Presently I caught sight of them as they streamed across the face of the moon, the high, excited clamor of their voices tingling through the night, and suddenly I saw, in one of those rare moments of insight, what it means to be wild and free. As they went over me, I was there with them, passing over the moonlit countryside, glorying with them in their strong-hearted journeying, exulting in its joy and splendor.

The haunting voices grew fainter and faded in distance, but I sat on, stirred by a memory of something beautiful and ancient and now lost—a forgotten freedom we must all once have shared with other wild things, which only they and the wilderness can still recall to us, so that life becomes again, for a time, the wonderful, sometimes frightening, but fiercely joyous adventure it was intended to be.

SUE HUBBELL

BECOMING FERAL

from *A Country Year* (1986)

Sue Hubbell (1935–   ) writes, "I am a beekeeper but I am also a writer, and some years ago I sat down at the typewriter to experiment with words, to try to tease out of the amorphous, chaotic and wordless part of myself the reason why I was staying on this hilltop in the Ozarks after my first husband, with whom I had started a beekeeping business, and I had divorced." The result was her first book, *A Country Year: Living the Questions,* which traces the natural history of her hilltop from one springtime to the next.

Born in Kalamazoo, Michigan, Hubbell married, had a son, Brian, and worked as a librarian at Brown University before she and her husband bought the 105-acre hilltop farm in southern Missouri that became the subject of her writing. *A Country Year* brought Hubbell to the attention of an old college friend, now her second husband. She presently splits her time between her Ozark apiary and Washington, D.C., where he lives. "I want to be with him in the city, but my Ozark hilltop and its wild things and wild places pull me all the time," she explains in her second book, *A Book of Bees* (1988).

Hoohoo-hoohoo . . . hoohoo-hoohooaww. My neighbor across the river is doing his barred owl imitation in hopes of rousing a turkey from the roost. It is turkey-hunting season, and at dawn the hunters are trying to outwit wild turkeys and I listen to them as I drink my coffee under the oak trees.

Hoohoo-hoohoo . . . hoohoo-hoohooaww.

GahgahGAHgah replies an imitation turkey from another direction. I know that neighbor, too. Yesterday he showed me the hand-held wooden box with which he made the noise that is supposed to sound like a turkey cock gobbling. It doesn't. After the turkey cocks are down from their roosts, the hunters, by imitating hen turkeys, try to call them close enough to shoot them. The barred owl across the river once showed me his turkey caller. He held it in his mouth and made a soft clucking noise with it.

"Now this is the really sexy one," he said, arching one eyebrow, *"Putput . . . putterputput."*

It is past dawn now, and I imagine both men are exasperated. I have not heard one real turkey yet this morning. The hunting season is set by the calendar but the turkeys breed by the weather, and the spring has been so wet and cold that their mating has been delayed this year. In the last few mornings I have started hearing turkeys gobbling occasionally, and it will be another week or two before a wise and wary turkey cock could be fooled by a man with a caller.

There are other birds out there this morning. The indigo buntings, who will be the first birds to sing in the dawn later on, have not yet returned to the Ozarks, but I can hear cardinals and Carolina chickadees. They wintered here, but today their songs are of springtime. There are chipping sparrows above me in the oak trees and field sparrows nearby. There are warblers, too; some of their songs are familiar, and others, those of the migrators, are not. I hear one of the most beautiful of birdsongs, that of the white-throated sparrow. He is supposed to sing "Old Sam Peabody, Peabody, Peabody." This is the cadence, to be sure, but it gives no hint of the lyrical clarity and sweetness of the descending notes of his song.

I slept outdoors last night because I could not bear to go in. The cabin, which only last winter seemed cozy and inviting, has begun to seem stuffy and limiting, so I spread a piece of plastic on the ground to keep off the damp, put my sleeping bag on it and dropped off to sleep watching the stars. Tazzie likes to be near me, and with me on the ground she could press right up to my back. But Andy is a conservative dog who worries a lot, and he thought it was unsound to sleep outside where there might be snakes and beetles. He whined uneasily as I settled in, and once during the night he woke me up, nuzzling me and whimpering, begging to be allowed to go inside to his rug. I think he may be more domesticated than I am. I wonder if I am becoming feral. Wild things and wild places pull me more strongly than they did a few years ago, and domesticity, dusting and cookery interest me not at all.

Sometimes I wonder where we older women fit into the social scheme of things once nest building has lost its charm. A generation ago Margaret Mead, who had a good enough personal answer to this question, wondered the same thing, and pointed out that in other times and other cultures we have had a role.

There are so many of us that it is tempting to think of us as a class. We are past our reproductive years. Men don't want us; they prefer younger women. It makes good biological sense for males to be attracted to females who are at an earlier point in their breeding years and who still want to build nests, and if that leaves us no longer able to lose ourselves in the pleasures and closeness of pairing, well, we have gained our Selves. We have another valuable thing, too. We have Time, or at least the awareness of it. We have lived long enough and seen enough to understand in a more than intellectual way that we will die, and so we have learned to live as though we are mortal, making our decisions with care and thought because we will not be able to make them again. Time for us will have an end; it is precious, and we have learned its value.

Yes, there are many of us, but we are all so different that I am uncomfortable with a sociobiological analysis, and I suspect that, as with Margaret Mead, the solution is a personal and individual one. Because our culture has assigned us no real role, we can make up our own. It is a good time to be a grown-up woman with individuality, strength and crotchets. We are wonderfully free. We live long. Our children are the independent adults we helped them to become, and though they may still want our love they do not need our care. Social rules are so flexible today that nothing we do is shocking. There are no political barriers to us anymore. Provided we stay healthy and can support ourselves, we can do anything, have anything and spend our talents any way that we please.

Hoohoo-hoohoo . . . hoohoo-hooaww.

The sun is up now, and it is too late for a barred owl. I know that man across the river, and I know he must be getting cross. He is probably sitting on a damp log, his feet and legs cold and cramped from keeping still. I also know the other hunter, the one with the wooden turkey caller. This week what both men want is a dead turkey.

I want a turkey too, but I want mine alive, and in a week I'll have my wish, hearing them gobbling at dawn. I want more, however. I want indigo buntings singing their couplets when I wake in the morning. I want to read *Joseph and His Brothers* again. I want oak leaves and dogwood blossoms and fireflies. I want to know how the land lies up Coon Hollow. I want Asher to find out what happens to moth-ear mites in the winter. I want to show Liddy and Brian the big rocks down in the creek hollow. I want to know much more about grand-daddy-longlegs. I want to write a novel. I want to go swimming naked in the hot sun down at the river.

That is why I have stopped sleeping inside. A house is too small, too confining. I want the whole world, and the stars too.

REBECCA GONZALES

THE SAFETY BEHIND ME

from *Slow Work to the Rhythm of Cicadas* (1985)

> Rebecca Gonzales (1946–   ) has been influenced as a poet
> by the rhythm of cicadas and the desert distances. Born in
> Laredo, Texas, she has lived since 1970 in the Beaumont
> area, where she teaches high school English.

Last night the house was too safe;
the heated air, stifling;
touches and topics, calculated, civilized.

Later, I couldn't sleep;
the digital clock kept me
waiting for each next moment.

In my robe and slippers,
I went outside and stood,
soaking the cold under our streetlight.

The houses closed in,
shouldering the night
from the glowing street and me.

But I wanted to be cold;
could have flung the safety behind me,
could have traded each moment

for the thump of fear in a marsh rabbit,
running to the sweet violence of a mate,
the direction of the next moment in the wind.

EDNA BRUSH PERKINS

THE FEEL OF THE OUTDOORS

from *The White Heart of Mojave* (1922)

> Edna Brush Perkins (1880–1930) was a middle-aged suf-
> fragette living in Cleveland with an epidemiologist husband
> and four sons when she and her friend Charlotte Hannahs
> Jordan heard the call of the wild and determinedly set out
> to respond. Her book *The White Heart of Mojave: An Adven-
> ture with the Outdoors of the Desert* is a chronicle of the
> women's pilgrimage from Chicago to Death Valley in an era
> when traveling on the desert for pleasure was "so novel an
> idea that everybody thought us insane." The book, by turns
> hilarious and reverent, is a testament to the power of earth's
> wild and lonely places to wake us up from the trance in-
> duced by living within four walls.
>
> The women's first trip by automobile from Los Angeles
> to Death Valley fell short of its goal when the road turned
> to "two ruts among the sagebrush." Undaunted, the pair
> returned nine months later, engaged a local guide, and fi-
> nally arrived in Death Valley in a wagon drawn by a horse
> and a mule. They spent January until April on the journey,
> concluding that "a lifetime is not enough to listen to the
> songs of the desolate places." Perkins and Jordan later trav-
> eled by camel across Algeria, and Perkins wrote about it in
> *A Red Carpet on the Sahara* (1925).

Beyond the walls and solid roofs of houses is the outdoors.
It is always on the doorstep. The sky, serene, or piled with
white, slow-moving clouds, or full of wind and purple
storm, is always overhead. But walls have an engrossing
quality. If there are many of them they assert themselves

and domineer. They insist on the unique importance of the contents of walls and would have you believe that the spaces above them, the slow procession of the seasons and the alternations of sunshine and rain, are accessories, pleasant or unpleasant, of walls,—indeed that they were made, and a bungling job, too, and to be disregarded as a bungling job should be, solely that walls might exist.

Perhaps your lawyer or your dentist has his office on the nineteenth floor of a modern skyscraper. While you wait for his ministrations you look out of his big window. Below you the roofs of the city spread for miles to blue hills or the bright sea. The smoke of tall chimneys rolls into the sky that fills all the space between you and the horizon and the sun; the smoke of hustling prosperity fans out, and floats, and mixes with the clouds, and becomes at last part of a majestic movement of something other than either smoke or clouds. Suddenly the roofs that covered only tables and chairs and power machines cover romance, a million romances rise and mingle like the smoke of the tall chimneys. They mix with the romance of the clouds and the hills. You are happy. Nothing is changed around you, but you are happy. You only know that the sun did it, and those far-off hills. When the man you are waiting for comes in you congratulate him on his fine view. Then the jealous walls assert themselves again; they want you to forget as soon as possible.

But you never quite forget. You visit the woods or the mountains or the sea in your vacation. You loaf along trout streams, or in red autumn woods with a gun in your hands for an excuse, or chase golf balls over green hills, or sail on the bay and get becalmed and do not care. For the pleasure of living outdoors you are willing to have your eyes smart from the smoke of the camp fire, and to be wet and cold, and to fight mosquitoes and flies. You like the feel of it, and you wait for that sudden sense of romance everywhere which is the touch of something big and simple and beautiful. It is always beyond the walls, that something, but most of us have been bullied by them so much that we have to go far away to find it; then we can bring it home and remember.

Charlotte and I knew the outdoors a little. Though we were middle-aged, mothers of families and deeply involved in the historic struggle for the vote, we sometimes looked at the sky. In our remote youth we had had a few brief experiences of the mountains and the woods; I had some not altogether contemptible peaks to my credit and she had canoed in the Canadian wilds, so when we decided that a vacation was due us we chose the outdoors. Our labors had been arduous, divided as they were between the clamorings of the young and our militant mission to free the world; we were thoroughly habituated to walls and set a high value on their contents. It was our habit to tell large and assorted audiences that freedom consists in casting a ballot at regular intervals and taking your rightful place in a great democracy; nor did it seem anomalous, as perhaps it should have, that our chiefest desire was to escape from every manifestation of democracy in the solitariness of some wild and lonely place far from city halls, smokestacks, national organizations, and streets of little houses all alike. For some time the desire had been cutting through our work with an edge of restlessness. We called it "Need for a Vacation," not knowing that every desire to withdraw from the crowd is a personal assertion and a protest against the struggle and worry, the bluff and banality and everlasting tail-chasing which goes on inside the walls of the stateliest statehouse and the two-room suite with bath. Our real craving was not for a play hour, but for the wild and lonely place and a different kind of freedom from that about which we had been preaching.

Our choice of the wild and lonely place was circumscribed by the fact that we had been offered the use of an automobile from Los Angeles. The automobile was a much appreciated gift, but we regretted that Los Angeles had to be the starting point because southern California is the blissful goal of the tired east and the tired east was what we needed to escape from. We left home without plans—too many plans in vacation are millstones hung around your neck—sure only that such places as Santa Barbara, Redlands, Riverside, and San Diego would be for us nothing more than points on the way to somewhere else. An atlas showed a great empty space just east of the Sierra Nevada Range and the San Bernadino Mountains vaguely designated as the Mojave Desert. It was surprising to find the greater part of southern California, the much-advertised home of the biggest fruit and flowers in the world, included in it. A few criss-cross lines indicated mountains; north of the Santa Fé Railroad, which crosses the Mojave on the way to the coast, the words Death Valley were printed between two groups of them; in the south a big white space similarly surrounded was the Imperial Valley; the names of a few towns sprangled out from the railroad—nothing else. Was the desert just a white space like that? The word had a mixed connotation, it suggested monotony, sterility, death—and also big open spaces, gold and blue sunsets, and fascination. We recollected that some author had written about the "terrible fascination" of the desert. The white blank on the map looked very wild and lonely. We went to Los Angeles on the Santa Fé in order to see what it might contain.

We looked at it. After leaving the high plateau of northern Arizona the railroad crosses the Colorado River and enters the lowlands of the Mojave Desert. That is the first glimpse the tourist has of California, but he hardly realizes that it is California, for it is so different from the pictures on the time-tables and hotel folders. At Needles he usually pulls down the window shades against the too-hot sun and forgets the dust and heat in the pages of the last best seller, or else he goes out on the California Limited which spares its passengers the dusty horrors of the desert by crossing the Mojave at night. His California, and ours when we left Chicago, consists of the charming bungalows with date palms in their dooryards and yellow roses climbing their porches, the square orange groves all brushed and combed for dress parade, the picturesque missions, and the white towns with streets shaded by feathery pepper trees west of the backbone of the Sierras, not the hundreds of miles of desolation east of them. Hour after hour we pounded through it in a hot monotony of yellow dust. Hour after hour great sweeps of blue-green brush led off to mountains blue and red against the sky. We passed black lava beds, and strange shining flats of baked clay, and clifflike rocks. It was very vast. The railroad seemed a tiny thread of life through an endless solitude. The train stopped at forlorn stations consisting of a few buildings stark on the coarse, gravelly sand. Sometimes a gang of swarthy Mexicans stopped work on the track to watch us go by, sometimes a house stood alone in the brush, sometimes a lonely automobile crawled along the highway beside the railroad. It was empty and vast, and over it all the sun poured a white flood.

In spite of the dust and glare a fascinated curiosity kept us looking out of the dirty windows all day. Occasionally dim wagon tracks led toward the mountains, some of which were high and set on wide, solid foundations. They were immovable, old, old mountains. Shadows cut sharply into the smooth brightness of their sides. Their colors changed and the sand ran between them like beckoning roads. "Come," it seemed to say, "and find what is hidden here." Once we saw a man with three burros loaded with cooking utensils and bedding. He was traveling across country through the sagebrush. Where could he be going?

Unconsciously I asked the question aloud and Charlotte answered:

"He is a prospector looking for a gold mine. Don't you see his pick on the second mule?"

"Please say burro," I pleaded. "It gives a better atmosphere. Besides it is not a mule, it's an ass."

"Those are the Old Dad Mountains over there, those big rosy ones. That's where he is going, up the long path of sand. He will camp there. Perhaps he is not a prospector, he may have a mine already."

"Of course he has one," I assented. "All the prospectors are dead. They died of thirst in Death Valley."

"My prospector did not. He is going to his mine. He tries to work it himself but it does not pay very well because he can't get enough out, and he can't sell it because too many booms have failed, and nobody will invest. So he goes up and down in the sun and has a good time."

Perhaps you could have a good time going up and down in the sun through those empty spaces that stretched so endlessly on either side of the track. I wondered if we might not go to the Imperial Valley and see that strange thing, the new Salton Sea, a lake in the desert; but Charlotte objected because that part of the white blank was partially under irrigation, too near the coast, and would be too civilized and full of ranches. I doubted much if the tired east went there for I thought that it was the desert like this, only hotter, worse. She declared that the tired east went everywhere that it could get to. Evidently it could not reach Mojave, for certainly it was not rushing around in automobiles trying to be happy, nor pouring the savings for its short holiday into the money bags of conscienceless hotel companies. Mojave was indeed a blank, a wild and lonely place.

"I think," Charlotte remarked after a time, "that we will go to Death Valley."

"Why?"

"Because I am tired of looking at the Twenty Mule Team Borax boxes and wondering what kind of place they came from that could have a name like that."

I thought it was not a sufficient reason for me to risk my life.

"I think," she said, "that it is the wildest and loneliest place of all. Nobody goes there except your prospectors, and you say they are all dead. Think of the gold and jewels they did not find lying around everywhere. Think of the hotness and brightness. It must be an awful, lonesome, sparkling place."

It must be! Those reasons appealed to me, but the idea

was a bit upsetting considering that we had started for a happy-go-lucky vacation, a little like playing with a kitten and having it turn into a tiger. Mojave was like a tiger, terrible and fascinating. From the windows of the Santa Fé train it was a savage, ruthless-looking country, naked in the sun. It repelled us and held us, we could not keep our eyes off it. They ached from straining to pierce the distances where the beckoning roads were lost in brightness. Mountains and valleys full of outdoors, nothing but outdoors! What was the feel of being alone in the sagebrush? How free the sweep of the wind must be, how hot the sun, how immense the deep night sky!

Thus the wild and lonely place was selected. A strange outdoors for a holiday truly, and we had an adventure with it.

IDAH MEACHAM STROBRIDGE

THE LURE OF THE DESERT
from *In Miners' Mirage-Land* (1904)

> Idah Meacham Strobridge (1855–1932) was captured by the lonely northwestern Nevada desert where she spent her girlhood, and although she finally moved to Los Angeles, the desert never released its hold on her. She wrote of her ecstatic communion with this harsh and desolate land, as well as of lost mines, desert wildlife, and prospectors, in three books and numerous articles. *In Miners' Mirage-Land,* *The Loom of the Desert* (1907), and *The Land of Purple Shadows*

(1909) were all privately printed in limited editions and hand-bound by her. Parts of her first book, which appeared a year after its kindred *Land of Little Rain* by Mary Austin, were originally published in the *Los Angeles Times* and the *San Francisco Chronicle.*

Idah Meacham was born in Moraga Valley, California, and when she was eight, moved with her family to Humboldt County, Nevada, where her father ranched and later operated the Humboldt House, a station stop on the Central Pacific Railroad. Idah attended Mills Seminary in Oakland, California, before marrying Samuel Strobridge in San Francisco and bearing three sons, all of whom died in infancy. When Samuel died four years after their marriage, Idah returned to Humboldt County, where she raised cattle, worked the Great West Gold Mine, and wrote short stories and poetry for periodicals. She used the pseudonym George Craiger, a combination of her parents' names, in her earliest writing. In about 1903 she moved to Los Angeles and built a house near where Mary Austin lived. From here she published her books and ran her Artemesia Bindery, named for her beloved sagebrush.

Except you are kindred with those who have speech with great spaces, and the Four Winds of the earth, and the infinite arch of God's sky, you shall not have understanding of the Desert's lure.

It is not the Desert's charm that calls one. What is it? I know not; only that there is a low, insistent voice calling—calling—calling. Not a loud voice. The Desert proclaiming itself, speaks gently. And we—every child of us who has laid on the breast of a mother while she rocked slowly, and hushed our fretting with a soft-sung lullaby song—we know how a low voice soothes and lulls one into sleep.

You are tired of the world's ways? Then, if you and the Desert have found each other, surely you will feel the drawing of your soul toward the eternal calm—the brooding peace that is there in the gray country.

Does the beautiful in Nature thrill you to your fingertips? When your eye is so trained that it may discover the beauty that dwells in that vast, still corner of the world, and your ear is attuned to catch the music of the plains or the anthems sung in deep cañons by the winds; when your heart finds comradeship in the mountains and the great sand-seas, the sun and the stars, and the huge cloud-drifts that the Desert winds set a-rolling round the world—when all these reach your heart by way of your eye and your ear, then you shall find one of the alluring ways that belongs to the Desert.

Do you seek for the marvelous? Or do you go a-quest for riches? Or simply desire to wander away into little known rifts in the wilderness? By these lures and a hundred others will the Desert draw you there. And once there, unprejudiced, the voice by and by will make itself heard as it whispers at your ear. And when you can lay your head on its breast, and hear its heart-beats, you will know a rest that is absolute and infinite. Then, you will understand those who yearly go a-searching for the mythical mines of mirage-land, and those who have lived apart from others for a lifetime, and are forgot by all their kindred and friends of a half-century ago. You will say: "It is the Desert's lure—I know—they cannot help it. And—yes!—it is worth all the penalty the gray land makes them pay!"

If you go to the Desert, and live there, you learn to love it. If you go away, you will never forget it for one instant in after life; it will be with you in memory forever and forever. And always will you hear the still voice that lures one, calling—and calling.

ELLA HIGGINSON

IN A VALLEY OF PEACE

from *When the Birds Go North Again* (1902)

Ella Higginson (c. 1860–1941) was a popular lyricist in her day. More than fifty composers set her words to music, and the early twentieth century's greatest singers—Caruso among them—performed them. She was born in Kansas, raised in eastern Oregon, and after her marriage to a pharmacist spent most of the rest of her life in Bellingham, Washington. She wrote one novel *(Mariella, of Out-West),* numerous award-winning short stories, and six collections of verse. Her poem "Four-Leaf Clover" is still taught to young people in the 4-H Club.

This long, green valley sloping to the sun,
With dimpling, silver waters loitering through;
The sky that bends above me, mild and blue;
The wide, still wheat-fields, yellowing one by one,
And all the peaceful sounds when day is done—
   I cannot bear their calm monotony!
   Great God! I want the thunder of the sea!
I want to feel the wild red lightnings run
Around, about me; hear the bellowing surf,
   And breathe the tempest's sibilant, sobbing breath;
   To front the elements, defying death,
And fling myself prone on the spray-beat turf,
   And hear the strong waves trampling wind and rain,
   Like herds of beasts upon the mighty plain.

CHINA GALLAND

RUNNING LAVA FALLS

from *Women in the Wilderness* (1980)

China Galland (1943–), in growing up, learned that "the
need to run wild, the sense of adventure and exploration,
the excitement in discovering the world of nature around
me were not acceptable in a grown woman." Still, she was
driven into the wilderness "to make sense of a life that didn't
fit." Now, she says, "I go into the wilderness and rediscover
the home within." She has raised three children and worked
as a river guide and university lecturer. A longtime student
of Tibetan Buddhism, she is presently a research associate at
the Graduate Theological Union in Berkeley. Her book
Women in the Wilderness discusses the history and politics of
women's relationship to the wilderness, and profiles women
adventurers of the past and present.

The tension this morning is like a wired fence sparking at
the slightest touch. Today we run Lava Falls. Water flow is
about fifteen hundred cubic feet per second, giving Lava a
solid ten rating on the scale of difficulty for rapids. Number
ten. Lava marks the outer limit.

Our plan for running it is to set ourselves up for the
"slot," a narrow section of water that shoots straight
through the falls and gives us our only chance of avoiding
major obstacles. The slot is only three feet in the midst of
a churning hundred-foot-wide expanse of falling water. We
have only seconds to make our move; a foot off on either
side in that fast current means that we miss and all hell
breaks loose.

Only six of us will paddle through Lava. Barb Dupuis, our paddleboat captain, thinks the only fair way to select our crew is to draw straws. We settle for twigs, breaking six off short as a sign of being a crew member. At least ten of us want to paddle. Though our chances of flipping the boat are high—fifty-fifty—my preference is to paddle, knowing that at least I'll be thrown clean, no "death lines" or gear to get tangled in, to trap me in a rapid underneath a capsized boat.

"Death lines" are loose long ends of the webbing used to tie the boat loads down. If a boat flips and a piece of webbing wraps around you underneath the boat it can easily become a "death line." When we tie the loads down this morning, we help with all possibilities in mind, checking carefully to see that all gear is secured and no webbing is left loose. The mist that covers much of our day-to-day life is burned off in the heat of the apparent risks we are taking. The possibility of death is no longer veiled or mere morbid consideration; it is valid and essential to take into account.

If we make the slot, Barb will yell the command "Drop!" as we go into the first enormous wave. Then we'll automatically pop back up, released from the pressure of thousands of gallons of water pouring over us, and paddle like fury until the rapid ends. We agree and quietly position ourselves in the raft.

We pull out into the current, back paddling to position ourselves before being swept over the falls. Though my heart is pounding, my breath is steady. We are poised, ready to spring. We drift closer. From the back of the raft where she is standing, directing our strokes, Barb yells "Drop!" and we hit the floor, keeping the weight low and central. I'm in the back next to Barb to help rudder as we make our dive. The front of the raft comes up and a solid wall of gray water comes pouring down on us from overhead. It feels as if we're capsizing end over end. I can't tell if I'm in the boat or out of it, and then in a split second I know that I'm out as the next twenty-five-foot wave engulfs me, plunging me beneath the surface.

I begin to panic but realize that I'm only wasting time. All there is to do is breathe whenever possible and relax in the middle of this intense turbulence. Nothing more. Nothing less. Time balloons, full and swollen; seconds expand into minutes; there is only the gray thundering water, the constant boiling, and my presence of mind. I look over my right shoulder and see an immense wave that will take me under again. I take a deep breath and give over to the forces of a wild river, an explosion of water. Twenty-five feet over my head, the wave tip curls, breaks, and crashes down on me, pummeling me into the vortex of the turbulence itself. Down, around, until the next moment, tossed up like a twig to the surface again. I am through the rapid. It has all happened within forty-five seconds.

I look around and see that the paddle boat has not capsized and is just upstream of me, midriver, close enough for me to swim to. Somehow I still have my paddle in my hand. Someone grabs it, pulling me to the boat, then grabs me by the seat of my pants, frantically catapulting me back into the raft. I'm safe. So is Barb, who washed out with me. They have pulled her back in just before me. We give a shout. We're all accounted for and the boat has not flipped.

Barb quickly assumes command again and orders us to bail with a frenzy. The boat is filled to the brim with water and is barely maneuverable. We have to pull into an eddy and empty it so that we aren't swept into the next rapid downstream uncontrolled. More important, we are the rescue boat for the last snout rig, which is just beginning to make its run. By the time we're able to pull into the eddy, they've made a beautiful run and have no need of us. We can relax. We pull to shore and turn the boat over, emptying hundreds of gallons of water back into the river.

I am left stripped, vulnerable, and bare. I feel transparent, like a child, unable to disguise my feelings. The pounding of my heart vibrates throughout my entire body. I am safe, there are friends holding me, laughing. I shake my head as though waking from a dream and let out a loud "whoopeeee!"

CLARICE SHORT

THE OLD ONE AND THE WIND

from *The Old One and the Wind* (1973)

Clarice Short (1910–1977) commented, "I have lived two
lives—that of the farmer and rancher and that of the scholar.
The poetry is the product of both." She was born in Ellin-
wood, Kansas, raised on the family farm in the Arkansas
Ozarks, and later involved herself in the operation of her
family's ranch in the New Mexico desert near Taos. She
received a B.A. and an M.A. from the University of Kansas
and a Ph.D. from Cornell University, and spent most of her
career teaching English at the University of Utah. She con-
tributed many articles and poems to journals; *The Old One
and the Wind* is her only published volume of poetry, and
seems to touch on what was closest to her life and heart.

She loves the wind.
There on the edge of the known world, at ninety,
In her tall house, any wildness in the elements
Is as welcome as an old friend.
When the surgically patched elms and sycamores
Crack off their heavy limbs in the freak snow storm
Of October, she rejoices; the massy hail
That drives craters into her groomed lawn
Stirs her sluggish heart to a riot of beating.

A cluster of cottonwood trees in the swale
Of the prairie, oasis now in a desert of wheat fields,
Is all that is left of the home place. No one
Is left to remember the days there with her:

The playhouse sheltered behind the cowshed,
The whirlwinds that made a column of corn shucks,
Winters when snow brushed out all the fences,
Springs when the white of the snow turned to daisies,
Wind-bent as were the urchins who picked them.

To her in her tall house in the tame town, the wind
That escapes the windbreaks of man's constructing
Blows from a distance beyond the young's conceiving,
Is rife with excitements of the world's beginning
And its end.

Her Solace:
How Nature Heals Us

 It seems instinctive for me when I'm feeling lonely or blue or wrestling with some especially troublesome problem to take a walk outside. Fresh air and the reassuring presence of nature can clear my head and loosen the knots my thoughts have tied. I'm not the only one who's ever felt this instinct; in my walk I join an age-old stream of pilgrims who have journeyed in times of trial and trouble to special places of healing power in nature. When human connections fail us, we return to the source, to the font of health and sanity, to our Mother.

This section contains accounts by and about women who have turned to nature to assuage grief, discouragement, loneliness, anger, pain, fatigue, or alienation, or as an antidote to the fragmenting frenzy of urban life. Some have gone for an afternoon, others for a week, a month, or a year. All have found comfort and refuge there, a steadying influence, a new sense of proportion, healing of physical ills, transcendence of psychic ills.

NANCY WOOD

MY HELP IS IN THE MOUNTAIN *AND* EARTH CURE ME

from *Hollering Sun* (1972)

Nancy Wood (1936–   ) is a writer and photographer who has long been fascinated with the heritage and culture of Native Americans. In her books *Hollering Sun* and *Many Winters* (1974), she presents her poetic interpretation of the Taos Pueblo Indian way of seeing and understanding, which obviously resonates with her own. She lives in Santa Fe, New Mexico.

My Help Is in the Mountain

My help is in the mountain
Where I take myself to heal
The earthly wounds
That people give to me.
I find a rock with sun on it
And a stream where the water runs gentle
And the trees which one by one give me company.
So must I stay for a long time
Until I have grown from the rock
And the stream is running through me
And I cannot tell myself from one tall tree.
Then I know that nothing touches me
Nor makes me run away.
My help is in the mountain
That I take away with me.

Earth Cure Me

Earth cure me. Earth receive my woe. Rock
strengthen me. Rock receive my weakness. Rain
wash my sadness away. Rain receive my doubt.
Sun make sweet my song. Sun receive the anger
from my heart.

WILLA CATHER

THE ANCIENT PEOPLE

from *The Song of the Lark* (1915)

Willa Cather (1873–1947) once told a Nebraska journalist,
"All my stories have been written with the material that was
gathered—no, God save us! not gathered but absorbed—
before I was fifteen years old." Born in Virginia, she moved
with her family to the Nebraska frontier when she was nine;
her years in this landscape were the rich soil out of which
her writing grew. The only other landscape that affected her
nearly as much was that of the Southwest, an area she visited
many times, initially to see her favorite brother, who was a
trainman for the Santa Fe. She graduated from the Univer-
sity of Nebraska and worked in Pittsburgh as a journalist
and then as a teacher before joining the staff of *McClure's*
magazine in New York in 1906. During her tenure there,
she met Sarah Orne Jewett, who was to become her dear
friend and mentor. After finishing her first novel, Cather left
McClure's in 1911 to concentrate on her writing, eventually
producing twelve novels.

NANCY WOOD

Cather's work has been praised for its lyrical and profound evocations of nature. Much of her writing calls into question the materialistic ideal of progress espoused by industrial society. The land is a central figure in her mature fiction; a primary theme is that if treated properly, the land is a source of well-being and—in the case of struggling young opera singer Thea Kronborg, protagonist of Cather's third and longest novel, *The Song of the Lark*—a source of deep solace. Kronborg has tried to transcend the limits of her upbringing in the frontier Colorado town of Moonstone by escaping to Chicago; when that attempt has seemingly failed, she finds respite in Panther Canyon in the Southwest.

I

The San Francisco Mountain lies in Northern Arizona, above Flagstaff, and its blue slopes and snowy summit entice the eye for a hundred miles across the desert. About its base lie the pine forests of the Navajos, where the great red-trunked trees live out their peaceful centuries in that sparkling air. The *piñons* and scrub begin only where the forest ends, where the country breaks into open, stony clearings and the surface of the earth cracks into deep canyons. The great pines stand at a considerable distance from each other. Each tree grows alone, murmurs alone, thinks alone. They do not intrude upon each other. The Navajos are not much in the habit of giving or of asking help. Their language is not a communicative one, and they never attempt an interchange of personality in speech. Over their forests there is the same inexorable reserve. Each tree has its exalted power to bear.

That was the first thing Thea Kronborg felt about the forest, as she drove through it one May morning in Henry Biltmer's democrat wagon—and it was the first great forest she had ever seen. She had got off the train at Flagstaff that morning, rolled off into the high, chill air when all the pines on the mountain were fired by sunrise, so that she seemed to fall from sleep directly into the forest.

Old Biltmer followed a faint wagon trail which ran

southeast, and which, as they traveled, continually dipped lower, falling away from the high plateau on the slope of which Flagstaff sits. The white peak of the mountain, the snow gorges above the timber, now disappeared from time to time as the road dropped and dropped, and the forest closed behind the wagon. More than the mountain disappeared as the forest closed thus. Thea seemed to be taking very little through the wood with her. The personality of which she was so tired seemed to let go of her. The high, sparkling air drank it up like blotting-paper. It was lost in the thrilling blue of the new sky and the song of the thin wind in the *piñons.* The old, fretted lines which marked one off, which defined her,—made her Thea Kronborg, Bowers's accompanist, a soprano with a faulty middle voice,— were all erased.

So far she had failed. Her two years in Chicago had not resulted in anything. She had failed with Harsanyi, and she had made no great progress with her voice. She had come to believe that whatever Bowers had taught her was of secondary importance, and that in the essential things she had made no advance. Her student life closed behind her, like the forest, and she doubted whether she could go back to it if she tried. Probably she would teach music in little country towns all her life. Failure was not so tragic as she would have supposed; she was tired enough not to care.

She was getting back to the earliest sources of gladness that she could remember. She had loved the sun, and the brilliant solitudes of sand and sun, long before these other things had come along to fasten themselves upon her and torment her. That night, when she clambered into her big German feather bed, she felt completely released from the enslaving desire to get on in the world. Darkness had once again the sweet wonder that it had in childhood.

II

Thea's life at the Ottenburg ranch was simple and full of light, like the days themselves. She awoke every morning when the first fierce shafts of sunlight darted through the curtainless windows of her room at the ranch house. After breakfast she took her lunch-basket and went down to the canyon. Usually she did not return until sunset.

Panther Canyon was like a thousand others—one of those abrupt fissures with which the earth in the Southwest is riddled; so abrupt that you might walk over the edge of any one of them on a dark night and never know what had happened to you. This canyon headed on the Ottenburg ranch, about a mile from the ranch house, and it was accessible only at its head. The canyon walls, for the first two hundred feet below the surface, were perpendicular cliffs, striped with even-running strata of rock. From there on to the bottom the sides were less abrupt, were shelving, and lightly fringed with *piñons* and dwarf cedars. The effect was that of a gentler canyon within a wilder one. The dead city lay at the point where the perpendicular outer wall ceased and the V-shaped inner gorge began. There a stratum of rock, softer than those above, had been hollowed out by the action of time until it was like a deep groove running along the sides of the canyon. In this hollow (like a great fold in the rock) the Ancient People had built their houses of yellowish stone and mortar. The overhanging cliff above made a roof two hundred feet thick. The hard stratum below was an everlasting floor. The houses stood along in a row, like the buildings in a city block, or like a barracks.

In both walls of the canyon the same streak of soft rock had been washed out, and the long horizontal groove had been built up with houses. The dead city had thus two streets, one set in either cliff, facing each other across the ravine, with a river of blue air between them.

The canyon twisted and wound like a snake, and these two streets went on for four miles or more, interrupted by the abrupt turnings of the gorge, but beginning again within each turn. The canyon had a dozen of these false endings near its head. Beyond, the windings were larger and less perceptible, and it went on for a hundred miles, too narrow, precipitous, and terrible for man to follow it. The Cliff Dwellers liked wide canyons, where the great cliffs caught the sun. Panther Canyon had been deserted for hundreds of years when the first Spanish missionaries came into Arizona, but the masonry of the houses was still wonderfully firm; had crumbled only where a landslide or a rolling boulder had torn it.

All the houses in the canyon were clean with the cleanness of sun-baked, wind-swept places, and they all smelled of the tough little cedars that twisted themselves into the very doorways. One of these rock-rooms Thea took for her own. Fred had told her how to make it comfortable. The day after she came old Henry brought over on one of the pack-ponies a roll of Navajo blankets that belonged to Fred, and Thea lined her cave with them. The room was not more than eight by ten feet, and she could touch the stone roof with her fingertips. This was her old idea: a nest in a high cliff, full of sun. All morning long the sun beat upon her cliff, while the ruins on the opposite side of the canyon were in shadow. In the afternoon, when she had the shade of two hundred feet of rock wall, the ruins on the other side of the gulf stood out in the blazing sunlight. Before her door ran the narrow, winding path that had been the street of the Ancient People. The yucca and niggerhead cactus grew everywhere. From her doorstep she looked out on the ocher-colored slope that ran down several hundred feet to the stream, and this hot rock was sparsely grown with dwarf trees. Their colors were so pale that the shadows of the little trees on the rock stood out sharper than the trees themselves. When Thea first came, the chokecherry bushes were in blossom, and the scent of them was almost sickeningly sweet after a shower. At the very bottom of the canyon, along the stream, there was a thread of bright, flickering, golden-green—cottonwood seedlings. They made a living, chattering screen behind which she took her bath every morning.

Thea went down to the stream by the Indian water trail.

She had found a bathing-pool with a sand bottom, where the creek was dammed by fallen trees. The climb back was long and steep, and when she reached her little house in the cliff she always felt fresh delight in its comfort and inaccessibility. By the time she got there, the woolly red-and-gray blankets were saturated with sunlight, and she sometimes fell asleep as soon as she stretched her body on their warm surfaces. She used to wonder at her own inactivity. She could lie there hour after hour in the sun and listen to the strident whir of the big locusts, and to the light, ironical laughter of the quaking asps. All her life she had been hurrying and sputtering, as if she had been born behind time and had been trying to catch up. Now, she reflected, as she drew herself out long upon the rugs, it was as if she were waiting for something to catch up with her. She had got to a place where she was out of the stream of meaningless activity and undirected effort.

Here she could lie for half a day undistracted, holding pleasant and incomplete conceptions in her mind—almost in her hands. They were scarcely clear enough to be called ideas. They had something to do with fragrance and color and sound, but almost nothing to do with words. She was singing very little now, but a song would go through her head all morning, as a spring keeps welling up, and it was like a pleasant sensation indefinitely prolonged. It was much more like a sensation than like an idea, or an act of remembering. Music had never come to her in that sensuous form before. It had always been a thing to be struggled with, had always brought anxiety and exaltation and chagrin—never content and indolence. Thea began to wonder whether people could not utterly lose the power to work, as they can lose their voice or their memory. She had always been a little drudge, hurrying from one task to another—as if it mattered! And now her power to think seemed converted into a power of sustained sensation. She could become a mere receptacle for heat, or become a color, like the bright lizards that darted about on the hot stones outside her door;

or she could become a continuous repetition of sound, like the cicadas.

III

The faculty of observation was never highly developed in Thea Kronborg. A great deal escaped her eye as she passed through the world. But the things which were for her, she saw; she experienced them physically and remembered them as if they had once been a part of herself. The roses she used to see in the florists' shops in Chicago were merely roses. But when she thought of the moonflowers that grew over Mrs. Tellamantez's door, it was as if she had been that vine and had opened up in white flowers every night. There were memories of light on the sand hills, of masses of prickly-pear blossoms she had found in the desert in early childhood, of the late afternoon sun pouring through the grape leaves and the mint bed in Mrs. Kohler's garden, which she would never lose. These recollections were a part of her mind and personality. In Chicago she had got almost nothing that went into her subconscious self and took root there. But here, in Panther Canyon, there were again things which seemed destined for her.

Panther Canyon was the home of innumerable swallows. They built nests in the wall far above the hollow groove in which Thea's own rock chamber lay. They seldom ventured above the rim of the canyon, to the flat, wind-swept tableland. Their world was the blue air-river between the canyon walls. In that blue gulf the arrow-shaped birds swam all day long, with only an occasional movement of the wings. The only sad thing about them was their timidity; the way in which they lived their lives between the echoing cliffs and never dared to rise out of the shadow of the canyon walls. As they swam past her door, Thea often felt how easy it would be to dream one's life out in some cleft in the world.

From the ancient dwelling there came always a dignified, unobtrusive sadness; now stronger, now fainter,—like the aromatic smell which the dwarf cedars gave out in the sun,—but always present, a part of the air one breathed. At night, when Thea dreamed about the canyon,—or in the early morning when she hurried toward it, anticipating it,— her conception of it was of yellow rocks baking in sunlight, the swallows, the cedar smell, and that peculiar sadness—a voice out of the past, not very loud, that went on saying a few simple things to the solitude eternally.

Standing up in her lodge, Thea could with her thumb nail dislodge flakes of carbon from the rock roof—the cooking-smoke of the Ancient People. They were that near! A timid, nest-building folk, like the swallows. How often Thea remembered Ray Kennedy's moralizing about the cliff cities. He used to say that he never felt the hardness of the human struggle or the sadness of history as he felt it among those ruins. He used to say, too, that it made one feel an obligation to do one's best. On the first day that Thea climbed the water trail she began to have intuitions about the women who had worn the path, and who had spent so great a part of their lives going up and down it. She found herself trying to walk as they must have walked, with a feeling in her feet and knees and loins which she had never known before,—which must have come up to her out of the accustomed dust of that rocky trail. She could feel the weight of an Indian baby hanging to her back as she climbed.

The empty houses, among which she wandered in the afternoon, the blanketed one in which she lay all morning, were haunted by certain fears and desires; feelings about warmth and cold and water and physical strength. It seemed to Thea that a certain understanding of those old people came up to her out of the rock shelf on which she lay; that certain feelings were transmitted to her, suggestions that were simple, insistent, and monotonous, like the beating of Indian drums. They were not expressible in words, but seemed rather to translate themselves into attitudes of body, into degrees of muscular tension or relaxation; the naked strength of youth, sharp as the sun-shafts; the crouching timorousness of age, the sullenness of women who waited for their captors. At the first turning of the canyon there was a half-ruined tower of yellow masonry, a watch-tower upon which the young men used to entice eagles and snare them with nets. Sometimes for a whole morning Thea could see the coppery breast and shoulders of an Indian youth there against the sky; see him throw the net, and watch the struggle with the eagle.

Old Henry Biltmer, at the ranch, had been a great deal among the Pueblo Indians who are the descendants of the Cliff-Dwellers. After supper he used to sit and smoke his pipe by the kitchen stove and talk to Thea about them. He had never found any one before who was interested in his ruins. Every Sunday the old man prowled about in the canyon, and he had come to know a good deal more about it than he could account for. He had gathered up a whole chestful of Cliff-Dweller relics which he meant to take back to Germany with him some day. He taught Thea how to find things among the ruins: grinding-stones, and drills and needles made of turkey-bones. There were fragments of pottery everywhere. Old Henry explained to her that the Ancient People had developed masonry and pottery far beyond any other crafts. After they had made houses for themselves, the next thing was to house the precious water. He explained to her how all their customs and ceremonies and their religion went back to water. The men provided the food, but water was the care of the women. The stupid women carried water for most of their lives; the cleverer ones made the vessels to hold it. Their pottery was their most direct appeal to water, the envelope and sheath of the precious element itself. The strongest Indian need was ex-pressed in those graceful jars, fashioned slowly by hand, without the aid of a wheel.

When Thea took her bath at the bottom of the canyon, in the sunny pool behind the screen of cottonwoods, she sometimes felt as if the water must have sovereign qualities, from having been the object of so much service and desire. That stream was the only living thing left of the drama that had been played out in the canyon centuries ago. In the rapid, restless heart of it, flowing swifter than the rest, there was a continuity of life that reached back into the old time. The glittering thread of current had a kind of lightly worn, loosely knit personality, graceful and laughing. Thea's bath came to have a ceremonial gravity. The atmosphere of the canyon was ritualistic.

One morning, as she was standing upright in the pool, splashing water between her shoulder-blades with a big sponge, something flashed through her mind that made her draw herself up and stand still until the water had quite dried upon her flushed skin. The stream and the broken pottery: what was any art but an effort to make a sheath, a mould in which to imprison for a moment the shining, elusive element which is life itself,—life hurrying past us and running away, too strong to stop, too sweet to lose? The Indian women had held it in their jars. In the sculpture she had seen in the Art Institute, it had been caught in a flash of arrested motion. In singing, one made a vessel of one's throat and nostrils and held it on one's breath, caught the stream in a scale of natural intervals.

IV

Thea had a superstitious feeling about the potsherds, and liked better to leave them in the dwellings where she found them. If she took a few bits back to her own lodge and hid them under the blankets, she did it guiltily, as if she were being watched. She was a guest in these houses, and ought to behave as such. Nearly every afternoon she went to the chambers which contained the most interesting fragments of pottery, sat and looked at them for a while. Some of them were beautifully decorated. This care, expended upon vessels that could not hold food or water any better for the additional labor put upon them, made her heart go out to those ancient potters. They had not only expressed their desire, but they had expressed it as beautifully as they could. Food, fire, water, and something else—even here, in this crack in the world, so far back in the night of the past! Down here at the beginning that painful thing was already stirring; the seed of sorrow, and of so much delight.

There were jars done in a delicate overlay, like pine cones; and there were many patterns in a low relief, like basket-work. Some of the pottery was decorated in color, red and brown, black and white, in graceful geometrical patterns. One day, on a fragment of a shallow bowl, she found a crested serpent's head, painted in red on terra-cotta. Again she found half a bowl with a broad band of white cliff-houses painted on a black ground. They were scarcely conventionalized at all; there they were in the black border, just as they stood in the rock before her. It brought her centuries nearer to these people to find that they saw their houses exactly as she saw them.

Yes, Ray Kennedy was right. All these things made one feel that one ought to do one's best, and help to fulfill some desire of the dust that slept there. A dream had been dreamed there long ago, in the night of ages, and the wind had whispered some promise to the sadness of the savage. In their own way, those people had felt the beginnings of what was to come. These potsherds were like fetters that bound one to a long chain of human endeavor.

Not only did the world seem older and richer to Thea now, but she herself seemed older. She had never been alone for so long before, or thought so much. Nothing had ever engrossed her so deeply as the daily contemplation of that line of pale-yellow houses tucked into the wrinkle of the cliff. Moonstone and Chicago had become vague. Here everything was simple and definite, as things had been in childhood. Her mind was like a ragbag into which she had been frantically thrusting whatever she could grab. And here she must throw this lumber away. The things that were really hers separated themselves from the rest. Her ideas were simplified, became sharper and clearer. She felt united and strong.

ABBIE HUSTON EVANS

THE BACK-ROAD
from *Outcrop* (1928)

> Abbie Huston Evans (1881–1983) was born in New Hampshire and grew up in Maine, whose landscape was to form the principal subject of her poetry. Her father was a Congregational minister, and she taught Sunday school. Among her pupils was Edna St. Vincent Millay, who later wrote in the foreword to Evans's first volume of poetry, *Outcrop*, "These are the poems of one more deeply and more constantly aware than most people are, of the many voices and faces of lively nature." Evans was educated at Radcliffe (B.A., M.A.), was a social worker in a Colorado mining camp during World War I, and taught dancing, art, and dramatics at the Settlement Music School in Philadelphia (1923–1953) and at the College Settlement Farm-Camp in Horsham, Pennsylvania (1953–1957). She created a small but enduring body of poems published in three widely spaced volumes and collected later, along with five new poems, in *Collected Poems* (1970).

Perhaps I needed something gray and brown
And did not know it,—something spent and bare,
That morning on the back-road, in November.
I may have stood in need of something bedded
Like the ledge beside me barnacled with lichen,
With a great wave of juniper breaking on it;
Or darkly needed something straight like cedars,
Black on the traveling cloud-fringe,—something steady,
Like slate-gray mountains in behind bare birches.

Perhaps I needed something bright and scarlet,
Like winter berries on the stone-gray bush
Beside the rock-pile,—something sweet and singing,
Like water in the gutter running down
From springs up in the pasture out of sight.

But if I needed these, I did not know it.
If you had told me that I wanted fulness,
Or life, or God, I should have nodded "Yes";
But not a bush of berries,—not a mountain!
—Yet so it was: fantastic needs like these,
Blind bottom hungers like the urge in roots,
Elbowed their way out, jostling me aside;
A need of steadiness, that caught at mountains,
A need of straightness, satisfied with cedars,
A need of brightness, cozened with a bush.

—Whatever it was I needed, know I found it!
The oak-tree standing with its feet in water
Behind me, with the wind hoarse in its top
Of paper, or the thousand-penciled bushes
Across the road, or alders black with catkins,
Fed no more deeply on the earth than I,—
Nor half so passionately, I must think,
As I, who, rooted in my tracks, appeased
Undreamed-of hungers with unlikeliest food,
The first at hand; amazed to find what sweetness
Can be wrung out of clay and flint,—amazed,
Like a starving man in a swamp, to find what relish
Is hid in grass, and bark, and roots, and acorns.

EDITH WARNER

JOURNAL ENTRIES

from *The House at Otowi Bridge* by **Peggy Pond Church**
(1959, 1960)

Edith Warner (1892–1951) came to New Mexico from
Pennsylvania at the midpoint of her life, choosing it almost
at random when for her ill health her doctor prescribed a
year of outdoor life without responsibilities. The land's in-
visible energies captured her, and over the next thirty years
this shy spinster became a legend, befriending and absorb-
ing the wisdom of the Indians of San Ildefonso Pueblo as
well as the brilliant scientists who gathered from all over the
world to develop the atomic bomb at Los Alamos. Her little
house stood beside the bridge over the Rio Grande that
connected the pueblo with Los Alamos; the tearoom she ran
there served as a sanctuary to the scientists in the years
before Hiroshima. Tilano, governor of the pueblo, came to
live with her and became her companion and helpmate.
"The knowledge that leads to power, and the wisdom that
grows from the service of the earth and the love of its beauty
existed side by side for her, as though they were the oppo-
site banks between which the great river flowed," wrote
Peggy Pond Church in her moving book *The House at Otowi
Bridge: The Story of Edith Warner and Los Alamos.*

Warner made an attempt to write about her life, but
abandoned it after the first few pages, feeling that it sounded
too hackneyed: "White woman moves West. Lives among
Indians." She did leave journal fragments, skillfully woven
by Church into her story; a series of Christmas letters from
1943 through 1950, reprinted in Church's book; and a few
published essays. Frank Waters's novel *The Woman at Otowi
Crossing* (1966, revised 1987) is a narrative of the growth

and meaning of the myth that grew up around this woman who embraced a simple life and cultivated her depths. The following journal entries give us some glimpse into those depths, so attuned to the healing power of earth and sky.

I ran away today, so sick I was of the kitchen and everlasting food. Constant walls and a roof do something to me at any time and when the aspens turn golden, I seethe inside until finally I revolt and leave everything.

The sun was just above Baldy when I walked to the Pueblo for the old white horse, but by the time I reached the trail leading to the top of Shumo, it was halfway up the heavens. Shumo has a round knoll on its top which is the highest spot in the valley, and I had to be on top of my world today. All the beauty of the valley lay below me. Beyond were mesas reaching westward to the Jemez with its masses of golden aspens. The whirring of a bird overhead and the rushing of the river far below me were the only sounds. If I were a leader of people on such a day I would send them out alone into the open.

This morning when I stood on the river bank, the sun was making all golden the edge of the clouds in the west. There was a blue sky above Shumo, but snowflakes were blown thick and fast from the canyon until they hid the mesas. As they shut out the world and made for me a hushed place in their midst, I was very near the source of things.

Yesterday when I woke there were clouds in the east and I was happy . . . Later the winds blew them away and I doubted. But by noon the snow had come and it fell until the earth was thickly covered. When darkness came, I went out into it—that softly falling whiteness in the hush of the night. This morning all was heavy with snow and from it rose a white veil about the foot of the mesa. I was alone in a world of snow and I was conscious only of what came to me from it.

This is a day when life and the world seem to be standing still—only time and the river flowing past the mesas. I cannot work. I go out into the sunshine to sit receptively for what there is in this stillness and calm. I am keenly aware that there is something. Just now it seemed to flow in a rhythm around me and then to enter me—something which comes in a hushed inflowing. All of me is still and yet alert, ready to become part of this wave that laps the shore on which I sit. Somehow I have no desire to name it or understand. It is enough that I should feel and be of it in moments such as this. And most of the hatred and ill will, the strained feeling is gone—I know not how.

No, it is not what Ouspensky experienced when he was drawn by the waves into them, becoming all—mountain, sea, sky, ship. I am I and earth is earth—mesa, sky, wind, rushing river. Each is an entity but the essence of the earth flows into me—perhaps of me into the earth. And to me it is more than a few seconds' experience. Nor is it any longer strange but natural, not ecstatic but satisfying. The detail of life becomes the scaffolding.

Even in these rushed days there is such peace between. There are moments when two eagle feathers can fill me with joy; when the last rays of the sun touch my forehead as I stand by the kitchen door; when the outline of To-tavi is marked in rhythm against a clear western sky; when even the wind is part of it all. Surely such moments do something to me. If not, it is because I hide beneath the pettiness. I have no apparent goal. I only know that I am living a day at a time as I feel the way.

Today the sun shines here, but the clouds hang low on the Sangre peaks and beyond Shumo. Again I have touched the fringe of the unknown and been drawn to it, not by my seeking, which is the only real way.

As I worked . . . there came without warning a flowing into me of that which I have come to associate with the gods. I went to the open door and looked up at the mountains with something akin to awe. It forced me out into the open where I could look up to those sacred high places on which humans do not dwell. Then it left me—perhaps to return to those sacred places.

I had almost forgotten how to lie curled on the ground or here on my couch, content just to look and feel and enjoy the thoughts that come. Rushing with things to be done crowding is such a waste of living. There need to be hours of this.

Twice within this week I have seen what must be meant only for the delight of the gods. I chanced to look up from my reading a bit ago, and went flying out to the river bank. My carved foothill was a shining thing of beauty. No artist could capture the gold that bathed it with wonder and set it apart. And while I looked in awe, from its earth-hold rose slowly a new color—a cloak of mauve only less bright than the gold that with a caressing movement wrapped itself about my golden hill. Only then could I look to faraway purple mountains and the Mesa which was quite black against a clouded sky. When I looked back to the hill the magic was gone. Can such beauty be and then not be? I think the gods must have taken back to themselves that godmade color—perhaps to paint themselves for an approaching ceremony. And I know that some of it came to stay with me.

Just now as I watched the ever-changing beauty, I saw a cloud pass over the earth on long gray stilts of rain. And then as I looked I saw its shape and knew that over the pueblo moved the Thunder Bird. With wings outspread he slowly passed, broad tail sweeping the thirsty earth. Down from his breast fell feathers of rain and out from his heart the lightning flashed its message to the people that the gods never forget. Thunder roared from his long black beak and all earth sounds were hushed. He has gone, leaving only his mark on the land, but I still see his broad wings stretched, and the white rain-feathers dropping from his breast. And any fear, lingering from those childhood days when I, unafraid, was made to fear lightning, has gone. Did it not come from his heart? If it should seek me out or find me wandering in its path, would it not take me back with it? I should not mind going so much if I could look down on beauty like earth's today.

I have been sitting here looking at the peaked ceiling of two gray and one brown, one rough and one smooth board—the only roof for which I have any affection—wondering why such heights and depths have been given me. There are days when I question the gods. And then come the things that make me catch my breath. There are moments when this crude house, my little pottery singing woman, my books and pictures are filled with something that sends out to me peace. Is it because of an ancient prayer that color and form and movement have come to mean so much more, or is it that the years bring an increased vision—no, a more understanding vision? Is it a natural gift that accompanies maturity, or is it a gift of the gods?

I am glad that the years of adjustment are over and that there has come to me this new relationship with all of earth. I know that I was never so aware of the river and the trees; that I never walked so eagerly looking for the new wild things growing. I know that I have had to grow sufficiently —no, to cast off enough of civilization's shackles so that the earth spirit could reach me.

This morning I stood on the river bank to pray. I knew then that the ancient ones were wise to pray for peace and beauty and not for specific gifts except fertility which is continued life. And I saw that if one has even a small degree of the ability to take into and unto himself the peace and beauty the gods surround him with, it is not necessary to ask for more.

INA COOLBRITH

LONGING

from *Songs from the Golden Gate* (1896)

Ina Coolbrith (1842–1928) was a woman with a remarkable history whose poems focused mainly on the theme of unhappiness abated in the simple pleasures of nature. Born into a Mormon family in Nauvoo, Illinois, she was christened Josephine Donna Smith and as a child came west to Los Angeles by wagon with her family. After a tumultuous four-year marriage she moved to San Francisco and adopted the pseudonym Ina Coolbrith. She established a literary reputation there, publishing three volumes of verse, and came to associate with the literary luminaries of the day: Mark Twain, Ambrose Bierce, John Muir, Bret Harte. She was selected Oakland's first librarian and in 1915 was named California's poet laureate, the first female laureate in America.

O foolish wisdom sought in books!
　　O aimless fret of household tasks!
O chains that bind the hand and mind—
　　A fuller life my spirit asks!

For there the grand hills, summer-crowned,
　　Slope greenly downward to the seas;
One hour of rest upon their breast
　　Were worth a year of days like these.

Their cool, soft green to ease the pain
　　Of eyes that ache o'er printed words;
This weary noise—the city's voice,
　　Lulled in the sound of bees and birds.

For Eden's life within me stirs,
  And scorns the shackles that I wear;
The man-life grand—pure soul, strong hand,
  The limb of steel, the heart of air!

And I could kiss, with longing wild,
  Earth's dear brown bosom, loved so much,
A grass-blade fanned across my hand,
  Would thrill me like a lover's touch.

The trees would talk with me; the flowers
  Their hidden meanings each make known—
The olden lore revived once more,
  When man's and nature's heart were one!

And as the pardoned pair might come
  Back to the garden God first framed,
And hear Him call at even-fall,
  And answer, "Here am I," unshamed—

So I, from out these toils, wherein
  The Eden-faith grows stained and dim,
Would walk, a child, through nature's wild,
  And hear His voice and answer Him.

TERRY TEMPEST WILLIAMS

THE BOWL

from *Coyote's Canyon* (1989)

Terry Tempest Williams (1955–   ) is a Utah native, natural-ist-in-residence at the Utah Museum of Natural History, and an accomplished storyteller. She is also an adjunct professor in the College of Education and Women's Studies at the University of Utah, where she received her master's degree in environmental education. "To ask a question and find a story about an episode of earth is to remember who we are," she writes in *Pieces of White Shell: A Journey to Navajoland* (1984). Elsewhere, she has written, "The natural world allows us to make peace with our own contradictory natures. We are returned to a balance of mind and spirit. We are healed." The following selection is from *Coyote's Canyon,* a collection of her stories inspired by southern Utah's desert canyons.

There was a woman who left the city, left her husband, and her children, left everything behind to retrieve her soul. She came to the desert after seeing her gaunt face in the mirror, the pallor that comes when everything is going out and nothing is coming in. She had noticed for the first time the furrows under her eyes that had been eroded by tears. She did not know the woman in the mirror. She took off her apron, folded it neatly in the drawer, left a note for her family, and closed the door behind her. She knew that her life and the lives of those she loved depended on it.

The woman returned to the place of her childhood, where she last remembered her true nature. She returned to the intimacy of a small canyon that for years had loomed large in her imagination, and there she set up camp. The walls were as she had recalled them, tall and streaked from rim to floor. The rock appeared as draped fabric as she placed her hand flat against its face. The wall was cold; the sun had not yet reached the wash. She began wading the shallow stream that ran down the center of the canyon, and chose not to be encumbered by anything. She shed her clothing, took out her hairpins, and squeezed the last lemon she had over her body. Running her hands over her breasts and throat and behind her neck, the woman shivered at her own bravery. This is how it should be, she thought. She was free and frightened and beautiful.

For days, the woman wandered in and out of the slick-rock maze. She drank from springs and ate the purple fruit of prickly pears. Her needs were met simply. Because she could not see herself, she was unaware of the changes—how her skin became taut and tan, the way in which her hair relaxed and curled itself. She even seemed to walk differently as her toes spread and gripped the sand.

All along the wash, clay balls had been thrown by a raging river. The woman picked one up, pulled off the pebbles until she had a mound of supple clay. She kneaded it as she walked, rubbed the clay between the palms of her hands, and watched it lengthen. She finally sat down on the moist sand and, with her fingers, continued moving up the string of clay. And then she began to coil it, around and around, pinching shut each rotation. She created a bowl.

The woman found other clay balls and put them inside the bowl. She had an idea of making dolls for her children, small clay figurines that she would let dry in the sun. Once again, she stopped walking and sat in the sand to work. She split each clay ball in two, which meant she had six small pieces to mold out of three balls she had found. One by one, tiny shapes took form. A girl with open arms above her head; three boys—one standing, one sitting, and one lying down (he was growing, she mused); and then a man and a woman facing each other. She had re-created her family.

With the few scraps left over she made desert animals: a lizard, a small bird, and a miniature coyote sitting on his haunches. The woman smiled as she looked over her menagerie. She clapped her hands to remove the dried clay and half expected to see them dance. Instead, it began to rain.

Within minutes, the wash began to swell. The woman put the clay creatures into the bowl and sought higher ground up a side canyon, where she found shelter under a large overhang. She was prepared to watch if a flash flood came. And it did. The clear water turned muddy as it began to rise, carrying with it the force of wild horses running with a thunderstorm behind them. The small stream, now a river, rose higher still, gouging into the sandy banks, hurling rocks, roots, and trees down stream. The woman wondered about the animals as she heard stirrings in the grasses and surmised they must be seeking refuge in the side canyons as she was—watching as she was. She pulled her legs in and wrapped her arms around her shins, resting her cheekbones against her knees. She closed her eyes and concentrated on the sound of water bursting through the silence of the canyon.

The roar of the flood gradually softened until it was replaced by birdsong. Swifts and swallows plucked the water for insects as frogs announced their return. The woman raised her head. With the bowl in both hands, she tried to get up, but slipped down the hillside, scraping the backs of her thighs on rabbitbrush and sage. She finally reached the wash with the bowl and its contents intact. And then she found herself with another problem: she sank up to her knees in the wet, red clay, only to find that the more she tried to pull her foot free, the deeper she sank with the other. Finally, letting go of her struggle, she put the bowl and her family aside, and wallowed in it. She fell sideways and rolled onto her stomach, then over onto her back. She was covered in slimy, wet clay, and it was delicious. She stretched her hands above her head, flexed her calves, and pointed her toes. The woman laughed hysterically until she became aware of her own echo.

Her body contracted.

She must get control of herself, she thought; what would her husband think? What kind of example was she setting for her children? And then she remembered—she was alone. She sat up and stared at the coiled bowl full of clay people. The woman took out the figurines and planted them in the wash. She placed the animals around them.

"They're on their own," she said out loud. And she walked back to the spring where she had drunk, filled up her bowl with water, and bathed.

The next morning, when the woman awoke, she noticed that the cottonwood branches swaying above her head had sprouted leaves.

She could go home now.

PAT MORA

LESSON 1 *and*
LESSON 2

from *Chants* (1984)

Pat Mora (1942–   ) bears the imprint of many years spent in the encompassing arms of vast stretches of desert. She says, "The desert, *mi madre,* is my stern teacher." Born in El Paso, Texas, and educated at Texas Western College (B.A.) and the University of Texas at El Paso (M.A.), Mora has published two award-winning volumes of poetry. She

now lives in Cincinnati, where she continues to write poetry
as well as children's books and essays.

Lesson 1

The desert is powerless
when thunder shakes the hot air
and unfamiliar raindrops slide
on rocks, sand, *mesquite,*
when unfamiliar raindrops overwhelm
her, distort her face.
But after the storm, she breathes deeply,
caressed by a fresh sweet calm.
My Mother smiles rainbows.

When I feel shaken, powerless
to stop my bruising sadness,
I hear My Mother whisper:

        Mi'ja

don't fear your hot tears
cry away the storm, then listen, listen.

Lesson 2

Small, white fairies dance
on the *Rio Grande.* Usually they swim
Deep through their days and nights
hiding from our eyes, but when the white
sun pulls them up, up
they leap about, tiny shimmering stars.

The desert says: feel the sun
luring you from your dark, sad waters,
burst through the surface

        dance

JEAN LIEDLOFF

THE GLADE

from *The Continuum Concept* (1977)

> Jean Liedloff is a writer, lecturer, and consultant who has
> focused on understanding the evolutionary origin of human
> well-being and learning how to restore it to the "normal"
> (alienated) member of Western civilization. She was born in
> New York and attended Cornell University, Florida South-
> ern College, and the New School for Social Research before
> making five expeditions deep into the South American jun-
> gle and living for a total of two and a half years with Stone
> Age peoples there. Her observations of their lives inspired
> her much-acclaimed book *The Continuum Concept: Allowing
> Human Nature to Work Successfully,* now translated into many
> languages. Her description of a childhood experience of
> enlightenment in the Maine woods points to the power of
> nature as a centering force.

I went to the South American jungles with no theory to
prove, no more than normal curiosity about the Indians and
only a vague sense that I might learn something of signifi-
cance. In Florence, on my first trip to Europe, I was invited
to join two Italian explorers on a diamond-hunting expedi-
tion in the region of Venezuela's Caroni River, a tributary
of the Orinoco. It was a last-minute invitation and I had
twenty minutes to decide, race to my hotel, pack, dash to
the station, and jump on the train as it was pulling away
from the platform.

It was very dramatic, but rather frightening when the
action suddenly subsided and I saw our compartment piled

with suitcases, reflected in the light through the dusty window, and realized I was on my way to a genuine jungle.

There had not been time to take account of my reasons for wanting to go, but my response had been instant and sure. It was not the idea of the diamonds I found irresistible, though digging one's fortune out of tropical riverbeds sounded far more attractive than any other work I could think of. It was the word *jungle* that held all the magic, perhaps because of something that happened when I was a child.

It was when I was eight and it seemed to have great importance. I still think of it as an experience of value, but like most such moments of enlightenment, it gave a glimpse of the existence of an order without revealing its construction, or how one could sustain a view of it in the muddle of day-to-day living. Most disappointing of all, the conviction that I had seen the elusive truth at last did little or nothing toward guiding my footsteps through the muddle. The brief vision was too fragile to survive the trip back to applicability. Although it had to contend with all my mundane motivations and, most disastrously, with the power of habit, perhaps it is worth mentioning, for it was a hint of that sense of rightness (for want of a less clumsy phrase) the search for which this book is about.

The incident happened during a nature walk in the Maine woods where I was at summer camp. I was last in line; I had fallen back a bit and was hurrying to catch up when, through the trees, I saw a glade. It had a lush fir tree at the far side and a knoll in the center covered in bright, almost luminous green moss. The rays of the afternoon sun slanted against the blue-black green of the pine forest. The little roof of visible sky was perfectly blue. The whole picture had a completeness, an all-there quality of such dense power that it stopped me in my tracks. I went to the edge and then, softly, as though into a magical or holy place, to the center, where I sat, then lay down with my cheek against the freshness of the moss. It is here, I thought, and I felt the anxiety that colored my life fall away. This, at last, was where things were as they ought to be. Everything was in its place—the tree, the earth underneath, the rock, the moss. In autumn, it would be right; in winter under the snow, it would be perfect in its wintriness. Spring would come again and miracle within miracle would unfold, each at its special pace, some things having died off, some sprouting in their first spring, but all of equal and utter rightness.

I felt I had discovered the missing center of things, the key to rightness itself, and must hold on to this knowledge which was so clear in that place. I was tempted for a moment to take a scrap of moss away with me, to keep as a reminder; but a rather grown-up thought prevented me. I suddenly feared that in treasuring an amulet of moss, I might lose the real prize: the insight I had had—that I might think my vision safe as long as I kept the moss, only to find one day that I had nothing but a pinch of dead vegetation.

So I took nothing, but promised myself I would remember The Glade every night before going to sleep and in that way never be far from its stabilizing power. I knew, even at eight, that the confusion of values thrust upon me by parents, teachers, other children, nannies, camp counselors, and others would only worsen as I grew up. The years would add complications and steer me into more and more impenetrable tangles of rights and wrongs, desirables and undesirables. I had already seen enough to know that. But if I could keep The Glade with me, I thought, I would never get lost.

That night in my camp bed I brought The Glade to mind and was filled with a sense of thankfulness, and renewed my vow to preserve my vision. And for years its quality was undiminished as I saw the knoll, the fir, the light, the wholeness, in my mind every night.

But as more years went by, I often found that I had forgotten The Glade for days, or weeks, at a time. I tried to recapture the sense of salvation that had formerly infused it. But my world widened. The simpler sort of good-girl-bad-girl values of the nursery had gradually been overrun by the often conflicting values of my sector of the culture and of my family, a mixture of Victorian virtues and graces with a strong bent toward individualism, liberal views, and artistic talents, and above all, high regard for a brilliant and original intellect, like my mother's.

By the time I was about fifteen, I realized with a hollow sadness (since I could not remember what I was mourning) that I had lost the meaning of The Glade. I recalled perfectly the woodland scene, but as I had feared when I abstained from taking the souvenir bit of moss, its significance had escaped. Instead, my mental picture of The Glade had become the empty amulet.

I lived with my grandmother, and when she died I decided to go to Europe though I had not finished college. My thoughts were not very clear during my grief, but because turning to my mother always ended in my being hurt, I felt I had to make a giant effort to get on my own feet. Nothing I was expected to want seemed worth having— jobs writing for fashion magazines, a career as a model, or further education.

In my cabin on the ship bound for France, I wept for fear I had gambled away everything familiar to me for a hope of something nameless. But I did not want to turn back.

I wandered about Paris sketching and writing poetry. I was offered a job as a model at Dior, but did not take it. I had connections on French *Vogue,* but did not use them except for occasional modeling jobs that entailed no commitment. But I felt more at home in that foreign country than I ever had in my native New York. I felt that I was on the right track, but I still could not have said what I was looking for. In the summer, I went to Italy, first to Venice, and then, after a visit to a villa in the Lombard countryside, to Florence. There I met the two young Italians who invited me to South America to hunt for diamonds. Again, as on my departure from America, I was frightened by the boldness of the step I was taking, but never for an instant considered retreat.

When at last the expedition began, after many preparations and delays, we traveled up the Carcupi River, a small unexplored tributary of the Caroni. In a month, we made considerable headway upriver in spite of the obstacles, mainly trees fallen across the water, through which we had to cut a passage for the canoe with axes and machetes, or waterfalls or rapids over which we portaged about a ton of matériel with the help of two Indians. The little river had halved in volume by the time we made a base camp to explore some tributary streamlets.

It was our first day of rest since we had entered the Carcupi. After breakfast the Italian leader and both Indians went off to look at the geological situation while the second Italian lolled gratefully in his hammock.

I took one of the two paperback books I had bought from a small selection of English titles at the Ciudad Bolivar airport and found a seat among the roots of a large tree that overhung the river. I read partway through the first chapter, not daydreaming but following the story with normal attentiveness, when suddenly I was struck with terrific force by a realization. "This is it! The Glade!" All the excitement of the little girl's insight came back. I had lost it, and now in a grown-up Glade, the biggest jungle on earth, it had returned. The mysteries of jungle life, the ways of its animals and plants, its dramatic storms and sunsets, its snakes, its orchids, its fascinating virginity, the hardness of making one's way in it, and the generosity of its beauty all made it appear even more actively and profoundly right. It was rightness on a grand scale. As we flew over, it had looked like a great green ocean, stretching to the horizon on every side, interlaced with waterways, raised high upon assertive mountains, offered to the sky on the open hands of plateaus. It vibrated in its every cell with life, with rightness—everchanging, ever-intact, and always perfect.

In my joy that day, I thought I had come to the end of my search, that my goal had been achieved: the clear view of things at their undiluted best. It was the "rightness" I had tried to discern through the bafflements of my childhood and—in the talks, discussions, arguments, often pursued until dawn, in the hope of a glimpse of it—in my adolescent years. It was The Glade, lost, found, and now recognized, this time forever. Around me, overhead, underfoot, everything was right, being born, living, dying and being replaced without a break in the order of it all.

I ran my hands lovingly over the great roots that held me like an armchair, and began to entertain the idea of staying in the jungle for the rest of my life.

JANET LEWIS

MEADOW TURF

from *Poems Old and New, 1918–1978* (1981)

Janet Lewis (1899–   ) was born in Chicago and graduated from the University of Chicago, but moved to Santa Fe for reasons of health in 1923. Here she enjoyed the friendship of the poet, critic, and teacher Ivor Winters, whom she married in 1926. In 1927 the couple moved to Palo Alto, California, where Winters joined the Stanford faculty. Lewis has had a long and distinguished career as a novelist and poet, drawing often on earth imagery in her writing.

Goldenrod, strawberry leaf, small
bristling aster, all,
Loosestrife, knife-bladed grasses,
lacing their roots, lacing
The life of the meadow into a deep embrace

Far underground, and all their shoots,
    wet at the base
With shining dew, dry-crested with sun,
Springing out of a mould years old;
Leaves, living and dead, whose stealing
Odors on the cold bright air shed healing—
Oh, heart, here is your healing, here among
The fragrant living and dead.

LAURA LEE DAVIDSON

THE MIRACLE OF RENEWAL

from *A Winter of Content* (1922)

Laura Lee Davidson (c. 1870–1949) was a Baltimore schoolteacher who decided to spend a year alone on an island in Canada's Lake of Many Islands. "I am tired to death," she declared to friends and family as her plans took shape. "I need rest for at least one year. I want to watch the procession of the seasons in some place that is not all paved streets, city smells and noise. Instead of the clang of car bells and the honk of automobile horns, I want to hear the winds sing across the ice fields, instead of the smell of asphalt and hot gasoline, I want the odor of wet earth in boggy places. I have loved the woods all my life; I long to see the year go round there just once before I die." So at summer's end in 1914 she and her gear were deposited on a small rocky island and she set up housekeeping in a one-room shack. In the selection that follows, she looks back over the year and what it has done for her.

My holiday is over. In a very few weeks I must go back to the city and take up my work—the same, yet never again to be the same. Here in the quiet of the woods I am trying to take stock of all that this year has done for me.

It has given me health. I have forgotten all about jerking nerves and aching muscles. I sleep all night like a stone; I eat plain food with relish; I walk and row mile after mile; I work rejoicing in my strength and glad to be alive.

There has been also the renewing of my mind, for my standards of values are changed. Things that once were of supreme importance seem now the veriest trifles. Things that once I took for granted, believing them the common due of mankind—like air and sunshine, warm fires and the kind faces of friends—are now the most valuable things in the world. What I have learned here of the life of birds and beasts, of insects and trees are the veriest primer facts of science to the naturalist—to me they are inestimably precious, the possessions of my mind, for, like Chicken Little, "I saw them with *my* eyes, and heard them with *my* ears." And I shall carry away a gallery of mind-pictures to be a solace and refreshment through all the years to come.

The camp is ready for its owner. I have spent many hours in cleaning, arranging, replacing, that she may find all as she left it ten months ago. The island lies neat and fair in the sunshine, reminding me of a good child that has been washed and dressed and seated on the doorstep to wait for company. Never have the woods looked so fair to me, or the wide lake, where the dragonflies are hawking to and fro over the water, so beautiful.

This is dragonfly season. Millions of them are darting through the air—great green and brown ones with a wing-spread of three to four inches; wee blue ones, like lances of sapphire light; little inch-long yellow ones, and beautiful, rusty red.

To-day I spent three hours on the dock watching one make that wonderful transition from the life amphibious to the life of the air. Noon came and went, food was forgotten while that miracle unfolded there before my very eyes.

I was tying the boat, when I saw what looked like a very large spider, crawling up from the water and out on a board. It moved with such effort and seemed so weak that I was tempted to put it out of its pain. But if I have learned nothing else in all these months in the woods, I have thoroughly learned to keep hands off the processes of nature. Too often have I seen my well-meant attempts to help things along end in disaster. So I gave the creature another glance and prepared to go about my business, when I noticed a slit in its humped back, and a head with great, dull beads of eyes pushing out through the opening. Then I sat down to watch, for I realized that this was birth and not death.

Very slowly the head emerged and the eyes began to glow like lamps of emerald light. A shapeless, pulpy body came working out and two feeble legs pushed forth and began groping for a firm hold. They fastened on the board and then, little by little and ever so slowly, the whole insect struggled out, and lay weak, almost inanimate, beside the empty case that had held it prisoner so long.

Two crumpled lumps on either side began to unfurl and show as wings. The long abdomen, curled round and under, like a snail-shell, began to uncurl and change to brilliant green, while drops of clear moisture gathered on its enameled sides and dripped from its tip. The transparent membrane of the wings, now held stiffly erect, began to show rainbow colors, as they fanned slowly in the warm air, and, at last, nearly three hours after the creature had crept out of the water, the great dragon-fly stood free, beside its cast-off body lying on the dock. And

> "Because the membraned wings,
> So wonderful, so wide,
> So sun-suffused, were things
> Like soul and nought beside,"

certain stupendous phrases rose in my mind and kept sounding through my thoughts.

"Behold, I show you a mystery. We shall not all sleep, but we shall all be changed."

There it stood, that living jewel, growing every moment more strong, more exquisite, waiting perhaps for some trumpet call of its life. Suddenly it stiffened, the great wings shot out horizontally, and with one joyous, upward bound, away it flashed, an embodied triumph, out across the shining water, straight up into the glory of the sun.

When I came to myself I was standing a-tiptoe gazing up after it, my breath was coming in gasps and I heard my own voice saying: "It is sown in weakness, it is raised in power. . . . Thanks be to God, which giveth us the victory."

Then, standing there under those trees, clothed in their new green and upspringing to the sky, and beside the lake, where the young ferns troop down to the water's edge, valiant little armies with banners, there came to me one of those strange flashes of understanding, that pierce for an instant the thick dullness of our minds, and give us a glimpse of the meaning of this life we live in blindness here.

I had seen those woods, all bare and dead, rise triumphant in a glorious spring. I had seen that lake grow dark and still and lie icebound through the strange sleep of winter. Its water now lay rippling in the sun.

Since my coming to Many Islands, one year ago, the Great War has broken forth, civilization has seemed to die, and the hearts of half the world have gone down into a grave.

But even to me has come the echo of the Great Voice that spoke to John, as he stood gazing on a new heaven and new earth:

"I am the beginning and the end," it said. "Behold I make all things new."

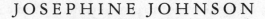

JOSEPHINE JOHNSON

ON A WINTER MORNING
from *Ohio* magazine (February 1990)

Josephine Johnson (1910–1990) came from a long line of farmers, was reared on a hundred-acre farm in south-central Missouri, and lived to the end of her days with a fervent attachment to the piece of Ohio land she and her husband bought in 1956. Love of nature, along with social concerns and a struggle with pessimism, was a theme throughout her writing career, during which she produced twelve books—novels; collections of poems, short stories, and essays; and an autobiography—and many essays published in periodicals. Her first novel, *Now in November* (1934), a celebration of the land and the family farm, won the 1935 Pulitzer Prize.

Her much later book *The Inland Island* (1969), at once a meditation on the natural year and a protest against militarism and the inhumanity of modern technology, was a wellspring of the modern environmental movement. Its setting is the thirty-seven acres of worn-out farmland near Cincinnati that she bought with her second husband, Grant Cannon, an editor of *Farm Quarterly*, with the intention of letting it go back to the wild in the midst of creeping suburban development, a small protest against Progress. She lived on there alone after her husband died and their three children were grown. The following essay, one of the last she wrote, seems to bear out Rachel Carson's words: "Those who dwell ... among the beauties and mysteries of the earth are never alone or weary of life."

I live alone in the country. I like it. The big kitchen in winter is full of potatoes and boots and sacks of seed. One can never be lonely in a room with a fifty-pound sack of sunflower seed. There it sits, large and comforting—a presence. One early morning in winter, I sat in the circle of lamplight in the kitchen, in that hour of silence before the sun rises, the hour of hot toast and coffee, when a sense of power and safety fills one; the soul is solid, and therefore momentarily kind.

In the kitchen is a blackboard for messages. This winter morning in huge chalk letters was printed NU. Just two letters alone on a big black board. Who is NU? Why was this word there on a cold winter morning when crystals covered all the windows, heavy crystals that stretched far, like a glittering beach, and ended in crystal cliffs?

Nu is the Egyptian god of the Beginning, the primal formlessness or chaos, from which was born the formal chaos of this world. After and out of the ancient Nu came the numina, the *lares* and *penates* who presided over the Roman homes, who gave dignity and meaning to the common tasks of life, shaping up, protecting the home and garden, standing over the cradle where the sick child lies. But what, I had been wondering, are the numina of those who live alone? There must be a kind god among them who explains us, solitaries, to the world of families, clumps and groups. Surely they who preside over the whole households do not desert the solitary dweller. Do they move stiffly, listlessly? Bless the one plate, without conviction? Yawn and nod? Would they not rather gather up their robes and blessings and go elsewhere where there appears to be something really going on? A richer and more populated life, warmer than the scratch of little bird feet in the frost.

But to each his own divinities. New gods arise when they are needed. I shall go back to NU and find one who will huddle with me around the sack of sunflower seed, preside over the wild flock of fowl outside. Teach the legal rights of trees, the nobility of hills; respect the beauty of singularity, the value of solitude.

Here in the circle of lamplight, warm, momentarily safe, the great sack of seed looming quietly in the corner, one counts blessings, honors at last an old companion of many years, Noah, Noah Webster, the great square and silent ark of words. Oh, my beloved Noah, when the fire comes, I will lumber through the smoke and gather your great bulk in my arms, the square heavy world of words, my "precious," and rush out to safety in the night and snow.

I thought this winter morning to begin at the beginning where I had never been before. What a smooth and orderly beginning! Two whole blank pages of excellent white paper in this edition—my second copy of the Second Edition, copyright 1959—such paper as one seldom sees in this world, precedes the portrait of Noah Webster. The serene portrait of an amazing man. "He knew the farm, the law, the city, the school, and politics. He knew the country as a whole. . . . For ten years he labored from point to point about the large circular table that held the dictionaries and grammars of twenty languages. . . . In 1828, at the age of seventy, he . . . published *An American Dictionary of the English Language*. . . ."

I sat in the lamplight in a big chair with this enormous achievement on my lap—or half on my knees and half on a small circular table—and turned the pages slowly from the very beginning, through Contents . . . Preface . . . Editorial Staff . . . and came to the organs of speech, the sounds . . . glottal stop, the whispering glottis, the epiglottis . . . the velin.

This was all extraordinary to me. It made me wonder if by seldom speaking out loud in this long winter had my own voice changed? If one does not exercise all these things, do the words emerge in soft, shapeless blobs, un-palatized, or sputtering with glottal stops? One night, I had heard the cats talking, a hot tarry sound. It was just before dawn. They spoke in sounds very like the human voice, with risings, fallings, inflections, clots and stops, such as we use. At times, it was a wailing pour of lava, then cooling off. In that odd gray hour, it seemed possible to learn and translate their language. Form the strange licorice into Arabic symbols and then English. There was a great deal of hate and warning in the sound. It had ended in a hissing and sputtering out.

Outside the earth was coming closer to the sun, but the moon still hung white in the west. It was cold. Very Cold. I tried to think of the self as part of a Whole, a cell of the universe. A universe always shedding, a rain of sheddings and shardings. I saw the little scraps of a silver-fish on the floor, flattened even flatter by some weight. There were these little white things, still fish-shaped, dry and transparent—our ancestors the *Lepisima saccharina,* the fishmoths who fascinate me, who inhabit the tub, who ap-pear as bookmarks dead in their haunts. Can the Whole do without them? Can it do without me? Then the refrig-erator hummed, the clock made tiny tonking clicks, the sunflower seed made a small sliding sound, and there was the dry grainy smell that brings back barns and bins and the moist soft feel of a horse's nose, lipping and snuffling in the oats.

I hefted the dictionary reverently back on its stand and practiced speaking whole sentences out loud. "Good things may come today," I said. "Good things can be winter borne. At least a First will come today," I said loudly, the many *s*'s and *t*'s making a hissing sound. I had read an article once many years ago, by a man who wrote that there were no Firsts—no first times, after middle age. Old age, he wrote, held no real events, no first love, first child, first job, first promotion, no more firsts that he considered of any note, or worth living for. He must have been a breathtak-ingly narrow man to state such a wide lie. Apart from all the great firsts that come at any age, and even sorrow and resignation have the light of illumination around them, the nimbus of first times, there are the thousand and one first times in the natural world, the large and small events, never seen before, or never heard, or never felt before. If we seal this world of ours under concrete, we will have sealed ourselves in an early tomb.

I turned off the light. Began to unwrap the windows. It takes a long time to do things in winter. To wrap the house at night and unwrap it in the morning. It takes four blankets and the eiderdown to "do" the kitchen; it takes a stepladder, clothes pins, loops over badly driven nails. But down came the blankets at last, great soft things, avalanches, falling into my arms, and I looked out on a winter world that had been going on all night without me.

There had been a great wind in the night. A small load of snow. Cold, cold this morning! Windows sealed with crystals. How the birds live I do not know. One would expect little feet and feathers all shattered like glass in the snow. But no, there they are—bright, jumpy, bending the weeds, husking seeds, peering and probing—as though that great belly of ice had not sunken itself in the night, a cold whale smothering over the land. The windows were whorled and furred with ice crystals. The pelt of a beautiful night beast pressed against the pane. And on the feeder I thought a wild black creature, a spiny furred Thing, had fallen and covered it completely. But the Thing was only a swarm of quarreling starlings piled on top of each other—a black starling animal.

Then a hawk came, a dark pigeon hawk. It pursued a junco in and out among the bare branches, a weaving of sharp wings. It gave up and perched, vibrating with cold and rage. I saw its barred tail and its darkness, the color of creek sludge in the summer, and knew it was no hawk I had seen before. The hills and trees and snow were swept of all birds by its knife wings—except for a sullen crow, who in its turn swept the hawk away.

The crow came close on this cold morning. A great crow, with a neck so large and sleek one imagined it might feel to touch like stroking the sleek black arch of a horse's neck. It watched the world, and I watched its eyes and tried very hard to imagine looking out from inside that shining head, imagine what it was thinking, feeling, its cells moving about in an orderly fashion as mine moved. But nothing came to me—or I went nowhere—so locked are we in our own frames, so locked we cannot even imagine the limitations of a crow.

Then the crow began to caw. The *effort* of cawing! The shoulders shoved forward, the caw shoved out like a vomit. Three times. Caw! Caw! Caw! Never more. Never less. First facing east, then facing west. Completely alone. Nobody answered. No other crow came.

Later in the morning, grosbeaks came. They sat in the higher branches with an oriental calm. Few birds sit still and brooding for so long. There was something Buddhist, monklike, in their black and yellow, something presiding in their high positions, and their waiting. The morning was white and empty around them.

I left the window and went to feed the stove. Winters seem colder and colder all the time. Thank God for Ben Franklin! Ben sits there like a big open-mouthed toad with iron wings. Flames flicker up from his grated teeth. More, more, he hisses quietly. He is always digesting, always dying down. Cones, twigs, paper logs do not last. I feed him squashed up news-balls, careful twists of yesterday's avarice and anger. Unfed, he starts slyly smoking. The gray underbelly of the log cracks open. Bundles of pine twigs burn like fiery nests from which fly up the burning owls that hatch from fiery cones. The flames hypnotize. Sometimes they speak a *tcht,* a chiding, irritable sound. Bronze colors have come into the blackened iron. Ben's small feet point north and south, carved and dainty, bearing his great weight like an elephant with claws.

It took much time to tend this fire before one learned. What people must go through to survive by wood alone in winter! I burned a newspaper with a fat man's picture on the front page, a local man of power. I swear I smelled bacon cooking for a long time after that. But it vanished finally in the resin smell of pine cones and the twigs of spruce and fir.

God knows what tiny beasts have been brought in, clinging for dear life to the cone and twig. (For life is very dear to insect things, a tiny eternal flame inside their crackly brittle heads. It's all they've got. No love, no hope of afterworlds, or pride, or joy.)

At night what scrawl and sprawl of little legs will begin a creep across the carpet, an assembly in the hearth rug. The eyes of spiders, black diamonds winking here and there around the room. Who knows what's hatching in the broken bark, what plans and mysteries in those exiled insect heads?

A friend sent me a saw shaped like a bow. It was in some ways a revelation. A magic saw. It cut through wood like a knife through butter. One day I cut wood for two hours. Mostly ash, that straight tree, with the mathematical limbs. Ash and locust—the locust never lets you forget it was once alive. Piled in the house, it smells of fresh pumpkin. The thorns live on and on.

I began to think of inventing the ideal tree. A tree that was spindle shaped, swelling in and out at regular intervals, the fat parts stove length, the thin parts taking only a moment of the saw.

I came back to the kitchen window at noon and heard a hawk crying very close. It was shouting Fair! Fair! Fair! Fair! over and over.

Outside in the snow, instead of a world swept clean by wings, was a strange and surprising sight. A great hawk was perched low in the nearest tree, ten feet from the house. Its breast was rust and white, and its beak and claws were gold. In the snow below, the sparrow and juncos and the redbirds went on feeding. Scratching and fluttering under its icy stare. The hawk was watching the ground, watching the dry grass humps and holes in the snow. It moved its head in a fierce and intent peering and then flew down, walked among the birds, pecked at nothing, flew up to the branch again. It cried Fair! Fair! Fair! angrily and then fell silent, watching.

The birds went on feeding, coming and going as usual, paying it less attention than they would the mice it sought. But how did they know? How did they know this huge hawk wanted mice, not birds—how did they know it would not change its mind from hunger?

Did they tell by the cry? By the fair, fair, fair—some known wild bugle sound of truce?

Well, it is time to erase NU from the blackboard and write instead: *What hawk was this?* . . . and *buy suet, apricots and bread.*

Life is full of Firsts and mysteries, and here we are, only halfway through one winter day.

JANE KENYON

DEPRESSION IN WINTER

from *The Boat of Quiet Hours* (1986)

Jane Kenyon (1947–   ) chronicles in her poetry the inner and outer weathers of her life in New Hampshire, illuminating the details and nuances of ordinary moments. Born in Ann Arbor and graduated from the University of Michigan, she has had her poems published in many magazines and three collections: *From Room to Room* (1978), *The Boat of Quiet Hours,* and *Let Evening Come* (1990).

There comes a little space between the south
side of a boulder
and the snow that fills the woods around it.
Sun heats the stone, reveals
a crescent of bare ground: brown ferns,
and tufts of needles like red hair,
acorns, a patch of moss, bright green. . . .

I sank with every step up to my knees,
throwing myself forward with a violence
of effort, greedy for unhappiness—
until by accident I found the stone,
with its secret porch of heat and light,
where something small could luxuriate, then
turned back down my path, chastened and calm.

Her Creatures:
Animal, Vegetable, and
Mineral Presences

To become aware of other creatures as in-
dividuals is to discover that life is a mansion
with many rooms. We humans see the world
out of the windows of our own small room and think
we've seen it all, but each species has its own window and
its own view. I watch my cat and wonder what the world
looks like to her. I'll never know (at least in this life), but
trying to imagine takes me out of my own small room and
stretches my boundaries. She can teach me a lot about
things like patience, contentment, and concentration, and
she can also provide me a kind of companionship people
can't. When a mother raccoon and her three cubs came
into our yard one night, my cat and I watched spellbound
for an hour as the coons sniffed and dug. I slept well that
night, feeling somehow less alone, reassured by the com-
pany of all the other-than-human lives stirring out there in
the darkness.

The selections in this section honor our fellow creatures. These writers bear witness to the fact that we are immeasurably enriched when we approach our nonhuman relations, domestic and wild, with reverence and respect. They express the pleasure to be found in living in harmony with animal, vegetable, and mineral presences.

DENISE LEVERTOV

COME INTO ANIMAL PRESENCE

from *Poems, 1960–1967* (1983)

Denise Levertov (1923–   ) frequently writes poetry cele-
brating the values of nature and nurture from a distinctively
feminine perspective, although she does not define herself
as a nature poet or a feminist. She has been visible as an
activist in the peace movement while teaching at a number
of universities. Born in London, she was educated mostly at
home, worked as a nurse during World War II, and became
an American citizen in 1955. She has published more than
a dozen volumes of poetry.

Come into animal presence.
No man is so guileless as
the serpent. The lonely white rabbit
on the roof is a star
twitching its ears at the rain.
The llama intricately
folding its hind legs to be seated
not disdains but mildly
disregards human approval.
What joy when the insouciant
armadillo glances at us and doesn't
quicken his trotting
across the track into the palm bush.

What is this joy? That no animal
falters, but knows what it must do?
That the snake has no blemish,
that the rabbit inspects his strange surroundings

in white star-silence? The llama
rests in dignity, the armadillo
has some intention to pursue in the palm forest.
Those who were sacred have remained so,
holiness does not dissolve, it is a presence
of bronze, only the sight that saw it
faltered and turned from it.
An old joy returns in holy presence.

ALICE WALKER

WHY DID THE BALINESE CHICKEN
CROSS THE ROAD?

from *Living by the Word* (1988)

Alice Walker (1944–   ), the eighth child of black share-
croppers in Eatonton, Georgia, has developed a transcen-
dent sympathy with nature and the earth's creatures,
apparent in much of her more recent writing. Educated at
Spelman and Sarah Lawrence colleges, Walker was deeply
involved in the civil rights movement for many years and has
explored the effects of racism and the resiliency of black
women in her fiction, poetry, and essays, most notably *The
Color Purple* (1982), winner of the 1983 Pulitzer Prize and
the American Book Award. Now she spends most of her
time in the small town of Navarro on the Mendocino coast
of California, where she works in her garden and runs Wild
Trees Press with her companion Robert Allen. (The books
they publish "have to be worth the trees.")

"Why do you keep putting off writing about me?" It is the voice of a chicken that asks this. Depending on where you are, you will laugh, or not laugh. Either response is appropriate. The longer I am a writer—so long now that my writing finger is periodically numb—the better I understand what writing is; what its function is; what it is supposed to do. I learn that the writer's pen is a microphone held up to the mouths of ancestors and even stones of long ago. That once given permission by the writer—a fool, and so why should one fear?—horses, dogs, rivers, and, yes, chickens can step forward and expound on their lives. The magic of this is not so much in the power of the microphone as in the ability of the nonhuman object or animal to *be* and the human animal to *perceive its being*.

This then is about a chicken I knew in Bali. I do not know her name or that of her parents and grandparents. I do not know where she was from originally. Suddenly on a day whose morning had been rainy, there she was, on the path in front of us (my own family, on our way back to our temporary shelter), trying to look for worms, trying to point out other possible food items to her three chicks, and trying at the same time to get herself and her young ones across the road.

It is one of those moments that will be engraved on my brain forever. For I really *saw* her. She was small and gray, flecked with black; so were her chicks. She had a healthy red comb and quick, light-brown eyes. She was that proud, chunky chicken shape that makes one feel always that chickens, and hens especially, have personality and *will*. Her steps were neat and quick and authoritative; and though she never touched her chicks, it was obvious she was shepherding them along. She clucked impatiently when, our feet falling ever nearer, one of them, especially self-absorbed and perhaps hard-headed, ceased to respond.

When my friend Joanne—also one of my editors at *Ms.* magazine for nearly fifteen years—knew I was going to Bali, she asked if I would consider writing about it. There was so much there to write about, after all: the beautiful Balinese, the spectacular countryside, the ancient myths, dances, and rituals; the food, the flowers, the fauna, too. When I returned, with no word on Bali, she asked again. I did not know how to tell her that my strongest experience on Bali had been to really be able to see, and identify with, a chicken. Joanne probably eats chicken, I thought.

I did, too.

In fact, just before going to Bali I had been fasting, drinking juices only, and wondering if I could give up the eating of meat. I had even been looking about in San Francisco for an animal rights organization to join (though it is the animal liberationists, who set animals free, who actually take my heart); in that way I hoped to meet others of my kind, i.e., those who are beginning to feel, or have always felt, that eating meat is cannibalism. On the day my companion pointed out such an organization, in an Australian magazine we found at a restaurant in Ubud, I was slow to speak, because I had a delicious piece of Balinese-style chicken satay in my mouth.

I have faced the distressing possibility that I may never be a "pure" vegetarian. There is the occasional stray drumstick or slice of prosciutto that somehow finds its way into my mouth, even though purchased meat no longer appears in my kitchen. Since Bali, nearly a year ago, I have eaten several large pieces of Georgia ham (a cherished delicacy from my childhood, as is fried chicken; it is hard to consider oneself Southern without it!) and several pieces of chicken prepared by a long-lost African friend from twenty years ago who, while visiting, tired of my incessant chopping of vegetables to stir-fry and eat over rice and therefore cooked a chicken and served it in protest. There have been three crab dinners and even one of shrimp.

I console myself by recognizing that this diet, in which ninety percent of what I eat is nonmeat and nondairy, though not pristinely vegetarian, is still completely different from and less barbarous than the one I was raised on—in which meat was a mainstay—and that perhaps if they knew or cared (and somehow I know they know and care), my chicken and fish sister/fellow travelers on the planet might give me credit for effort.

I wonder.

Perhaps I will win this struggle, too, though. I can never *not* know that the chicken I absolutely *saw* is a sister (this recognition gives a whole different meaning to the expression "you chicks"), and that her love of her children definitely resembles my love of mine. Sometimes I cast my quandary about it all in the form of a philosophical chicken joke: Why did the Balinese chicken cross the road? I know the answer is, To try to get both of us to the other side.

It is not so much a question of whether the lion will one day lie down with the lamb, but whether human beings will ever be able to lie down with any creature or being at all.

LOIS CRISLER

LIFE WITH A WOLF PACK

from *Arctic Wild* (1958)

Lois Crisler (1896–1971) and her husband, Cris, lived in the
Brooks Range of Alaska for a year and a half, filming the
wolves and the caribou migration for a major Hollywood
studio. Each of the two summers they were there, they
raised a litter of wolf pups taken from parents in the wild.
Her book *Arctic Wild* about this period and her later book
Captive Wild (1968) contain some of the most detailed and
careful observations of wolf behavior yet recorded and dis-
pel a number of myths about the creatures. Lois was born
in Spokane and taught English at the University of Washing-
ton before her marriage and subsequent experience with a
wilderness life.

The wolves, our companions, were more mysterious and
wonderful than we had dreamed. We had lost a sense of
wolf-mystery on one level to find it on a deeper level. The
mystery and uncertainty that had half veiled Trigger and
Lady at first were replaced by the greater mysteries of na-
ture. How trivial was our old question, would the wolves
turn on us unpredictably! We discerned real questions now,
not man-made ones concocted of fear and myth. There
were answers we should never know; perhaps no one
would. There were questions we should always wonder
about. That dead wolf near the den, for instance.

Cris had come across it a hundred yards from the den
where the pups were found. He had not examined it, except
to note that it must have died that spring. In a mating duel?
If so, was it male or female? The body answered one ques-

tion merely by being there: are wolves cannibals? The dead wolf lay untouched.

The main fact about wolves had grown upon us slowly. Wolves have what it takes to live together in peace.

For one thing, they communicate lavishly. By gestures—the smile, for instance—and by sounds, from the big social howls to the conversational whimpers. They even seek to control by sounds first, not by biting. A full-grown wolf will plead with you not to take his possessions. And you in turn can plead with a wolf. He glances at your eyes, desists from what displeased you and walks off as if indifferent.

They have the big three peace enablers: social observingness (that wonderful wolf attentiveness turned upon social nuances), social concern, and what we used to call feral generosity. Now we realized it was deeper than that. It is social responsibility. We were to see more of it as our wolves grew older. But already we had seen wolves, both male and female, instantly take over responsibility for feeding and protecting from us pups not their own.

Wolves will do the same for dog pups. Disgorge for them too. Our male wolf Coonie, whom we reared later, kidnaped a dog pup, not to kill but to care for. Wolves are crazy about puppies.

Also they feel concern for an animal in trouble even when they cannot do anything for it. A dog got his nose full of porcupine quills on our walk one day. All the way home the wolf Alatna hovered anxious-eyed around his face, whimpering when the dog cried in trying to tramp the quills out. The other dogs with us ran along indifferently.

A new dog was chained and crying. All night a wolf stayed near him, whimpering a little when he cried. The other dogs slept.

A young dog wandered off, on our daily walk. The wolf with us ran to me, cried up to my face, then standing beside me looked searchingly around, call-howling again and again. When the dog sauntered into view the wolf bounded to him and kissed him, overjoyed.

Incidentally, as to this unexpected business of losing each other, wolves are gazehounds and will eagerly overpass a trail and lose it. When Trigger and Tootch ran a caribou, the dog followed the zigzag scent trail. The wolf raised his head and ran straight toward the prey.

The hardest wolf behavior for humans to fathom is the "species quality." The wolf is gentlehearted. Not noble, not cowardly, just nonfighting. Trigger and Lady did not defend the wolf pups from Tootch. The pups' parents did not defend them from the men stealing them from the den. The first time Alatna witnessed a dog fight she was frantically upset. She would have jumped on any innocent bystander, but she did not, as a dog would have done, join the fight; she tried to end it. She did not know what to do; she stammered, as it were, in her actions. At last, incredibly, she pulled the aggressor off by the tail! (The socially observant wolf was never to err about who started a fight.)

The gentleness of wolves is often mentioned in early American accounts—gentleness both as nonbelligerence and as limited flight reaction. Captain Lewis of the Lewis and Clark expedition said that in the neighborhood of buffalo killed by Indians they saw a great many wolves: "they were fat and extremely gentle." He added that Captain Clark killed one of them with a short staff, gentleness being, it would seem, no part of the Captain's own nature.

Gentleness may be appearing in our species. But the deadly words of Konrad Lorenz still characterize our species quality. "Latent in all mankind are the terrible drives of a very irascible ape."

It is almost as hard for us to sense our own species quality as it is to sense our species smell. We have an ape-fretfulness as well as irascibility. I caught a momentary glimpse of our species quality, so profoundly different from the species quality of wolves, the first time I returned to a city after living with wolves on the tundra. Suddenly, for just a little while, I was conscious of our species as a visitor from another planet might be conscious of it. The nervous faces; the fidgety, trifling, meaningless moves and objects;

all the mincing paraphernalia of our weakly, thin-skinned, fetuslike species. I thought of the wide clean tundra, hundreds of miles of it, and the baggageless, purposeful, radiant pups that ranged that tundra with us.

In a reasonable world these peaceful predators would be the most cherished object of study by our race, trying to unlearn war. Why then do people hate wolves and seek to exterminate them? Probably for the same reasons as they do people. It takes a psychiatrist to say why. Lester Pearson in his Nobel Peace Prize lecture at Oslo quotes the Canadian psychiatrist Dr. G. H. Stevenson, whose words apply equally well to our liking for war and for scapegoat programs of wolf extermination.

> People are so easily led into quarrelsome attitudes by national leaders. We men like war. . . . We like the excitement of it, its thrill and glamour, its freedom from restraint. *We like its opportunities for socially approved violence.* [The italics are mine.] . . . This psychological weakness is a constant menace to peaceful behavior. We need to be protected against this weakness, and against the leaders who capitalize on this weakness.

The ambivalent ape likes to be irascible but righteous. And professional wolf haters—Olaus Murie's phrase—capitalize on this weakness of ours. Wolves are not a menace to the wilds but orgies of wolf hate are. Wolves themselves are a balance wheel of nature.

Besides this basic flaw in ourselves, this orgiastic zeal, there are two minor reasons why we indulge in wolf hating. One is that wolves have had a bad press, from Red Riding Hood on. Automatically the museum information card by the fossil wolf skeletons from the La Brea pits in Los Angeles goes on to assert, "a savage creature," "these grim predators."

The other reason is that North American wolves have been tarred with the reputation of their European and Asiatic cousins, though American wolves have never normally been killers of man—perhaps because this continent was so rich in varied food supplies. There are authentic cases of unprovoked attack by wolves on man in America, but they are few.

One incident that is in all the books occurred back of our cabin in the Olympic Mountains. Down the steep slippery trail came a ranger, twenty feet at a jump in places, fleeing two wolves that had treed him twice. The male proved to have a broken jaw, perhaps kicked by an elk. His helplessness may have inclined him toward weakly prey. But the wolves had not closed in; they were wary.

Typical of the usual stories are these, of human and caribou kills.

The driver of a borrowed dog team was killed. By wolves, said the owner of the team. Investigation indicated that the dogs had killed the man and that the owner blamed wolves to avoid putting his dogs to death.

A myth-wolf tale can be made from real-wolf behaviorisms merely by suppressing a crucial fact. A wolf detaches himself from his pack—odd!—and follows a dog team home. That night he tangles with a male dog tied outside the shed housing the team. (Why tied outside?) A tale of menace. Until you learn there was a bitch in heat in the team.

In all sincerity a myth-wolf tale was made from observed facts when caribou wintered near Yellowknife, in 1953. Local people slaughtered about five thousand, butchering many on open lakes. Airplane passengers excitedly reported the lakes littered with "wolf kills."

To a human alone in the wilderness the question remains serious: will wolves attack? A month after our arrival in Alaska, the answer was put into our hands as we stood by the frozen Yukon, partly surrounded by a pack of ten wolves. We were a little scared because the only wolves we knew then were myth wolves.

In the long, still, chill April twilight as we sat in the umbrella tent—new, then—there came a sound we had never heard before, the howl of a wolf. Thrilled, we stepped outdoors. Impulsively I imitated the sound, pouring out my wilderness loneliness.

I was answered. Not by one voice but by a wild weird pandemonium of deep-pitched voices. We stood awestruck. Each wolf opened up medium high. At once its voice broke with a yodel break to a low note which it held and held, a long, unvarying Oooo, while other wolves joined in, overlaid it with their own deep Oooo's, each on a different note. The wild deep medley of chords, broken by Wooo's entering, the absence of treble, made a strange, savage, heart stirring uproar. It was the hunting howl, as we know now.

It ended. We stole to the river bank. Trotting upriver toward us on the white ice came nine dark forms. In front of us they spread in a loose semicircle, watching us. One or two lay down, one or two trotted to touch noses with them. (Wolf socialness! We did not read it. And were the resting wolves pregnant? The other two their mates?)

Apprehensively I glanced into the black spruces at my left. A crush-crush of paws neared in there, a tenth wolf. The tent back of us seemed frail shelter.

"Should I throw them the meat?" I whispered. (Throw the baby from the troika.) The day before we had received a carton of raw meat in a supply drop from a bush pilot.

"No!" whispered Cris sternly. "Howl again."

This time I was too close, the wolves were not deceived. Besides—we did not understand it then—they had their howl out; wolves don't howl at random. One or two answered briefly but the main result of my howl was that the wolves rose and in desultory fashion trotted away upriver on their night's hunt. Not, of course, in the military file of myth.

But surely that tenth wolf had been after our meat? It would be easy to say he was. It is easy to misunderstand a wild animal's actions. The real story was told by his tracks in the snow. Coming up the wooded bank instead of the river, he was within thirty feet of us before he noticed us.

He had backtracked hastily and joined the other wolves on the ice.

Myth wolves would have made a meal of us. For real wolves, humans weren't the dish.

MARGARET MURIE

WILDLIFE IN THE HOME

from *Wapiti Wilderness* (1966)

Margaret (Mardy) Murie (1902–   ) knows what it means to live intimately with wildlife. Her husband, Olaus, was a field biologist for the U.S. Biological Survey (now the Fish and Wildlife Service) for twenty-six years, a job that sent him first into the wilds of western Alaska to study caribou, and later to Jackson Hole, Wyoming, to study the life history of the largest elk herd in the world. Mardy accompanied and worked closely with him on many of his field trips, even when it meant bringing along infants and toddlers as their family grew to include three children. During these years she developed the deep concern for wild creatures and country that still motivates her.

Born in Seattle and raised in Fairbanks, Alaska, she attended Reed College in Oregon, Simmons College in Boston, and was the first woman to graduate from the University of Alaska (with a degree in English). Two months later she married Olaus, and the two spent their honeymoon on a dog-sled trip into the caribou study area. Her memoir *Two in the Far North* (1962) documents this early part of her life; *Wapiti Wilderness,* with some chapters by her and some by Olaus, describes facets of their lives together in Jackson Hole, where she still makes her home. Olaus eventually left the Biological Survey to become director and then president of the Wilderness Society; after his death in 1963, Mardy continued working in the cause of conservation. She is now supporting campaigns to reintroduce the wolf to Yellowstone National Park and to preserve the caribou calving area in the Arctic National Wildlife Refuge from disturbance by oil drilling; but she enjoys most just chatting with visitors who drop by her log house.

We did not just live in Jackson Hole; we lived with a work. Olaus did not leave at 8 A.M. and return at 5 P.M. He lived with his study every hour, and, consciously or not, the family fitted into the pattern.

In our first autumn in the valley Olaus had to be away for three weeks, learning range plants and range-utilization methods at the Forest Service experiment station in Utah. At the same time Adolph was up in Glacier Park studying a certain species of mouse for his Ph.D. dissertation at the University of Michigan. He needed live mice of the same species—*Peromyscus,* the white-footed mouse—from another region, and so, before leaving for the East and school, young Billy Sheldon was live-trapping these on the Elk Refuge and bringing them in to me each day in tin cans tied to the horn of his pony's saddle. Olaus had built a wood and metal-screen cage before he left for Utah. I was to collect the mice, and when he returned he would ship them to Adolph. I had my instructions about rolled oats, apples, and potatoes to be put in for food.

All day I kept myself busy with the two babies, trying not to feel too lonely. There was plenty to do: carrying water from the nearby irrigation ditch, washing baby clothes on a washboard in the tin tubs on the back porch (Olaus had also built a wash bench for the two tubs before he left); keeping an eye on Martin as he played with his toys in the sand and sagebrush around the house; and in spare moments typing Olaus's report on the studies of the caribou of Alaska and Yukon Territory, a government report which would later be his doctoral thesis at the University of Michigan.

When I had tucked Martin into bed each night and given Joanne her last feeding, I was ready for some rest myself. Then the mice began.

Peromyscus are nocturnal. All day, while the noises of the household went on about them, they slept, curled in the big heap of cotton in one corner of the box. With darkness they came forth, to play, to cavort, ceaselessly jumping from one corner to another. I put the box in the kitchen and closed the door and tried to sleep. No use—the more mice Billy brought, the more decibels. How could such small creatures make so much noise? It was like a steady hailstorm. One night I remembered that nailed high to the back wall of the house, on the back porch, was a wooden box. I carried the mouse cage out and hoisted it to the top of this and went to bed, desperate for sleep. Wonderful quiet. I was just losing myself in velvety blackness when there was a loud thump, and another one, on the porch. Wearily I donned slippers and robe and went out. As I opened the door, a big black cat streaked down the steps. Of course! I had forgotten that Inez my sweet neighbor had been complaining about a cat hanging around their place.

I was quite determined to have some sleep that night and I had an inspiration. I carried the cage in and down the steps from the kitchen into the basement below. Before Olaus had gone he had stacked a good supply of cordwood there. I managed to lift the cage to the top of the neat stack and returned to bed. Five minutes later there was a roll of thunder from the basement which brought me to my feet trembling. Flashlight in hand, I went down in trepidation. The cage was still on top, but half of the wood was in a heap in the middle of the floor and the cat was clawing desperately to get back out through the crack under the tiny basement window.

Real peace came only with Olaus's return, whereupon

he shipped off the mice. I was so glad to see him come back from town empty-handed. But he was laughing. "I thought I was going to have to bring those mice back to you! Butch Lloyd didn't know about sending live mice through the mail. He looked up all his books, and finally said: 'Well, they send young chicks through the mail every spring. I guess there's no reason we can't send mice!' So he took them, thank goodness!"

Olaus went on into the big living room to finish unpacking his suitcase. He lifted out a cardboard box, held it up to his ear. "What's that?" I said apprehensively.

"Oh, it's just one of those Uinta ground squirrels. It was already hibernating and I want to sort of observe it during the winter. I thought we could keep it in that back bedroom where there's no heat, where we have things stored. I'll just transfer him to a little bigger box."

Two or three weeks later, when winter had really arrived and we were busily stoking the kitchen range, the wood-burning heater in the corner of the living room, and on most evenings the fireplace also, Olaus looked at the thermometer one evening and said: "You know, I think it's going to go to twenty below before morning. I just wonder if I shouldn't put a little something on top of that squirrel, just enough to raise the temperature a few degrees. How about this pillow?"

He picked up a round silk-covered rust-colored pillow from the couch. "That's the only decent sofa pillow we have, you know," I said.

"Yes, I know, but nothing will touch it; it will only be lying on top of the box."

In the morning Olaus said: "Guess I'll go see whether that squirrel is really still hibernating, or frozen stiff."

A moment later he returned to the kitchen, pillow in hand and a very sheepish grin on his face. There was a hole the size of a teacup in the middle of the rust-colored silk. "Gosh, Mardy, I wouldn't have believed just a pillow could raise the temperature enough to wake that critter up. I went in there and lifted the pillow off to see how the thing was, and there was no squirrel in the hay in the box; then I felt something wiggling inside the pillow in my hand!"

This incident ended as would hundreds of other similar ones through all the ensuing years—in a gale of laughter. Since I could practically never get really angry at Olaus, and absolutely never stay angry with him, and since he was so dedicated to his work that every project or experiment he thought important was bound to go on despite anything or anybody, it was far better just to relax and take it all as it came.

One of the things which came next was elk skulls boiling on the kitchen stove. This was after we had moved to the new house; lovely clean-wood-shavings- and paint-smelling new house. I had been in town all afternoon and hurried up the front steps with thoughts of how quickly I could make a meat loaf for dinner, opened the door, and was nearly knocked down by a terrific odor—indescribable. I shouted up the stairs: "What on earth happened?"

Olaus appeared at the head of the stairs. "Nothing happened. What do you mean?"

"I mean that horrible smell, of course. What is it?"

"Oh, does that smell? It's just some elk skulls I had to boil; you know, it's the only way I can get all the meat off, to make a good specimen. These are some that show the *necrotic stomatitis* in the jawbones, you know. I thought it would be a good time to do it while you were not using the stove."

"Where are the children?"

"Well, they went over to the Grants'."

"Where is your mother?"

"Oh, she's in her room. I guess she did say something about a smell."

And this was not the last time. Skulls had to be boiled. But after three or four more years Olaus called in the Nelson brothers and had a museum-garage built behind the house, and the museum room had a stove in it big enough to hold an old-fashioned wash boiler.

There were other things, just as startling if not as odoriferous. Olaus had that big room upstairs, but he didn't always confine his operations to it; things were likely to be laid down most anywhere, if he were thinking hard about some problem. More than once I went into my kitchen to mix a cake or start a meal, and was confronted with a glass vial of some kind of internal parasites of elk, in formaldehyde, sitting on the windowsill over the sink. The children, from age two on, knew all about Daddy's "smeldehyde" and that it was not for them.

Even the museum building and the study upstairs were not enough when Olaus came to the stage in the writing of the elk report where he had to compare antlers. I had learned to recognize a certain half-humorous questioning smile. "Mardy, I just don't know where I can set those things while I measure them. It's winter, you know."

"Yes, I know, and I know what you're thinking, too. The living room."

In retrospect it seems to me we barked our shins and stabbled ourselves on and fell over elk antlers for a week, but perhaps it was only a few days. By pushing the couch and all the big chairs back flat against the wall, we were able to get the antlers set up all along both sides of the room and across the hearth at the end, and Grandma and the children were warned to pick their way carefully.

It was not just because we were raising a family that I had insisted on the heaviest grade of inlaid linoleum for all the floors.

I think that almost every bird or mammal known to the valley was inside or outside our house over the years, dead or alive. One of the first things Olaus did after we moved into the new house in town was to build a roomy pen or cage, walled and roofed with chicken wire, at the back of the lot and near the willows. The first occupant I recall was a kit fox which some friend sent him from Colorado, and while we still had her someone brought in a coyote pup.

Meanwhile the children were growing; and they were Olaus's children. Martin had a pet skunk in the big cage for a while. Joanne had a baby ground squirrel in a box of cotton behind the kitchen range; she even tried to raise some baby mice she and Alma Ruth had found out on the Refuge, but that ended sadly because Donald, age two, thought they were something for him to play with.

It was not only what the children and Olaus brought in; anyone in the valley who found a crippled animal or bird, or a sick one, promptly brought it to us. One autumn I was away on a short trip to visit my family over in Okanogan. I had been back home only a few minutes and was unpacking my bag; might as well carry these clothes down to the laundry room right now. I dashed downstairs and into the laundry room, put the clothes in the hamper, heard a strange sound just behind me, and turned. There, perched on top of my drying rack, sat a very large great horned owl clicking his beak at me. I fled, and at the bottom of the stairs met Olaus: "Gee whiz, I didn't think you'd be going downstairs so soon! Charlie Nelson found that owl by the road; one wing seemed to be injured."

After that we had a horned lark free in the house until he was able to fly, and then someone brought in a piñon jay, a species not known in Jackson Hole, and this one seemed to be injured in some way; he was let loose in the basement. But one day as I came up from the laundry I noticed him perched on one of the hundreds of elk skulls Olaus had ranged on shelves in the front part of the basement, deftly lifting the teeth out with his clever bill. I began to look around a bit; there on one end of a shelf was an open shoe box, one third full of elk teeth! The piñon jay went back to the wilds, and Olaus spent a good many hours trying to fit teeth back where they belonged.

EDNA ST. VINCENT MILLAY

THE FAWN

from *Collected Poems* (1956)

Edna St. Vincent Millay (1892–1950), an ardent feminist and antiwar activist, wrote poems of contemporary relevance about feminism, injustice, the beauty of nature, and the idiocy of environmental pollution and war. Her appreciation of nature is open, quiet, passionate. Born in the small coastal town of Rockland, Maine, she was educated at Vassar and lived an artist's life in Greenwich Village and in Europe for many years before marrying and settling on an upland farm in the Berkshires on the New York–Massachusetts border, where she tended her garden and wrote poetry. The farm, known as Steepletop, is now the site of the Millay Colony for the Arts founded by her sister Norma Millay Ellis.

There it was I saw what I shall never forget
And never retrieve.
Monstrous and beautiful to human eyes, hard to believe,
He lay, yet there he lay,
Asleep on the moss, his head on his polished cleft small
    ebony hooves,
The child of the doe, the dappled child of the deer.

Surely his mother had never said, "Lie here
Till I return," so spotty and plain to see
On the green moss lay he.
His eyes had opened; he considered me.

I would have given more than I care to say
To thrifty ears, might I have had him for my friend
One moment only of that forest day:

Might I have had the acceptance, not the love
Of those clear eyes;
Might I have been for him the bough above
Or the root beneath his forest bed,
A part of the forest, seen without surprise.

Was it alarm, or was it the wind of my fear lest he
    depart
That jerked him to his jointy knees,
And sent him crashing off, leaping and stumbling
On his new legs, between the stems of the white trees?

HOPE RYDEN

TO BUILD A DAM

from *Lily Pond* (1989)

Hope Ryden, during a distinguished career as a documen-
tary filmmaker, photographer, and writer, has taken a spe-
cial interest in the protection of North American wildlife. A
caring and careful observer, Ryden has sympathetically doc-
umented the lives of bobcats, coyotes, wild horses, bald
eagles, deer, and beavers, in five books for adults and eight
for youngsters. Born in St. Paul, Minnesota, and graduated

from the University of Iowa, she lives in New York City when she's not in the field.

Ryden first became interested in beavers when she wrote a cover story for the *New York Times Magazine* suggesting the beaver be named New York's state animal, a suggestion the state legislature promptly followed. Her book *Lily Pond* tells the story of a pair of wild beavers and their offspring, whose activities Ryden watched for four years at Lily Pond and other nearby ponds they built in New York's Harriman State Park. Through Ryden's eyes, we come to appreciate the beavers' intelligence, skill, and sociability, and to deplore the destructive acts of humans toward them. Of note is her struggle on several occasions with the question of whether or not to extend a helping hand to the beavers. Ryden was sometimes accompanied on her trips to the pond by naturalist John Miller, now her husband.

Building a dam is not an easy thing to do. I say this from firsthand experience. One afternoon, while exploring New Pond, John and I decided to look for burrows on the far bank. To get there, we took a short cut across the dam that Laurel and the Skipper had built. But the fresh mud on its crest had not settled, nor had the structure been in place long enough to give rise to rooted plants that would hold it together, and so it failed to support our weight. When we were half-way across, a section collapsed. I was not so much upset over the dousing we got—which I felt we deserved—as I was over the damage we had done to the beavers' new dam.

"We ought to try to fix this thing before the Skipper and Laurel wake up," I suggested to John.

And so, after making a trip to my cabin for hoes, we pulled on our hip boots and waded out to the break we had made. In fairness to John, I must say that he did not think much of my idea, being convinced that the beavers would take care of the big break all by themselves. I knew he was right, but an urge to slosh about in a beaver pond had been growing in me (being a spectator all the time can pall), and repairing the dam we had damaged seemed just the excuse to satisfy it. And so we waded in with our hoes and tried to bring up bottom mud.

It didn't take long to discover how difficult a task we had set for ourselves. The pond bottom was rock hard, the ground having been inundated for too short a time to have softened.

"They must be getting their mud from somewhere other than here by the dam," John finally said. And so we began testing various places for muckiness.

"I found a patch," I called, after considerable hoe-pounding.

John joined me in trying to raise my find to the surface, but the stuff was unmanageable. It dissolved, and clouded the water as we tried to get hold of it.

"What about sticks?" I asked. "Maybe we should just try to push some sticks into the breach."

That idea proved no more workable. Water rushed over and under our haphazard placement of forked and branching lumber. In the end, we gave up trying to repair the dam and waited to see how the beavers would do it.

Their efficiency in accomplishing this feat was downright embarrassing. Within minutes of waking, the Skipper and Laurel were hard at work removing our poorly placed sticks and creating a more satisfactory arrangement of them. A long straight one was maneuvered to lie lengthwise across the breach. Then both animals scoured the shore for buttressing material. Several long polelike branches were towed to the break and heaved over it, so that they came to rest in an upright position on the backside of the dam. To secure these in place, the beavers held and guided them with their front hands, while pile-driving them with their mouths.

Afterward the Skipper packed finer material—branching twigs and bottom debris—against this picket work, while Laurel made repeated trips for bottom mud, which she obtained from a place John and I never would have found. Apparently, the two had dredged a tunnel under a small island, land that had not yet become submerged in the rising pond. Into this waterfilled tunnel Laurel repeatedly dived, and each time she surfaced she came up with an armload of fresh mud pressed tightly to her chest. The walls of the deep tunnel, not being in the grip of roots, had quickly softened, and so it was from here that the beavers mined all the mud they needed to cement and seal their dam.

I noticed that the order in which materials were used to fix a breached dam differed significantly from that used by the Lily Pond beavers in creating Square Pond from scratch. To stop fast-moving water, the Skipper and Laurel began with heavy lumber and only later used mud to fill in chinks and seal their repair. By contrast, the Lily Pond beavers, in containing a shallow, sluggish flood, first pushed up mud to form a long ridge. They then added fine twigs and decaying leaves to this. Not until several days had passed and the water they raised threatened to erode the soft structure did they back it with upright sticks.

In applying two different strategies to stem two different flow rates, the beavers seemed to have invoked some choice. Perhaps beaver kits serve long apprenticeships to acquaint them with the many ways that water behaves and to allow them time and freedom to experiment with different methods of dealing with what looks to us to be simple flow. To understand precisely what I mean, you would do well to pull on a pair of hip boots and try to mend a beaver dam.

HELEN HOOVER

TWO CREATURES OF THE LONG-SHADOWED FOREST

from *The Long-Shadowed Forest* (1963)

Helen Hoover (1910–1984) and her artist husband, Adrian, renounced city life in 1954 and moved to a cabin on a Minnesota lake forty-five miles from town on a one-way road, where they spent their first nine years without a car. The Hoovers were genuine pioneers, experiencing intense physical hardships but richly appreciating the natural beauty around them. Helen conveyed their respect for nature when she wrote, "When Ade and I had the opportunity of receiving electric power and telephone service at the cost of felling a swath through our old trees, we decided in favor of the trees." She was born in Greenfield, Ohio, and attended Ohio University, where she studied chemistry, and the University of Chicago, where she studied biology. She worked as a research metallurgist for the International Harvester Company in Chicago and held patents for agricultural implement disks.

After the move to Minnesota, Hoover wrote women's fiction under the name Jennifer Price, but most of her writing, published largely in magazines, was about wild and human life in the North Woods. Her husband illustrated the series of books she wrote chronicling their progress from greenhorns to seasoned woodspeople: *The Long-Shadowed Forest, The Gift of the Deer* (1966), *A Place in the Woods* (1969), and *The Years of the Forest* (1973). Her nature writing is distinguished by its accuracy, grace, optimism, lack of sentimentality, and expression of abiding love for the earth and its creatures, as conveyed in the following selection.

The weasel is the most beautiful and efficient mousetrap on earth, and does not deserve its ugly reputation. Its killing of more than it can eat is an attempt to procure food which may be stored and eaten later. Adult weasels need one-third of their weight in meat daily and the young, which number up to a dozen in a litter, one-half of theirs. That weasels are intelligent and resourceful enough to deserve anyone's respect was demonstrated to us by Walter, our adaptable weasel.

On a mid-December afternoon the screaming of blue jays told me that something was amiss in the yard. The center of the disturbance was the ermine we named Walter. Twisted into a fur rope, he was making acrobatic attempts to get suet from a cage hung on a cedar bole. Not having much success, he dropped down and bounded gracefully to the doorstep.

He was only a foot long and very dashing in his snow-white coat, accented by his black tailtip and the candy-pink lining of his rounded ears. His glittering black eyes peered past me. Then he sniffed, audibly and ecstatically, and licked the corners of his mouth with a fuschia-colored tongue. Walter was trying to tell me that, if I would kindly withdraw, he would be happy to go in and take care of the meat thawing in the kitchen.

If this was the crafty, ferocious weasel of ill-repute, he concealed his true nature adequately. He looked alert, eager, straightforward. He gave me an impression of intelligent interest that I had not seen before in any animal.

I wanted to know him better. Like all other wild things, his whole existence was directed by hunger and fear. By satisfying his hunger, I might overcome his fear. I tossed a bit of meat. He snatched it and flashed away, feather-light on his dainty paws.

Gradually we gained mutual confidence until he took meat from my bare hand with care and daintiness. When he occasionally mistook a finger for food, he pulled hard, then sat back and looked puzzled, as though he could not understand why this particular bit of meat was attached to me.

Never did he show any tendency toward biting. From this point, I made no effort to train him, that I might learn how he would use his new and strange situation.

Walter was soon busy moving from the deep woods, a matter of finding storehouses and shelters under stumps, outbuildings, boulders, and brush piles near the house. He laboriously transferred one item of personal property, a meaty bone that was twice his length and weighed several times his three ounces.

He took suet and ground beef to each of seven storehouses. He liked frankfurters, potted meat, butter, and bacon, and a can containing remnants of boned chicken was a treasure to be carried home in his mouth. He arched his neck as proudly as a carousel horse as he held his head high to keep his pattering front feet clear of the dangling can. But he preferred red meat, especially moose meat, given us by our Indian friends. Ade insists that Walter is the only weasel ever to eat anything as large as a moose.

My appearance outside after dark was a signal for Walter's head to emerge jack-in-the-box-like from one of his doorways in the snow, whence he hurried to the step to wait for a handout. When I did not go out, he attracted my attention by running up and down on the screen door.

Walter's life, from one of ease, became filled with deadly peril when his larger cousin and arch-enemy, the fisher, arrived. This fellow had all the suppleness and agility of the ermine, was forty inches long, weighed ten pounds, and could leap twenty feet—altogether a formidable adversary for little Walter. Even a female, perhaps two feet long and half as heavy as the male, would have been menacing to him.

The fisher began his campaign by systematically digging out Walter's storehouses and eating the contents. Then he concentrated on digging out Walter, who abandoned his open paths and found new ways to cross the yard: twisting routes under woodpiles, brush, any cover.

The fisher hunted at night, so Walter came daily for one large meal. When the fisher's night prowling did not yield

Walter into his jaws he began to forage by day. Walter promptly began to come at night, scratching briefly on the screen and waiting for me under the woodshed. At last the fisher began to prowl at any time during the twenty-four hours.

Walter did not appear for four days and a fresh snowfall was unmarked by his small tracks. We decided sadly that our ermine had come to the violent end of almost every wild thing.

In the small hours of the next morning I was awakened by a touch on my face. Walter, trembling pitifully, crouched on my eiderdown, his face gashed from brow to nosetip and his right eye black and swollen shut. One of the fisher's raids had been a near thing.

After he had eaten ravenously, Walter went straight to the inside of the kitchen door—remarkable because he had previously approached it only from the outside. When I opened it, he crouched on the sill, tense and fearful. I stepped into the blue-bright moonlight and opened my robe to throw a shadow across the step. In this sheltering dark, Walter shot into the night. He came regularly while his wounds were healing, sliding through some small opening under the foundation (which we never exactly located), and timed his later visits with the hours when the moon-shadows darkened the doorway, but he would not stay inside.

Walter loved his freedom and his own wild way of life more than any pampered security we could offer him. Because of his courage and rapid adjustments, he still roams the forest, the only sign of his brush with death a twisted line of fur beside his nose.

The fisher that was the villain of Walter's story is, when considered from his own standpoint, quite as fine as the ermine. Everywhere wild creatures demonstrate that nothing is good or bad of itself, that circumstances and viewpoint too easily lead to attitudes of judgment that should have no part in the evaluation of the things of the earth.

The fisher retires to remote and dense evergreen wilderness, where men seldom stay long. Consequently, the little that is known of it in the wild state has largely been deduced from observations of tracks on the snow. Because the country in which our cabin stands has rocky hills for den sites, and an abundance of small animals for food, and because we try hard not to disturb the wilderness quiet, fishers drop in on us every now and then.

A fisher is an outstandingly beautiful animal. More than a third of its length is fluffy, tapering tail. Usually its coat is so dark a brown that it seems black, with long, upstanding, pale guard hairs about the head and shoulders, that give it a frosted look. Sometimes the fur is a light or reddish brown and, in 1960, a cream-colored mutant was accidentally trapped a few miles from here. The fisher's body has the elongated form and agile grace of the weasel and mink. Its legs are short, especially the front ones, and powerful haunches foretell great leaping power. Its face is the slender face of the weasel, with the same interested eyes, small ears deep in fur, and sensitive pointed snout. Usually there is a small white throat patch.

By night the fisher is as fearfully exquisite as a creature out of dreams. Moving about in the cold light of the stars, moon, or aurora borealis, it is a mysterious, fluid part of the half-dark. The frosty hairs that give it daytime fluffiness are invisible and, smooth and sleek and sinuous, it flows and poses, a shadow darker than all other shadows, its eyes like emeralds exploding into flame. It glides in the unearthly beauty that belongs to the untamed land and its children.

My first daytime view of a fisher came when I was sitting on the step, admiring the beautiful stripings and rich red wash on the rump of an eastern chipmunk that was standing in my left hand and gobbling corn out of my right. I sensed movement in front of me. Crouched not ten feet away, a big male fisher glared at the little animal in my hands.

Very steadily I stood up, carrying the chippy along. Startled, it almost jumped away, but caught sight of the fisher and collapsed in fear in my hands.

When I moved forward a step, the fisher rose on his

haunches and hissed, but he gave ground and leaped to an observation position some five feet up the trunk of a small tree. He clung there much the way a black bear does—one foreleg wrapped higher than the other while he peered around the bole to see whether he might safely come down or should seek shelter higher up. When I made no other move, he inched himself down backwards—although they can literally flow head downward—and trotted away without haste, giving me an occasional over-the-shoulder glance.

The quivering of the frightened chipmunk stopped. I looked down to see it calmly stuffing its cheek pouches as though nothing had occurred.

During the past eight years, Ade and I have seen many fishers and even persuaded some of the more hunger-driven to feed from our hands. Always they took food with care not to touch our fingers. However, a trapped or cornered fisher will defend itself and its freedom ferociously.

I will accept the fisher as an animal that bears within it some of the same unquenchable spirit of wildness as the timber wolf, an animal that adds joy to my days because of its beauty and grace, that sometimes stirs in me an eerie whisper of ancient hauntings as it moves like a bodiless shadow in the moonlight or pads ever so softly across the roof in deep night.

MAXINE KUMIN

TURNING THE GARDEN IN MIDDLE AGE

from *Nurture* (1989)

Maxine Kumin (1925–   ) writes in *In Deep: Country Essays* (1987) that she finds the impulse for poems "in the vivid turn of the seasons, in the dailiness of growing things, in the quite primitive satisfaction of putting up vegetables and fruits, gathering wild nuts and mushrooms, raising meat for the table, collecting sap for sweetening." She was born in Philadelphia, earned a B.A. and an M.A. from Radcliffe, bore and raised three children, and now lives with her engineer husband on a farm in New Hampshire. She is best known for her carefully crafted poetry, having won the Pulitzer Prize in 1973 for *Up Country: Poems of New England* (1972), but she also has written children's books, novels, short stories, essays, and articles, and has taught writing at a number of colleges and universities.

They have lain a long time, these two:
parsnip with his beard on his foot,
pudding stone with fool's gold in her ear
until, under the thrust of my fork,
earthlock lets go. Mineral
and marrow are flung loose in May
still clinging together as if
they had intended this embrace.

I think then of skulls picked clean
underground, and the long bones
of animals overturned in the woods

and the gorgeous insurgency
of these smart green weeds
erect now in every furrow
that lure me once more
to set seeds in the loam.

ANNA BOTSFORD COMSTOCK

A LITTLE NOMAD

from *Ways of the Six-Footed* (1903)

Anna Botsford Comstock (1854–1930) was a key figure in
the nature study movement of the late 1800s and early
1900s, the aim of which was to introduce children to the
outdoors. She earned a B.S. degree in natural history from
Cornell University, and later married her zoology professor,
John Henry Comstock. She illustrated and aided her hus-
band in writing three college textbooks on insects before
writing her own book of insect stories, *Ways of the Six-Footed*.
In her preface to the latter book, she explains that she wrote
it not to present new facts about the ten insects whose stories
she tells, but rather to give a sense, from her own observa-
tion and experience, of the "dignity and grandeur" of their
"great silent struggle for adjustment and supremacy." Her
later books include *How to Know the Butterflies* (with J. H.
Comstock, 1904), *How to Keep Bees* (1905), *The Pet Book*
(1914), and *Trees at Leisure* (1916).

Comstock exerted her broadest influence through her
consolidation of her earlier works into the 900-page *Hand-
book of Nature Study* (1911), a teaching guide for elementary

teachers that enjoyed a long life, through twenty-four print-
ings and translation into eight languages. She also founded
and helped edit *Nature Study Review,* a national journal for
teachers of natural history; initiated an experimental nature
study program in the Westchester County schools; and
taught nature study at Cornell, where in 1920 she became
the first woman to earn the rank of full professor at that
university. In 1923 she was named one of America's twelve
greatest women by the League of Women Voters. Comstock
was a determinedly cheerful woman, and her books, lec-
tures, and magazine essays typically include a strong dose of
personal anecdote while emphasizing the value of all life and
the importance of understanding the interrelationships
among creatures.

One warm August morning I followed a certain restful,
woodsy path which soon led me to a partially wooded hill-
side. I found a shady resting-place under a pair of twin
maple trees, where I settled contentedly in the grass with
some downy young sumacs for neighbors. The blue waters
of the lake twinkled up at me through the tree-boles, and
a blue sky beamed down on me through the tree-tops. The
breeze, playing softly with the leaves above me, and the soft
swish of the water on the rocks below united in a soothing
song, to which a cicada from his high perch was doing his
best to perform a worthy obligato. I was tired of a world of
work and care; and as I turned my footsteps toward this cosy
nook I said to myself, "I will go where I can be alone." Vain
decision and absurd desire! I had just arranged for myself
a tree-trunk chair-back and was enjoying the nice bark
upholstery when a grandfather graybeard came teetering
along on his stilts, letting his body down at rhythmic inter-
vals to feel of my hand with his palpi to discover if per-
chance I were good to eat. Then a red squirrel darted up
a young ash tree in front of me, the dark stripe on his side
where the red and white meet being particularly vivid and
dashing; at first he sneezed and coughed his displeasure at
my intrusion and then sprang his rattle so suddenly that I

wondered if it might be that squirrels have secreted in them storage batteries that may be switched at will from action to sound. Then a great butterfly, a tiger swallowtail, came careening down through a hole in my leaf canopy and alighted on a sunlit bush near me; there, in utter luxuriousness, he slowly opened and shut his wings in obvious enjoyment of his sun-bath. While watching him I noticed that the maple sapling, on which he was resting, was in a bad way; its leaves were riddled with holes, varying in size from that of a bird shot to that of a small bean.

Now while I was tired of a world that lectured and talked and argued and did many other noisy things that wore on one's nerves, I was by no means tired of the great silent world that did things and made no fuss about doing them. So, when my butterfly drifted away, I lazily began to investigate the cause of the dilapidation of the maple leaves. There I found, as I suspected at first glance, a little nomad named the Maple-leaf Cutter, which pitches its tent on leafy plains and whose acquaintance I had made several years ago when I was employed to make its family portraits.

I plucked a leaf that had several oval holes in it and also several oval rings marked by a tracing of bare veins and translucent leaf tissue; then I noticed an oval bit of leaf wrong side up on the upper surface of the leaf. A glance at this through my lens showed that it was made fast to its place by several bundles of glistening white silk. With a knife point I tore asunder these ropes and lifted the wee tent and found fastened to its under surface another bit of the leaf identical in shape but somewhat smaller. Suddenly from an opening between the two an inquiring head was thrust out with an air that said plainly, "Who's there?" I tore the two pieces of leaf apart to get a better view of the little inmate. He was a stocky, brownish caterpillar, about one-sixth of an inch long, with shields on his thoracic segments that shone like polished bronze and an anal shield that was dull purple. His several simple eyes were in two such compact groups that they gave the impression of two keen, beady, black eyes, and I had a feeling that he was inspecting me through the lens. He was very unhappy and squirmy when removed from his cover, and he backed so vigorously that he backed half his length out of the rear end of his tent before he felt safe, and then remained very still. His loosened tent was lying bottom side up on the leaf; and owing to my clumsy proportions I was obliged to leave the labor of righting it to him; he gave it his immediate attention and went at it in a most workmanlike manner. He crawled halfway out upon the leaf and by a dexterous lift of the rear end of his body he brought the tent down right side up and at once began pegging it down. To do this he moved his lower lip around and around on the leaf surface to make fast, then spun his rope up and lifting his head fastened it to the edge of the tent; this process he repeated many times, but with great rapidity, and when the fastening was finished it was well worth seeing. He had spun his silken cords so they formed an X. This arrangement allowed him room to fasten many lines to the leaf and tent, and since they were crossed in the middle they had the strength of many twisted strands. He put his first fastening at one side of his tent and then hastened to put another on the opposite side, and thus made secure he took his time for putting down the remainder of his ropes.

While watching him spin, I mused on his history as revealed in its earlier chapters by that truly great scientist, Dr. Fitch, and added to in its later chapters by our own Dr. Lintner,—two men of whom New York is so justly proud. This history was as follows: Last May a tiny moth (*Paraclemensia acerifoliella*) sought out this maple sapling; she was a beautiful little creature with a wing expanse of a little more than a half inch; her front wings and thorax were steel-blue, and her hind wings and abdomen were pale, smoky brown; these hind wings were bordered with a wide, fine fringe; across both sets of wings glinted and gleamed a purple iridescence like that on the surface of a bit of mother-of-pearl. On her head, between her antennæ, she wore a little cap of orange feathers, this color combination of orange and steel-blue proving her to be a moth of fine discrimination in the matter of dress. This pretty mother moth laid an egg upon the leaf which I held in my hand; from that egg hatched my wee caterpillar, and began life, I suspect, as a true leaf-miner. However, this is a guess of my own, inspired by the appearance of the leaf. Anyway, he did not remain a miner long, but soon cut out a bit of the leaf and pulled it over him and pegged it down; beneath it he pastured on the green leaf-tissues in safety, and in this retreat he shed his skin. With added growth came the need for more commodious quarters; so he cut another oval piece from the leaf, as much larger than his tent as he could reach without coming entirely out of his cover; before he cut it completely free he ingeniously fastened one side of it to the leaf with silk so that he would not fall, cradle and all, to the ground. He then used this fastening as a hinge as he came part way out of his tent, took a good hold of the leaf with his sharp claws, and flipped the loosened piece over his back and fastened it down over fresh feeding-ground. What was previously his tent was then a rug beneath him; his new pasture was a margin of about one-twelfth inch that lay between the edges of his rug and his tent; for he was ever averse to exposing his precious person to lurking enemies more than was strictly necessary. Before he shed his skin again he may have needed a new pasture; if so, he struck his tent and walked off with it on his back, looking like a Lilliputian mud-turtle, and finally fastened it on a new site. He had already several times gone through this process of upsetting his house, for he had two rugs beneath him and two tents above him of graduated sizes. And I knew that some time in the near future he would peg down his largest tent more securely than he had ever done before, and there in this safe shelter would change to a pupa. When the leaf that had been the range of this small nomad fell in the autumn he would go with it; and wrapped in his tent rugs he would sleep his winter sleep under the snow until he should awaken next spring, no longer a tenter on leafy plains, but a true child of the air.

I tore off a bit of the leaf on which my little friend had

settled, and went over and pinned it to a leaf still on the bush. It may have been an absurd thing to do, but by this time I was shamelessly, nay, intrepidly sentimental, and I did not wish that little chap to starve because of my inborn tendency to meddle with other people's affairs. I then fell from bad to worse and began to moralize; for when a naturalist falls to moralizing science weeps. I meditated thus, "I came here to get away from puzzling problems, and yet here they are all around me; the problems of the little nomad; the problems of the poor, leaf-lacerated maple; and if I look in other directions I will find more in plenty." But for some sweet reason I did not feel about problems as I did when I ran away and hid from the noisy world two hours before. I was filled with a new sense of the dignity and grandeur of this great silent struggle for adjustment and supremacy which was going on around me. I felt inspired to go back and serenely do my own little part as well as I could, trusting that somehow, somewhere, and to Some One the net proceeds of struggle are greater than the cost.

MARY LEISTER

DRAMA ON A WOODEN FENCE

from *Wildlings* (1976)

> Mary Leister (1917–) writes of the square half-mile of
> land she inhabits in Howard County, Maryland, that "what
> happens to this small section of the living earth and to the
> life it nurtures is the daily interest and the continuing adven-
> ture of my life." She learned to love the wildlings of fields,
> marshes, streams, and woodlands while growing up on the
> family farm in the foothills of Pennsylvania's Allegheny
> Mountains. Years later, married to an electronics engineer,
> she combined her deep interests in wildlife, reading, and
> writing in a successful career writing articles for outdoor and
> children's magazines, and essays for the *Baltimore Sun.* Her
> *Sun* essays have been collected in two exquisite books, *Wild-
> lings* and *Seasons of Heron Pond* (1981). Leister notes, "With
> a deep belief in the interrelatedness, the oneness, of all
> life—and believing that, possibly, everything is alive—I
> write of animals, and plants, and weather, and water, and
> earth that others may learn to love all those things that share
> our small planet, and accord them the right to grow and
> to be."

The fence should have been painted early in the spring but
other tasks and other interests had pushed the job aside.
Summer had been a succession of rainy or steamy days, and
it was not until a glorious October afternoon that I began
to paint the scarred old pickets.

Being a perfectionist only in certain well-defined direc-
tions, I painted the fence, to my own satisfaction at least,
while letting the October day keep my five senses busy and

my gypsying mind wandering on a hundred vagrant trails.

Even the odor of paint could not prevent the nutty smells of the close-by woods or the fruity smells of the apple trees or the ripe Autumn smells of the weeds and grasses from reaching my nostrils.

Bob Whites whistled their anxious covey-calls from the orchards and the hills. Blue jays screamed and scolded and pounded sunflower seeds into the crevices of white oak bark. Gray squirrels chattered and quacked and bounced frost-ripened hickory nuts down the dark limbs to the ground.

The dogwoods were purple-leaved and scarlet-berried along the edges of the woods. Shadows shifted and flowed on the grass when cool-tipped breezes lifted their leaves. A thousand milkweed silks drifted on the light-drenched air.

And then a gravid, green-bronze mantis nearly four inches long landed on the unpainted plank at the top of the fence and brought my attention closer to my job.

She wandered restlessly back and forth along the top of the fence for several minutes. Suddenly she became aware of me. She stalked to the edge of the fence and peered down at my kneeling form. She cocked her green-button head first to one side and then to the other and stared at me with an intensity that made me acutely self-conscious. Could she see the whole of me? I wondered. If not, how much could she see with those great compound eyes? Was she studying me? Was she mystified by this untypical, non-food-gathering, non-shelter-building activity of mine? Was she trying to classify me?

I try not to be anthropomorphic, especially when considering a consciousness so foreign as that of an insect, but this mantis was something else. For two full hours she followed me along the fence, never more than two feet behind me, usually close at my side, not taking her eyes from me the entire time. She scrutinized every move I made, stared at my face and my paint-spattered coveralls, and seemed to interest herself in what I was doing, which included scrupulously not painting the top of the fence.

For two hours neither she nor I had looked at another creature, but now I saw, a few feet ahead of us, a small dark spider begin to build its frail web in the angle between the topmost plank and a fencepost. It spun swiftly and in less than twenty minutes it had suspended three fine lines and hung a sticky trap within them.

Building completed, it had scarcely retired to an upper corner when a housefly blundered into the snare. The spider dashed to the spot, tied down the struggling captive with a few well-placed strands of silk, and began to dine, first clipping off the pale wings and allowing them to spiral to the ground.

When the spider had finished its meal it sat back and wiped its face with its front legs.

Now, up behind the complacent spider crept the praying mantis. She stalked upon her four angular legs with sinister intent. Her head was up, her eyes were fixed upon the spider. She held her short, saw-toothed front legs folded below her face in a worshipful attitude. She was ready for the kill.

With a graceful motion so swift I'm not sure I saw it, the mantis reached forward and grasped the spider in her spiny arms. I know I witnessed no *coup de grâce,* but perhaps the knife-sharp grip stunned the little spider. At any rate, the mantis proceeded at once to eat it, from the edges in, as though it were a slice of watermelon.

When she had completed her meal, the mantis, in turn, washed her saw-tooth weapons and her face. Cat-like, she cleaned her front feet with her mouth, then rubbed them over her face and over her eyes again and again. When she had bathed, she took one more look at me, then spread her green-bronze wings and flew heavily off, dropping into the yellow chrysanthemums below the fence.

I confess that I watched these episodes in complete fascination with no thought to rescue either fly or spider. I considered that to really complete the drama a pigeon should fly down and eat the mantis; I, in turn, should eat the pigeon; then some larger animal should leap the fence and swallow me. Nothing of the sort occurred, however, and the food chain, for the time being, ended there.

But two questions press at the back of my mind: First, why did the mantis stay with me all that long afternoon? and, second, did the mantis feel that she had eaten only a spider, or did she realize she had also eaten a fly?

DIANA KAPPEL-SMITH

DANCE OF GIANTS

from *Wintering* (1984)

Diana Kappel-Smith (1951–) came to farming in Vermont with the skills and vision of both an artist and a scientist. Her book *Wintering*, decorated with her own fine illustrations, represents her attempt to get out of her own skin and inside the lives of the plants and animals in the fields and forests around her as fall turns to winter and winter to spring. "I need," she writes, "to enter the secret rooms of winter with the same curious urgency with which I enter dreams." Kappel-Smith was born in Connecticut and earned a B.S. in biology from the University of Vermont before going to live in an old farmhouse in Wolcott, Vermont. She married a neighbor and took up full-time farming on a 275-acre farm, bore a son, divorced, and stayed on the farm until 1985 to write and farm. Now she lives in Connecticut and works full-time as a writer. Her second book, *Night Life: Nature from Dusk to Dawn,* appeared in 1990, and she is at work on a third book of natural history essays, *Desert Pieces.*

After two nights without a freeze the maple seeds began to sprout on the slope by the Pond in the Woods. I only noticed them because there were sudden white squiggles among the dark leaves on the ground; newborn roots feeling the way out of their winged seeds like sensitive fingers. Some curved over sticks, other luckier ones had already penetrated the wet leaf-covered soil. Most of the embryonic leaves were still furled in the seed, but some of them were edged partly out, swollen and turning green, like insects in splitting husks struggling to be free.

A week later I found a cache of maple seeds farther up the slope. They had been packed away carefully last autumn in a six-inch-wide hollow and were laid round and round in a neat pattern, and even then at the end of April they were frozen, succulent, and crisp, laced with ice crystals. Red squirrel? Chipmunk? Something had rifled the hoard and the leaves were stirred up and seed fragments were scattered, but almost anything could have stumbled on them as I did, grateful for the discovery.

The sun was warm on the slope and the spring beauties had opened their pink stars overnight. Red and green dappled trout-lily leaves slanted up, and here and there a flower stem emerged among them coiled like a snake, ready to strike the eye with its yellow tongues.

Lying in the dry leaves, which rustled like paper, I had the old urge to stay put; if I stayed just there for another month I could see the trees dance. Passing through as I do, I can only trace the passage of that dance and can only imagine the flow, the reeling and bowing.

In these maples and birch and beech the branches reach out year after year, running skyward like the fingers of rivulets when water is poured on dry ground. Water is at the heart of their form; they have the shape of river systems seen from space, or veins of blood, or nerves. Standing there, buds swollen, with a wash of deep red over them, they seem as lambent and as alive and as ready as anything on earth could be.

The annual running-out of the branch ends begins in

May and will continue in slowing pace even into August, but the birth of the leaves themselves takes little more than a week, and in good weather even less time than that, so that in the movements of the tree dance this emergence of leaves would be seen as a flash, a flick, like the sudden unclenching of fisted hands.

Plants' movements are unmuddied by temporizing thought but are complex enough for all of that. In spite of years of biochemical research no one has managed to explain how they do most of their moving without the medium of nerve and muscle. Most of the time we zip around here too fast to notice that they are moving at all.

Movement is relative: a hummingbird goes by us in a blur; heart pulsing at more than 75 beats per second, metabolic core heat set at 105°F, flying along at fifty miles per hour . . . even the fastest human runner moves, from a hummingbird's perspective, as ponderously as a tortoise.

Plants choreograph their clenches and reaches in response to a great many things, but only while their tissues are still soft and young. Past midsummer the twigs and leaves stiffen and their position lignifies and becomes a permanent statement, like a photograph. Most plants move because of differences in growth rate between one bit of tissue and another, or because of shifts in water pressure within each fluid cell. Movement in plants is either an expression of growth itself, or an exercise in hydraulics, or a combination of both.

The newborn maple root is already intelligent about gravity, light, and water. It corkscrews, seeking an opening in which to poke down. Even in pitch-darkness a seedling orients itself by gravity, the shoot going up toward light, and the root twisting down to spread its absorbent network, hairy as a beard, between the crumbs of the soil. Once there it senses the presence of water and grows faster on its drier side, so that it curves and curves again to penetrate the wettest earth.

There is an odd little plant called dodder, and in the summertime the wildflowers that I pick are often twined with it. It is very pretty, leafless, tangled but graceful, like a snarl of fishing line drawn by a poet. It is a parasite. Its fine curling stems are pinkish and its flowers are a foam of white, but I can never quite escape from the knowledge, having read it once somewhere, that it can smell. It can smell a desirable host from inches away and will swing toward this good smell until it reaches its goal. The way it bends toward is the same way that any plant bends toward what it wants the most; by growing fastest on the side of itself that is farthest away from what it wants. So it curves. Its shape is the trace, the wake, of its motion.

In June the tendrils of my pea vines will hook the chicken wire I have put there for them, and, responding to the touch of this wire, they will spiral in a matter of hours and then stiffen. In October I will have to pluck these stiff coils off, themselves as hard as brittle wire, though the plants they held up to the sun are long dead and rotted away. The bog on the west hill has sundews that slam shut on ants and tiny flies in less than a half second. Maples with a patch of their bark gnawed away by a wintering porcupine hurry to send pale caramel-colored bulges of new flesh over the wound. Trees grown in the open are thicker of trunk because the wind has blown them, and they choose to thicken in the parts of themselves most stressed by their own bending. Trees in a dense woods where the wind can't push them are as thin as wands.

Look: I am watching this now as if I were putting together the countless still pictures I have accumulated, the befores and the afters and the durings, into one quick dance so that I can watch it happen, for once! I am tired of going into the woods in May and June and seeing leaves in mid-uncurl, ferns with a fist ready to punch air, twigs pointed like gleaming arrows. They look as though they had stopped their fling because I had stumbled on their private dance and was tactless enough to want to watch.

I have noticed that the bottom twigs of maples grow only an inch or two a year and that the top twigs may grow a foot or more in the same season, so that if one could see this month of their growth as a single convulsion it would be like the upward leap of a flame, as if someone had turned up the wick on an oil lamp. As they leap up the twigs wriggle. They make a hormone in their growing tips that flows back to where the cells are expanding, and it accumulates to the shadiest side of the twig and stimulates the expansion there, so that each twig bends independently toward the light. They turn in to each other and away, and in again until they have trembled to a stop in the spot most lit. Each single leaf does this same light-seeking dither, too, so that they seem to lurch and adjust like hands hefting a ball. The air around me suddenly fills with green commotion; the pond is lost from view, the air clogged with flutter, the path home closed with writhing leaves and with saplings and brush shuddering upward from their roots like sunbursts. Now the ferns careen from the ground, rolling upward and letting fly leaflets like the many limbs of Vishnu, until at last their tips flick over, wavelike, and a new green surf inhabits the shading ground. If you look up at the end of May here, the leaves are an almost perfect mosaic, there are few swatches left of the sky; they have become a web for the capture of the sun.

This seethe if actually seen in full boil could well terrify me beyond recall; except that I know that it isn't me they are after. I am as benign and unwanted as a rock.

I come back to the papery leaves, the spring beauties, the sun which reaches me here, now, unfiltered. The twigs, leaves, flowers, and ferns that are on their way are already formed, were made last summer and packed away in scales and sheaths; all they have to do is to expand like balloons, and then their branch tips will begin their hurry to make more.

As I went down the slope again, I reached into my pocket for some of the maple seeds that I had taken from the frozen hollow, and opened several and ate them; they were crisp and green and bitter. I know what you could become, I thought. I have seen you three centuries hence, massive as a god, pushing your ferment of leaves until you shade a quarter of an acre. I thought about the tribal warriors who ate the hearts of their enemies so that they would absorb the strength and intelligence of the adversary; you are hardly my enemy, O trees, but I want your grace.

BARBARA MEYN

CHANGING

from *The Abalone Heart* (1988)

Barbara Meyn (1923–   ) is a collector of natural objects and observations with a strong environmentalist conscience. She was born on her grandfather's farm south of Ukiah, California, and grew up there and in Eureka, attending Humboldt State College and earning a B.A. in English from the University of California at Berkeley. She has worked as a newspaperwoman, teacher, and writer, has been an environmental activist for many years, and helped found *Green Fuse,* a poetry journal dedicated to the preservation of the planet. She self-published her first book of poetry, *Blue Heron on Humbug Creek,* in 1981. She now lives on Humbug Creek in northeastern Sonoma County with her husband.

It happens quietly. A maple seed
blown here by a sudden, random wind
sprouts beneath the bedroom wall,
grows before I quite know how it grew,
tops the eaves, seeking afternoon

as well as morning sun, and fills my life.
Leaves unfold like ragged green umbrellas
waiting for an April rain.

I tell myself it's just another tree
that could have been dug up when it was small
and planted farther from the house.
If I don't cut it soon, if I keep on
watching while it reaches for the sky,
delighting in its gray, sinewy trunk,
the soft touch of leaves when I walk by,
the way it gathers light on winter days
and pours it generously through the glass,
it won't be long until it moves
my house off its foundation.

The room is full of curious, precious things,
skin of mole, hawk feathers, moth cocoons,
deer's-foot rattle, dry seed pods
of zygadene, racemes of saxifrage.
And now across the walls maple leaves
sign to me in shadows. Though the tree
is not yet in the room, in the dark
I hear it whisper, know it's coming in.

ANNE LABASTILLE

AMONG MY CLOSEST FRIENDS
from *Woodswoman* (1976)

Anne LaBastille (1938–) has with determination and per-
severance built a wilderness home in New York's Adiron-
dack Park and a life as an award-winning wildlife ecologist
and writer. She was born in New York City and raised in
suburban Montclair, New Jersey, an only child whose inter-
est in the outdoors was not encouraged by her parents and
did not find an outlet until she took a job at an Adirondack
summer resort as a teenager. Eventually she earned a B.S.
in wildlife conservation from Cornell University, married
the resort's owner, earned an M.S. from Colorado State,
divorced, and received her doctorate from Cornell. After
her divorce, she bought twenty-two acres of land on a lake
in the Adirondacks a mile and a half from the nearest dirt
road, and built a log cabin, an adventure described in her
book *Woodswoman*. When civilization seemed to be en-
croaching too much, she retreated farther into the woods
and built a second, smaller cabin modeled on Thoreau's
cabin at Walden Pond, as recounted in her 1987 book,
Beyond Black Bear Lake.

While LaBastille shuns a romantic view of nature in
favor of a scientist's tough-mindedness, she is not without a
deep appreciation and fellow feeling for her wilderness
neighbors, including the trees. She writes that despite the
constant demands of nature, "I share a feeling of continuity,
contentment, and oneness with the natural world, with life
itself, in my surroundings of tall pines, clear lakes, flying
squirrels, trailless peaks, shy deer, clean air, bullfrogs, black
flies, and trilliums."

During those first weeks and months at the cabin my close and constant companions were trees. I became intimately acquainted with every tree inside a 400-foot radius. What at first seemed like a dense stand of random temperate-zone vegetation—maples, spruces, hemlocks, beeches, birches, and pines—gradually introduced itself as an orderly congregation of unique individuals.

The "Four Sisters," a neatly spaced row of red spruces, stood practically within spitting distance of my sleeping loft. A trio of the same species clustered behind and above the dock, acting as friendly navigational aids against night skies. An enormous white pine leaned above the outhouse and another rose straight as a lighthouse on the point near the rocks. A forest of young firs graced the high shoreline from the side of the cabin almost down to the creek. Five more prodigious spruces loomed from a wet pocket of ground beyond the woodshed, while under them a few spindly youngsters stretched for the sun. I came to touch them all through trimming, pruning, clearing, cutting, admiring, and listening.

The first trees I got to know, and later draw strength from, were the mature, towering red spruces and white pines. These were highly skilled veterans, seasoned in survival techniques. They had started fortuitously as seedlings upon rich, sun-dappled patches of earth. They had escaped being nibbled by snowshoe hares, mice, grouse, or deer. They had shouldered past their siblings and finally pushed above the forest canopy into the free blue sky where swallows wheeled in summer and snowflakes whirled in winter. Here *all* the sunlight on any given day was theirs to activate the chlorophyll-laden needles, and *all* the rain of any given storm was theirs to wash the thick branches. These trees had survived attacks of smuts, aphids, mites, molds, beetles, galls, caterpillars, viruses, and the other miniature, life-robbing enemies of the plant world. They had also escaped being scratched by falling limbs, ripped by bears' claws, chafed by trunks, or rubbed by deer antlers. Likewise they had been unscathed by forest fires and bypassed by hurricanes. And so, in 1964, a goodly 300 years after their germination, they towered as invincible individuals of great character, lending dignity and beauty to my land.

I developed an amazing awareness of these trees. First, I noticed their noises. In wind, the spruces gave off a somber, deep, sad whoosh, while the pines made a higher, happier softer sough. After my initial surprise at the differences in sound between these two species, I began listening to other kinds of trees. Balsam firs made a short, precise, polite swishing; red and sugar maples gave an impatient rustling; yellow birches, a gentle, restful sighing.

Of course these strains of sound can be explained by the size, shape, flexibility, and thickness of leaf or needle. They can also be explained by the wind itself. I noticed distinct variations produced by the fresh westerly breezes, fierce north fronts, petulant south zephyrs, or stormy east winds. But the sound of the forest is more than this—just as a symphony is more than the sizes and shapes of the instruments, air pressure or touch which activate them to make music, and the players.

Next I discovered a whole assortment of tree scents. On hot, dry summer days, the balsams, spruces, and pines acted like giant sticks of incense, giving off a redolence which filled the air inside and outside the cabin. The carpet of dead needles, the dry duff, the trickles of pitch, the sun-warmed bark itself, all gave off subtle odors. The live needles tanged the air with what old-time doctors called "balsamifers."

The presence of this restorative odor is what made the Adirondacks a mecca for tubercular patients in the late 1800s and early 1900s. Whether the "balsamifers" did the curing, or the clean cold air, the long rests, the inspiring views, and the presence of such medical prophets as Dr. E. L. Trudeau, many mortally sick patients recovered in the Adirondacks. I know three men, all in their spry eighties, who came here to die in their thirties. They believe, as did Trudeau, pioneer tuberculosis researcher, that the resinous aromas produced by the evergreen forests helped cure them. Recent scientific studies have, in fact, revealed that the turpentine vapor exuded by conifers has a purifying effect on the local atmosphere and plays a part in keeping Adirondack air remarkably pure and healthy.

Another beautiful sensory experience happened to me in my forest of young balsam firs. On late summer afternoons, I saw the sun come slanting between the trunks. The light gave a glorious golden glow to the dense, dark copse. I began trimming off dead branches as high as I could reach with an axe. Whenever I nicked the bark of a trunk, I'd carefully daub moist earth on the wound to lessen sap flow and prevent the entry of disease organisms or insects. Off and on all summer I trimmed the balsam boles farther and farther away from the cabin until I achieved the desired effect. Then on a still September evening I perched on the porch railing, picking pitch from my palms, and watched the setting sun illuminate my fir forest. The sun shafts were straight diagonals of gold-washed air. As far as I could see, the balsam boles were straight black bars which threw black shadows onto the burnished-copper ground, golden-green moss, and bronzed fallen logs. My little forest had become a study in light and shadow, a stained glass window of gold and green panes with black bars, back-lit by the setting sun.

I experienced another quality of light on a dismal, dripping November day. It had rained for a week and the forest was totally drenched. My giant spruce trunks were soaked to charcoal-gray, their branches grizzly-green, the balsam boles inky-black, the ground tarry-brown, the pines pewter-gray. As Thomas Hardy wrote, "The whole world dripped in browns and duns." About eleven o'clock in the morning, the quality of light surrounding the cabin and trees was so watery that I might have been submerged somewhere in the North Atlantic. Each gust of rain felt like the surge of a swell, and the soggy forest looked like a stand of seaweed.

As I became more tuned into trees, I began to admire the enormous white pine near the path to the outhouse. I even oriented the entrance of the outhouse so that I could gaze at this tall, furrowed tree while sitting there. It was much better than reading *Time* magazine. In strong winds, the trunk would sway in a sinuous motion which combined the suppleness of a snake with the strength of an elephant. No rigidity to that pine. The thick bark, its multiple rings of wood, the very heart of the trunk all moved with a fluidity more animallike than plant. I drew closer to the tree and eventually came to stand against the trunk in order to watch those tons of wood bending lithely above my head. The grace and rhythm almost hypnotized me. . . .

On my trips back and forth to the outhouse, I took more and more enjoyment from touching the great white pine. One morning, with my arms wrapped around the trunk, I began to feel a sense of peace and well-being. I held on for over fifteen minutes, chasing extraneous thoughts from my mind. The rough bark was pressed hard against my skin. It was as though the tree was pouring its life-force into my body. When I stepped away from the white pine, I had the definite feeling that we had exchanged some form of life energy. . . .

I feel this communion, this strange attunement, most readily with large white pines, a little less with big spruces, sugar maples, beeches, or oaks. Clearly white pines and I are on the same wavelength. What I give back to the trees I cannot imagine. I hope they receive something, because trees are among my closest friends.

HILDEGARD FLANNER

THE OLD CHERRY TREE

from *Brief Cherishing* (1985)

> Hildegard Flanner (1899–1987) wrote, "I'm devoted to plants and have given a great deal of my life to them but I'm not a botanist. I am at the mercy of plants." She was born near Indianapolis, Indiana, and was educated at Sweet Briar College in Virginia and the University of California at Berkeley. She married the artist and architect Frederick Monhoff, who illustrated many of her books, and they made their home in southern California before moving to the Napa Valley of northern California, the subject of *Brief Cherishing: A Napa Valley Harvest.* An ardent conservationist and dedicated regionalist, younger sister to Janet Flanner of *The New Yorker,* she also wrote poetry, essays, articles, book reviews, and one-act plays.

Together with a few human beings, dead and living, and their achievements, trees are what I most love and revere. In my life and my concerns I have defended trees that are threatened and praised them when they are ignored; for their sakes I have made enemies of friends and neighbors. The knowledge that in a western canyon I am the owner of very tall straight redwoods and firs gives me pride of citizenship beyond anything I might accomplish by my own efforts. I have taken a serious kind of joy and a delightful kind of peace in their shade, and at night I have watched the shaggy white planets pass above their dark branches. I have loved trees, I have planted trees and have been excited to grow a tree from seed and discover the first minute sign of unfolding life that will, some distant year, become a rooted tower or a spreading bower of rustling foliage. I am fortunate to live where native trees are numerous and where horticulture is popular and every rural family has an orchard.

Our own orchard is old and contains many trees that are dilapidated, but even the most dilapidated have been safe for years because each time I look at them, aware of their crookedness and awkward appearance, I also see some odd curve of bough or improvisation of flowering that make sudden poetry of them and of their trashiness. They are thus protected, although they should, under good management, be sensibly discarded and replaced. Yet the more dubious they look the more they resemble the paintings of Oriental masters and suggest the fresh enduring emotions of the ancient anthologies. Perhaps there is universal truth in implying that real meaning is wrung out at the last moment, and the last moment must be prolonged. Whose duty is that? Really not mine. Yet I have discerned it. I am involved in its total meaning, of tree and of human. Still, as I myself grow older and, alas, much older, the image of new young trees in place of the old ones creeps temptingly into my mind. It is a troubling image and its disturbance, just now, settles on the spirit of a woman wandering and trying to think in an old orchard.

If I could have the sense and courage to take down a decrepit tree in spite of its fanatical habit of reminding me of the brave words of General Su Wu written down 2,000 years ago as he sadly embraced his wife for the last time, and in spite of its mad annual impulse to bloom and bear and spill bushels of amethyst prunes and rosy apples on the ground, it might be for me a spiritual rejuvenation and consequently even a beneficial thing for the flesh as well. But conscience is tyrannical. It is a womanly vice. I have become the guardian not of my own but of whatever other life remains in the earth I possess. It is hard to be wise and natural. Although my husband is no longer living I can guess what he might wish to do. To remove a tree that had lasted too long and replace it might well please him. This thought is a poignant incentive, also a consolation for the choice I foresee as melancholy and difficult, whenever it must be made.

The decision I am afraid of, on a mild February morning of our western spring, is one for advice from a clinical priest. It is beyond horticulture. It becomes moral. In my mind it faces and fights itself and I am torn. Must I continue to identify myself with the aged, no longer serviceable and eccentric trees, or do I dare to relate myself to young trees with futures, good looks and green chances of tonic sap? My orchard, by usual standards, is conspicuously shabby. This hurts me. And as I look around I notice a few unrewarding cherry trees.

To get a cherry in our orchard has meant to rise early, before birds or worms are awake, and snatch at a fruit or two as day breaks. One summer, in order to enjoy the large luscious black Bings, my husband ordered a nylon net he saw advertised in an agricultural supply magazine. The advertisement promised protection to fruit from marauding birds and complete accessibility for the picker. If all of this was true, we were not the ones to demonstrate it. As we hoisted the net on poles to the top of the tree the clinging mesh snagged on every twig on the way up; then, as we squinted into the sun and gave helpful and confusing suggestions to each other on how to free the net to slide down as directed, we found that it could descend only by being profanely and scrupulously removed from twig to clutching twig. However, the picture as given of happy people congratulating each other outside the net while the cherries waxed abnormally big and the birds fretted on the next tree—in the advertisement they were scowling—this fine fiction was worth keeping in mind until suddenly and utterly we tied ourselves in. The next step was just to ripen along with the cherries in boredom and frustration, while the birds jeered nastily. This very personal recollection comes back to me as I find myself standing under a cherry tree, not the one that lassoed us, but a very old pie-cherry tree, largest and surely the oldest inhabitant of the orchard. Indeed, where is there in the entire valley a cherry tree so old and so big? It is a tree known in the neighborhood, and when we first came here to live friendly strangers drove up our hill and requested, "Just a few cherries, please, from the old tree, enough for the wife to make one pie."

Now so much of the tree is fallen or dead that there is scarcely enough fruit for a robin to make one cherry tart. I get none myself, even on tiptoe or a ladder. And the trifle of birdsong it holds is nothing to give regard to. Neither has it grown ancient with picturesque aspects. All of its gifts are gone. Even the child with a little basket passes by. It is too large, you see, to be forgotten, yet neglect is its fate today. And so I talk to myself as I look up and see no buds swelling toward wide-open blossoms where the bees should soon be rolling. From something so unpromising, what is to be expected? Why is it so difficult for me to say, "It is time, old cherry tree"?

This happens to be the day on which my son is preparing a level space where there will be built a storehouse for tools and equipment. I welcome this plan as one to maintain order. Not only his powerful tractor, but various archaic automobiles considered by him too beautiful and valuable to go to the dump, can now be respectably housed, particularly that very sacred hot-chili-red truck that usurps the sight of grace and elegance where my tallest bamboo has established its feather culms. This is a day of orchard and premises keeping and its purposes begin to take hold of me. I look up at the cherry and assess what I see. Crippled and lumpy, here and there split, beheaded of several heads, and to all appearances so nearly dead that there seems no way to say it is alive. Then I look up at the sky and straighten, as if to think of other things. A good clear morning to be alive myself. And John has opened the deer gate and is driving the loud clanging tractor into the orchard toward the work that makes ready for his storehouse.

"Oh, John," I call. He doesn't hear above the roar of the machine. Without thinking I reach out and touch the subject I was about to speak of. I touch not only a tree of bark and wood but with tingling certainty in my fingers I touch an entire century. At this spot there stood a house which no longer exists. The spring that served its occupants still serves us from its cold stone trough at the edge of the nearby woods. And a county clerk had written the first deed to this property, dated 1878, in script almost too lace-like to read or believe. It was then that the tree was planted and began to work for men and birds and until this spring it has never stopped working. It was always the first to bloom and ripen, always prompt no matter that the weather might delay, still it brought on its sweet sparkling globes of fruit. For 100 years of faithfulness there should be a reward. Hang the old tree with garlands, strike up the fiddle. But I am caught up in another momentum. Again I call, "Oh, John!" He can't hear, there is too much noise. I go closer. "Maybe it's time," I shout, and he yells, "What is it?" How hard it is now for me to be positive and loud, quick and wise. But I must not take time to be careful. I am committed. "Time to take down the old cherry tree," I shriek.

I know that decisions like this should be made in quietness and deliberately. We should live slowly, even timidly, in imagination with all the possible results of the irrevocable. Once down, there would never be an up to this deed. I exercise a frightening power. It is not exactly a choice between life and death because life is already attacked by mean and obvious details of the end. However, the power of termination is awesome. Naturally, it chokes me. I cough. Kings, tyrants, judges—how have they arrived at that last fatal word that condemns life without feeling their own lives threatened, shredded and about to come apart? But don't be silly, I say to myself. What are you talking about? Just get on with what there is to do. Isn't this the mistake you have always been making? Too much emphasis on the wrong thing while you let the right thing drift? "John!" I shriek again. "Time to take down the old cherry tree!"

"Yes, yes," he says easily, "I can hear you," and I

become aware that he has turned off the noise of the tractor and also that in the interval of silence I can hear the demented sound of the ranging peacock that forages in the foothills and ravines near our place. It always seems to be a sound of mental stress and at this moment it is right for my state of mind.

I am surprised by hesitation on John's part. "I don't think I can cut it down, it's too big," he says. "I'll have to push it down." Again he seems doubtful. "If I can."

And the tractor starts again. Then for a while he is busy with his work of leveling nearby, but as I stand watching he begins to look at the old cherry tree in a calculating way. I suspect that he welcomes my decision to get rid of a tree so dominant yet unproductive in this place, and he must be astonished. He circles and comes closer. I cringe and brace myself for the shock to my nerves and my conscience. John backs his tractor and then goes forward with an awful clang. He hits the old cherry with a loud dull crash. It does not budge. It does not even quiver. He backs away. Again he charges forward and collides with the tree. It stands without shaking. It is only I who grow weak. I shake and feel sick. Perhaps I am wrong to condemn a creature so full of strength in spite of the many signs of being done with strength. Again the tractor charges and without effect. I would prefer to leave now, to go back to the house and hide behind closed doors where I could neither see nor hear; but it was I who started this turmoil and I must remain to see it through.

At this moment my 13-year-old grandson, Danny, arrives and stands near me, watching. "Your father is wasting a lot of good gas," I scream. "Diesel," he screams in return. "Fuel," I scream back at him, as the attack continues. Backing and charging, backing and colliding, the tractor roars and hits, and at last the old cherry tree begins to tremble. But it stands. I suffer and watch in a nauseating agony of indecision. Should I save the body while some secret obstinacy still holds it up? Or is it better to let the savage shocks continue? Suddenly John begins a new maneuver. He backs, then closes into the attack at an angle, tilts the sharp, wide blade of the tractor and digs it into the earth. Again he does this, and again, until the action of the bellowing machine and the chaos and the frightful uproar become a kind of violent choreography. I stand riveted and overcome by what I have started in the quiet orchard. Finally the tilted blade snags on a massive root. The root holds.

The contest goes on. My son will not give up. The old tree will not give up. The tractor will not give up. The boy and I stand and wait and the diabolic ballet goes on and on. The tractor, although a monolith, has been converted into a maniac of circling and twisting power. In its fierceness it is serpentine. At last, at last! With a heavy snap, a sound of fatal resignation, the root breaks. And the tree still stands! The tractor attacks it for the final time. And when the old cherry tree falls there goes down with it a century of hopes and many kinds of weather, sun and drought, of good rain and poor rain, of good pies and poor pies, and 100 years of countless round white flowers opening and coming apart and drifting down while early-rising and late-loitering birds and bees came and went and always, at the right cloistered moment there was the invisible sap slowly storming up through the trunk and into the tips of the branches, just as it was rising in a million other trees at the eternal hour given for ascension.

While I stand and have no voice to speak John nonchalantly gets down from his tractor and walks over to the fallen tree. He begins to peel off patches of thick bark. "Termites," he says. I do not want to see them. "More termites," he announces. I hate the sight of them. I stay where I am. Then he pulls off another, larger patch of bark. "Look here!" he cries. There is a company of small lizards, eight in all, spending the winter in the shelter of the cherry tree. John collects them and quickly puts them all down Danny's back. The boy rolls his eyes and draws up his shoulders but does not flinch.

I retrieve the young saurians and put them in the grass. Then I go to the prostrate tree to hunt for more, as if this intimacy with small creatures might reduce the magnitude of the old giant's final resignation. There seem to be no more lizards, but I find neat necklaces of empty holes, the precise work of woodpeckers whose echoing labors I have often heard. Then John, in the cavity left nearby, finds a beautiful little snake of a dark rich skin, a young gopher snake whose presence close to the tree appears to indicate dependence and community. John holds the snake for a moment and we watch as it flashes its rapid tongue in the sunlight. Then he puts it down and we see it take off, small and solitary. We are left alone with the fallen tree. It is stripped of everything, except its misshapen size, and its weighty bulk so lately upright and adamant. There it lies.

John gets his power-saw and starts methodically cutting branches for firewood. So soon does the drama and ordeal of destruction become the routine of plain use. Dazedly I pick up a few small logs. "Are you out of wood at your house?" he inquires.

"No," I answer, "This is ritual. I want a few pieces of the old cherry for my bedroom fireplace."

He tells me, "It won't burn yet. It has too much sap."

"Too much sap!" I exclaim and hastily drop the wood. "Is it still alive?"

"Well, what do you think? You saw how the old girl fought back."

His personification of the old tree horrifies me and I begin to cry.

John gives me a well-controlled look. "You're queer," he comments.

With difficulty I inquire, "What's the diameter?"

"Three feet at least, I guess. Big for an orchard tree." And he goes to work again.

In wretchedness I pick up the pieces of wood and hug them, small logs of smooth bark ornamented with delicate silver-green medallions of lichen. I carry them ashamedly to my bedroom porch. When I lay them down I know that I will never burn them, ever, no matter how long I keep them to lose their sap. They are too elegant, they have too much meaning. I shall never wish to warm myself at their melancholy and accusing blaze.

I return to the orchard. It is a still, empty place now. John has driven his tractor back through the deer gate, and Danny has gone with him. I stand and stare at the remains of the old cherry, the limbs in a heap, thick bark strewn, the powerful roots split and twisted. Now no one else will know if I give in to tears as I realize that there must always be new questions in my mind about the imperfection of my decision to remove the old tree. I have learned, too late, that there is more to life than what is visible. The greater strength had been underground and out of sight, and I had grossly, stupidly, not even guessed it was there. You fool, you made a wrong choice and you only proved that decisions are hell, a fact you've known since tormented childhood when it was not possible to be sure whether vanilla or strawberry or chocolate was the right choice, or whether to wear the sash with rosebuds woven into the silk or the blue satin one or the one with Roman stripes. I observe how tough the roots are and how strong and sharp and that they point up with a kind of spiraling hiss into the placid noon sky. How dreadfully eloquent they look, expressing all that I felt for them. It is not easy to stand alone with them.

Something prods me into an attempt to understand that the moment holds a finality beyond agitation. In weariness I can only decide that an urban-minded person would take this with helpful sanity, and I shall never be an urban-minded person. "For you they pulled out oak, fir, madrone and manzanita," I say to the roots. "It was a long time ago. Do you remember?"

For many minutes I stand here where the first axe wound and the first gouge of the plowshare cut into this very ground at my feet where the old cherry tree has just been knocked over. Now I hear the tractor again. It is down in the vineyard. "All right," I say, "It's true that I am queer. I talk to trees. I talk to roots. It's true they can't answer. But they have a lot to say. Look at them!" And I myself look at the roots where they lie on top of their trash, full of fierce power in every slashed point that thrusts up, full of a cherry tree voice, full of a forest voice, the forest that fell to make room for an orchard 100 years ago.

I start back to the house. "Just to get out of earshot," I tell myself.

KATHARINE SCHERMAN

ICEBERG

from *Spring on an Arctic Island* (1956)

Katharine Scherman (1915–   ), a native New Yorker, was an amateur ornithologist with some knowledge of wilderness camping when she and her husband, Axel, and a friend organized a six-week scientific expedition in the summer of 1954 to Bylot Island, 450 miles north of the Arctic Circle in Canada. "None of us had been in the far north, and we had a consuming curiosity about the humans and animals that can live in such inhospitable surroundings," she writes in her personal record of the journey, *Spring on an Arctic Island.* She and seven others—five of them trained scientists—stayed through the flowering and breeding season, observing, while "the creatures of the arctic unfolded themselves to us gradually, like characters in a novel." Educated at Swarthmore, Scherman wrote for *Life* magazine for several years before she began writing books, among them biographies for juveniles, a history cum natural history of Iceland, a history of early Christian Ireland, and another of France in the Merovingian period.

When Axel and I looked out of our tent the next morning the first sight that caught our eyes was the iceberg. It had broken off from some distant arctic glacier, gone tearing and grinding down the land to the ocean and sailed through storms and sun and fog, to come to rest finally in the quiet, ice-locked harbor of Eclipse Sound. Its long journey had scarred it. One part was an overturned galley, its keel high in the air, the other a mass of twisted turrets like a nightmare castle. It lay about a mile offshore—or maybe five. Distances were deceiving in the all-pervading flat whiteness.

We had never seen an iceberg before. Yet it was of all phenomena the essential symbol of the arctic. We thought we would like to go closer to it. Ned Ames, the enthusiastic young mountaineer, had an even better thought. "Let's climb it," he said.

Soon, carrying lunch, crampons, ropes and ice axes, we were trekking lightheartedly over the sun-bright sea ice. In small cracks the water shone intensely blue-green. We leaped them easily. Not knowing the ways of sea ice, we roped up at the larger cracks and jumped one at a time, leaving wide margins on both sides.

The iceberg loomed tremendous over us as we neared. It was much bigger than we had realized, dangerously steep and seamed with broad dark-green cracks. It gave off a chill breath and even in the hot sun we shivered. When we were within a hundred yards the monster suddenly thundered at us from deep inside.

"Go away," it said clearly. We stopped instantly. But nothing happened, so we went nearer, setting our feet down as gingerly as if we were walking on china. The iceberg was surrounded by a deep moat of melted ice. The only way to get on it was over a narrow snow bridge, visibly melting in the sun.

We sat down on the snow to eat lunch and think it over. At our backs was the cold breath of the unfriendly ice monster. But the sun was brilliant, the sky was deep blue and the snow gleamed. We felt adventurous, so we put on our crampons and roped up. Ned, as an experienced glacier climber, went first. The soft snow bridge held him, and he tried to cut steps in the sheer wall of the iceberg. The ice chipped off in small flat flakes and the steps were no more than shallow depressions. Pared down and hardened by fierce winter winds, our iceberg was solid as oak. Ned managed to scrape his way up to an easier slope on its lower lip, and we scrambled up after him. We found ourselves on a ledge fifteen feet above the sea. Over us leaned a slim, graceful tower of glare ice fifty feet high, shaped by wind and sleet into beautiful curves and carved with delicate ridges. Architecturally it was a very elegant iceberg, but absolutely unassailable. We walked around our little promontory. On all sides it sloped precipitously into dark open water.

At such close quarters with the sea giant we were stricken with awed respect and a sudden fear. It seemed a tremendous live force beneath us and above us. We could feel the titanic power that had torn it from its moorings and tumbled it into the sea.

"Wouldn't it be funny," said Ned in a small voice, "if this thing gave a sigh and slowly rolled over." We laughed uncomfortably and immediately started to get off it.

Axel and I descended first, groping for footholds and slipping on the ice. Ned decided to make it easier for himself and hacked at the top steps with his ice ax. As he gave the third stroke there was a terrible roar from right underneath him. We stood absolutely still for a moment, shocked into immobility. Ned's light words seemed suddenly to be written across the sky. Then Ned slid rapidly down the wall and we retreated as fast as we dared, not looking behind us.

You can sometimes knock over those tall, narrow icebergs with one well-placed bullet from a thirty-thirty, Pete Murdoch told us later, casually. Then he laughed. He knew, as we did, that we had been in no real danger.

Eskimos often climb frozen-in icebergs to reconnoiter for seals. Eight ninths of an iceberg is under water, and ours was safely locked in unmoving bay ice.

However, we had known the fear that an immense physical force inspires. Safe our iceberg might be—but we were humble before it.

Her Rape:
How Nature Has
Been Abused

On a visit to the Oberlin Art Museum in Oberlin, Ohio, I came across a striking bronze figure entitled "Nature Revealing Herself to Science." Nature is a woman swathed in a length of cloth that drapes over her head, crosses and is knotted at her belly, and falls to her feet, clinging revealingly to her hips and legs. She is lifting the cloth at her shoulders to bare her perfectly proportioned bronze breasts. Absent from the scene but seemingly present in the sculptor's imagination is a leering scientist, clipboard in hand. This imagery is an accurate representation of historical attitudes: Francis Bacon, the principal founder of modern science, described nature as a woman and defined science as a quest to capture her, subdue her, and wrest her secrets from her. Similarly, during our country's settlement, men sought to open up "virgin" territory and exploit the land, its creatures, and native peoples, seeing the earth as theirs to subdue and use.

Given the prevalence of this imagery even today, it's not surprising that many writers—women and men alike—have seen the despoilment of Mother Earth in sexual terms.

Some of the writers in this section draw close parallels between the abusive treatment of women and the abusive treatment of the earth. Others keen and grieve and sound the alarm about the destruction of our planet without specific reference to sexual metaphors. All feel deeply the threat to earth's integrity posed by a technological culture thrown out of balance by an excessively masculine ethos, a culture that takes from the earth without giving back, that values control and conquest more than compassion and communion, that sees the world in fragments rather than as a whole cloth.

JUDITH MCCOMBS

THE MAN

from *Against Nature: Wilderness Poems* (1979)

Judith McCombs (1939–) explores in her volume *Against Nature: Wilderness Poems* the extent to which our "expensive techniques of survival, / [our] comforts, [our] ideas" distance us from nature and ensure that "no matter how far in we go, how long / we are what we are / unnatural, human." In a number of articles, she has written about a "women's nature myth" emerging in the work of women nature writers who conceive of nature as equivalent to the female self. Born in Virginia and educated at the University of Chicago (B.A., M.A.), she taught college English for nearly twenty years. She now lives in Silver Spring, Maryland, and works full-time writing poetry, fiction, and scholarly books.

See, a small space in the woods,
green overgrown with green,
shadows trees brush entangled
At the edge of the clearing a man
a white man, middle-aged, aging
just his face stands out in the dimness
"dominion over every living thing"
a hunter's jacket, hunter's cap
He lifts the spear of his rifle barrel
aims
with cold, hard, arthritic hands
16 years on the line, finally made foreman,
finally inspector, finally retired
The cold, square, aging jaws of the man

are barely flushed, a tingle of fear
or pleasure as he aims

diagonally across the clearing
into the black furry mass of the bear
She sits on her haunches, back to a stump,
an ancient, massive, dog-nosed brute
pawing the dogs
who yap & skitter away
(My mother's mother, huge in her dress,
sits in the creek, swatting the water & laughing)
She is warm, stupid; she smells of bear
an abundance of flesh, stumpy limbs,
stone of a head & little pig eyes
teats where she rears, in the black close fur
She smells like my mother/my mother's mother
she does not understand
she won't get away

The man with the rifle aiming
confers with the other shadowy men
ranging the edge of the clearing
Each in position: they have agreed
which one will have her/whose turn it is
One of them covers the kill

My mother does not understand
rears, paws, shakes her head & its wattles of fur
thinking she's won

Afterwards the body is hoisted
"a sack full of lard" on inaccurate scales
is hung, dressed, weighed on accurate scales
The skull (unshattered, unhurt) is found eligible
for Boone & Crockett official measuring
The head is stuffed & mounted
                              safe on the walls
where every evening he enters, approaches

fires recoils fires into the small stupid eyes
"the thrill of a lifetime" my mother

MARY AUSTIN

THE LAST ANTELOPE

from *Lost Borders* (1909)

Mary Austin, introduced earlier (in "Her Pleasures"), was
painfully aware of what she describes in "The Last Ante-
lope" as "that spirit which goes before cities like an exhala-
tion and dries up the gossamer and the dew," having seen
the once-verdant Owens Valley sucked dry by a thirsty Los
Angeles. "The Last Antelope" contrasts a vanishing way of
being in relationship to nature with the way that was to
prevail. It comes from a collection of some of Austin's finest
stories, portraying souls marked by the land the Indians
called Lost Borders—the high California desert east of the
Sierra.

There were seven notches in the juniper by the Lone Tree
Spring for the seven seasons that Little Pete had summered
there, feeding his flocks in the hollow of the Ceriso. The
first time of coming he had struck his ax into the trunk,
meaning to make firewood, but thought better of it, and
thereafter chipped it in sheer friendliness, as one claps an
old acquaintance, for by the time the flock has worked up
the treeless windy stretch from the Little Antelope to the

Ceriso, even a lone juniper has a friendly look. And Little Pete was a friendly man, though shy of demeanor, so that with the best will in the world for wagging his tongue, he could scarcely pass the time of day with good countenance; the soul of a jolly companion with the front and bearing of one of his own sheep.

He loved his dogs as brothers; he was near akin to the wild things; he communed with the huddled hills, and held intercourse with the stars, saying things to them in his heart that his tongue stumbled over and refused. He knew his sheep by name, and had respect to signs and seasons; his lips moved softly as he walked, making no sound. Well—what would you? a man must have fellowship in some sort.

Whoso goes a-shepherding in the desert hills comes to be at one with his companions, growing brutish or converting them. Little Pete humanized his sheep. He perceived lovable qualities in them, and differentiated the natures and dispositions of inanimate things.

Not much of this presented itself on slight acquaintance, for, in fact, he looked to be of rather less account than his own dogs. He was undersized and hairy, and had a roving eye; probably he washed once a year at the shearing as the sheep were washed. About his body he wore a twist of sheepskin with the wool outward, holding in place the tatters of his clothing. On hot days when he wreathed leaves about his head, and wove him a pent of twigs among the scrub in the middle of his flock, he looked a faun or some wood creature come out of pagan times, though no pagan, as was clearly shown by the medal of the Sacred Heart that hung on his hairy chest, worn open to all weathers. Where he went about sheep camps and shearings there were sly laughter and tapping of foreheads, but those who kept the tale of his flocks spoke well of him and increased his wage.

Little Pete kept to the same round year by year, breaking away from La Liebre after the spring shearing, south around the foot of Piños, swinging out to the desert in the wake of the quick, strong rains, thence to Little Antelope in July to drink a bottle for *Le Quatorze,* and so to the Ceriso by the time the poppy fires were burned quite out and the quail trooped at noon about the tepid pools. The Ceriso is not properly mesa nor valley, but a long-healed crater miles wide, rimmed about with the jagged edge of the old cone.

It rises steeply from the tilted mesa, overlooked by Black Mountain, darkly red as the red cattle that graze among the honey-colored hills. These are blunt and rounded, tumbling all down from the great crater and the mesa edge toward the long, dim valley of Little Antelope. Its outward slope is confused with the outlines of the hills, tumuli of blind cones, and the old lava flow that breaks away from it by the west gap and the ravine of the spring; within, its walls are deeply guttered by the torrent of winter rains.

In its cup-like hollow, the sink of its waters, salt and bitter as all pools without an outlet, waxes and wanes within a wide margin of bleaching reeds. Nothing taller shows in all the Ceriso, and the wind among them fills all the hollow with an eerie whispering. One spring rills down by the gorge of an old flow on the side toward Little Antelope, and, but for the lone juniper that stood by it, there is never a tree until you come to the foot of Black Mountain.

The flock of Little Pete, a maverick strayed from some rodeo, a prospector going up to Black Mountain, and a solitary antelope were all that passed through the Ceriso at any time. The antelope had the best right. He came as of old habit; he had come when the lightfoot herds ranged from here to the sweet, mist-watered cañons of the Coast Range, and the bucks went up to the windy mesas what time the young ran with their mothers, nose to flank. They had ceased before the keen edge of slaughter that defines the frontier of men.

All that a tardy law had saved to the district of Little Antelope was the buck that came up the ravine of the Lone Tree Spring at the set time of the year when Little Pete fed his flock in the Ceriso, and Pete averred that they were glad to see each other. True enough, they were each the friendliest thing the other found there; for though the law ran as far as the antelope ranged, there were hill-dwellers who took no account of it—namely, the coyotes. They hunted the buck in season and out, bayed him down from the feeding grounds, fended him from the pool, pursued him by relay races, ambushed him in the pitfalls of the black rock.

There were seven coyotes ranging the east side of the Ceriso at the time when Little Pete first struck his ax into the juniper tree, slinking, sly-footed, and evil-eyed. Many an evening the shepherd watched them running lightly in the hollow of the crater, the flash-flash of the antelope's white rump signaling the progress of the chase. But always the buck outran or outwitted them, taking to the high, broken ridges where no split foot could follow his seven-leagued bounds. Many a morning Little Pete, tending his cooking pot by a quavering sagebrush fire, saw the antelope feeding down toward the Lone Tree Spring, and looked his sentiments. The coyotes had spoken theirs all night with derisive voices; never was there any love lost between a shepherd and a coyote. The pronghorn's chief recommendation to an acquaintance was that he could outdo them.

After the third summer, Pete began to perceive a reciprocal friendliness in the antelope. Early mornings the shepherd saw him rising from his lair, or came often upon the warm pressed hollow where he had lain within cry of his coyote-scaring fire. When it was midday in the misty hollow and the shadows drawn close, stuck tight under the juniper and the sage, they went each to his nooning in his own fashion, but in the half light they drew near together.

Since the beginning of the law the antelope had half forgotten his fear of man. He looked upon the shepherd with steadfastness, he smelled the smell of his garments which was the smell of sheep and the unhandled earth, and the smell of wood smoke was in his hair. They had companionship without speech; they conferred favors silently after the manner of those who understand one another. The antelope led to the best feeding grounds, and Pete kept the sheep from muddying the spring until the buck had drunk. When the coyotes skulked in the scrub by night to deride him, the shepherd mocked them in their own tongue, and promised them the best of his lambs for the killing; but to hear afar off their hunting howl stirred him out of sleep to curse with great heartiness. At such times he thought of the antelope and wished him well.

Beginning with the west gap opposite the Lone Tree Spring about the first of August, Pete would feed all around the broken rim of the crater, up the gullies and down, and clean through the hollow of it in a matter of two months, or if the winter had been a wet one, a little longer, and in seven years the man and the antelope grew to know each other very well. Where the flock fed the buck fed, keeping farthest from the dogs, and at last he came to lie down with it.

That was after a season of scant rains, when the feed was poor and the antelope's flank grew thin; the rabbits had trooped down to the irrigated lands, and the coyotes, made more keen by hunger, pressed him hard. One of those smoky, yawning days when the sky hugged the earth, and all sound fell back from a woolly atmosphere and broke dully in the scrub, about the usual hour of their running between twilight and mid-afternoon, the coyotes drove the tall buck, winded, desperate, and foredone, to refuge among the silly sheep, where for fear of the dogs and the man the howlers dared not come. He stood at bay there, fronting the shepherd, brought up against a crisis greatly needing the help of speech.

Well—he had nearly as much gift in that matter as Little Pete. Those two silent ones understood each other; some assurance, the warrant of a free-given faith, passed between them. The buck lowered his head and eased the sharp throbbing of his ribs; the dogs drew in the scattered flocks; they moved, keeping a little cleared space nearest the buck; he moved with them; he began to feed. Thereafter the heart of Little Pete warmed humanly toward the antelope, and the coyotes began to be very personal in their abuse. That same night they drew off the shepherd's dogs by a ruse and stole two of his lambs.

The same seasons that made the friendliness of the antelope and Little Pete wore the face of the shepherd into a keener likeness to the weathered hills, and the juniper flourishing greenly by the spring bade fair to outlast them both. The line of plowed lands stretched out mile by mile from the lower valley, and a solitary homesteader built him a cabin at the foot of the Ceriso.

In seven years a coyote may learn somewhat; those of the Ceriso learned the ways of Little Pete and the antelope. Trust them to have noted, as the years moved, that the buck's flanks were lean and his step less free. Put it that the antelope was old, and that he made truce with the shepherd to hide the failing of his powers; then if he came earlier or stayed later than the flock, it would go hard with him. But as if he knew their mind in the matter, the antelope delayed his coming until the salt pool shrunk to its innermost ring of reeds, and the sun-cured grasses crisped along the slope. It seemed the brute sense waked between him and the man to make each aware of the other's nearness. Often as Little Pete drove in by the west gap he would sight the prongs of the buck rising over the barrier of black rocks at the head of the ravine. Together they passed out of the crater, keeping fellowship as far as the frontier of evergreen oaks. Here Little Pete turned in by the cattle fences to come at La Liebre from the north, and the antelope, avoiding all man-trails, growing daily more remote, passed into the wooded hills on unguessed errands of his own.

Twice the homesteader saw the antelope go up to the Ceriso at that set time of the year. The third summer when he sighted him, a whitish speck moving steadily against the fawn-colored background of the hills, the homesteader took down his rifle and made haste into the crater. At that time his cabin stood on the remotest edge of settlement, and the grip of the law was loosened in so long a reach.

"In the end the coyotes will get him. Better that he fall to me," said the homesteader. But, in fact, he was prompted by the love of mastery, which for the most part moves men into new lands, whose creatures they conceive given over into their hands.

The coyote that kept the watch at the head of the ravine saw him come, and lifted up his voice in the long-drawn dolorous whine that warned the other watchers in their unseen stations in the scrub. The homesteader heard also, and let a curse softly under his breath, for besides that they might scare his quarry, he coveted the howler's ears, in which the law upheld him. Never a tip nor a tail of one showed above the sage when he had come up into the Ceriso.

The afternoon wore on; the homesteader hid in the reeds, and the coyotes had forgotten him. Away to the left in a windless blur of dust the sheep of Little Pete trailed up toward the crater's rim. The leader, watching by the spring, caught a jackrabbit and was eating it quietly behind the black rock.

In the meantime the last antelope came lightly and securely by the gully, by the black rock and the lone juniper, into the Ceriso. The friendliness of the antelope for Little Pete betrayed him. He came with some sense of home, expecting the flock and protection of man-presence. He strayed witlessly into the open, his ears set to catch the jangle of the bells. What he heard was the snick of the breech-bolt as the homesteader threw up the sight of his rifle, and a small demoniac cry that ran from gutter to gutter of the crater rim, impossible to gauge for numbers or distance.

At that moment Little Pete worried the flock up the outward slope where the ruin of the old lava flows gave sharply back the wrangle of the bells. Three weeks he had won up from the Little Antelope, and three by way of the Sand Flat, where there was great scarcity of water, and in all that time none of his kind had hailed him. His heart warmed toward the juniper tree and the antelope whose hoofprints he found in the white dust of the mesa trail. Men had small respect by Little Pete, women he had no time for:

the antelope was the noblest thing he had ever loved. The sheep poured through the gap and spread fanwise down the gully; behind them Little Pete twirled his staff, and made merry wordless noises in his throat in anticipation of friendliness. "Ehu!" he cried when he heard the hunting howl, "but they are at their tricks again," and then in English he voiced a volley of broken, inconsequential oaths, for he saw what the howlers were about.

One imputes a sixth sense to that son of a thief misnamed the coyote, to make up for speech—persuasion, concerted movement—in short, the human faculty. How else do they manage the terrible relay races by which they make quarry of the fleetest-footed? It was so they plotted the antelope's last running in the Ceriso: two to start the chase from the black rock toward the red scar of a winter torrent, two to leave the mouth of the wash when the first were winded, one to fend the ravine that led up to the broken ridges, one to start out of the scrub at the base of a smooth upward sweep, and, running parallel to it, keep the buck well into the open; all these when their first spurt was done to cross leisurely to new stations to take up another turn. Round they went in the hollow of the crater, velvet-footed and sly even in full chase, and biding their time. It was a good running, but it was almost done when away by the west gap the buck heard the voice of Little Pete raised in adjuration and the friendly blether of the sheep. Thin spirals of dust flared upward from the moving flocks and signaled truce to chase. He broke for it with wide panting bounds and many a missed step picked up with incredible eagerness, the thin rim of his nostrils oozing blood. The coyotes saw and closed in about him, chopping quick and hard. Sharp ears and sharp muzzles cast up at his throat, and were whelmed in a press of gray flanks. One yelped, one went limping from a kick, and one went past him, returning with a spring upon the heaving shoulder, and the man in the reeds beside the bitter water rose up and fired.

All the luck of that day's hunting went to the homesteader, for he had killed an antelope and a coyote with one shot, and though he had a bad quarter of an hour with a wild and loathly shepherd, who he feared might denounce him to the law, in the end he made off with the last antelope, swung limp and graceless across his shoulder. The coyotes came back to the killing ground when they had watched him safely down the ravine, and were consoled with what they found. As they pulled the body of the dead leader about before they began upon it, they noticed that the homesteader had taken the ears of that also.

Little Pete lay in the grass and wept simply; the tears made pallid traces in the season's grime. He suffered the torture, the question extraordinary of bereavement. If he had not lingered so long in the meadow of Los Robles, if he had moved faster on the Sand Flat trail—but, in fact, he had come up against the inevitable. He had been breathed upon by that spirit which goes before cities like an exhalation and dries up the gossamer and the dew.

From that day the heart had gone out of the Ceriso. It was a desolate hollow, reddish-hued and dim, with brackish waters, and moreover the feed was poor. His eyes could not forget their trick of roving the valley at all hours; he looked by the rill of the spring for hoofprints that were not there.

Fronting the west gap there was a spot where he would not feed, where the grass stood up stiff and black with what had dried upon it. He kept the flocks to the ridgy slopes where the limited horizon permitted one to believe the crater was not quite empty. His heart shook in the night to hear the long-drawn hunting howl, and shook again remembering that he had nothing to be fearing for. After three weeks he passed out on the other side and came that way no more. The juniper tree stood greenly by the spring until the homesteader cut it down for firewood. Nothing taller than the rattling reeds stirs in all the hollow of the Ceriso.

SUSAN GRIFFIN

THE HUNT *and* **USE**

from *Woman and Nature* (1978)

> The following two excerpts from *Woman and Nature* con-
> tinue the dialogue begun in the Prologue (reprinted earlier
> in this anthology). "The Hunt" is from the section in which
> Griffin lists and protests against the unnatural divisions that
> must proceed from a thought that opposes male and female,
> body and mind, heaven and earth. "Use" is from the section
> that sketches the history of scientific, religious, and philo-
> sophical notions about nature and matter, juxtaposes them
> chronologically with a history of ideas about women, and
> explores the manifestations of these notions as they have
> been applied to land and to women's bodies.

The Hunt

She has captured his heart. She has overcome him. He
cannot tear his eyes away. He is burning with passion. He
cannot live without her. He pursues her. She makes him
pursue her. The faster she runs, the stronger his desire. He
will overtake her. He will make her his own. He will have
her. (The boy chases the doe and her yearling for nearly
two hours. She keeps running despite her wounds. He pur-
sues her through pastures, over fences, groves of trees,
crossing the road, up hills, volleys of rifle shots sounding,
until perhaps twenty bullets are embedded in her body.)
She has no mercy. She has dressed to excite his desire. She
has no scruples. She has painted herself for him. She makes
supple movements to entice him. She is without a soul.

Beneath her painted face is flesh, are bones. She reveals only part of herself to him. She is wild. She flees whenever he approaches. She is teasing him. (Finally, she is defeated and falls and he sees that half of her head has been blown off, that one leg is gone, her abdomen split from her tail to her head, and her organs hang outside her body. Then four men encircle the fawn and harvest her too.) He is an easy target, he says. He says he is pierced. Love has shot him through, he says. He is a familiar mark. Riddled. Stripped to the bone. He is conquered, he says. (The boys, fond of hunting hare, search in particular for pregnant females.) He is fighting for his life. He faces annihilation in her, he says. He is losing himself to her, he says. Now, he must conquer her wildness, he says, he must tame her before she drives him wild, he says. (Once catching their prey, they step on her back, breaking it, and they call this "dancing on the hare.") Thus he goes on his knees to her. Thus he wins her over, he tells her he wants her. He makes her his own. He encloses her. He encircles her. He puts her under lock and key. He protects her. (Approaching the great mammals, the hunters make little sounds which they know will make the elephants form a defensive circle.) And once she is his, he prizes his delight. He feasts his eyes on her. He adorns her luxuriantly. He gives her ivory. He gives her perfume. (The older matriarchs stand to the outside of the circle to protect the calves and younger mothers.) He covers her with the skins of mink, beaver, muskrat, seal, raccoon, otter, ermine, fox, the feathers of ostriches, osprey, egret, ibis. (The hunters then encircle that circle and fire first into the bodies of the matriarchs. When these older elephants fall, the younger panic, yet unwilling to leave the bodies of their dead mothers, they make easy targets.) And thus he makes her soft. He makes her calm. He makes her grateful to him. He has tamed her, he says. She is content to be his, he says. (In the winter, if a single wolf has leaped over the walls of the city and terrorized the streets, the hunters go out in a band to rid the forest of the whole pack.) Her voice is now soothing to him. Her eyes no longer blaze, but look on him serenely. When he calls to her, she gives herself to him. Her ferocity lies under him. (The body of the great whale is strapped with explosives.) Now nothing of the old beast remains in her. (Eastern Bison, extinct 1825; Spectacled Cormorant, extinct 1852; Cape Lion, extinct 1865; Bonin Night Heron, extinct 1889; Barbary Lion, extinct 1922; Great Auk, extinct 1944.) And he can trust her wholly with himself. So he is blazing when he enters her, and she is consumed. (Florida Key Deer, vanishing; Wild Indian Buffalo, vanishing; Great Sable Antelope, vanishing.) Because she is his, she offers no resistance. She is a place of rest for him. A place of his making. And when his flesh begins to yield and his skin melts into her, he becomes soft, and he is without fear; he does not lose himself; though something in him gives way, he is not lost in her, because she is his now: he has captured her.

Use

He breaks the wilderness. He clears the land of trees, brush, weed. The land is brought under his control; he has turned waste into a garden. Into her soil he places his plow. He labors. He plants. He sows. By the sweat of his brow, he makes her yield. She opens her broad lap to him. She smiles on him. She prepares him a feast. She gives up her treasures to him. She makes him grow rich. She yields. She conceives. Her lap is fertile. Out of her dark interior, life arises. What she does to his seed is a mystery to him. He counts her yielding as a miracle. He sees her workings as effortless. Whatever she brings forth he calls his own. He has made her conceive. His land is a mother. She smiles on the joys of her children. She feeds him generously. Again and again, in his hunger, he returns to her. Again and again she gives to him. She is his mother. Her powers are a mystery to him. Silently she works miracles for him. Yet, just as silently, she withholds from him. Without reason, she refuses to yield. She is fickle. She dries up. She is bitter. She scorns him. He is determined he will master her. He will make her produce at will. He will devise ways to plant what he wants in her, to make her yield more to him. He deciphers the secrets of the soil. (He knows why she brings forth.) He recites the story of the carbon cycle. (He masters the properties of chlorophyll.) He recites the story of the nitrogen cycle. (He brings nitrogen out of the air.) He determines the composition of the soil. (Over and over he can plant the same plot of land with the same crop.) He says that the soil is a lifeless place of storage, he says that the soil is what is tilled by farmers. He says that the land need no longer lie fallow. That what went on in her quietude is no longer a secret, that the ways of the land can be managed. That the farmer can ask whatever he wishes of the land. (He replaces the fungi, bacteria, earthworms, insects, decay.) He names all that is necessary, nitrogen, phosphorus, potassium, and these he says he can make. He increases the weight of kernels of barley with potash; he makes a more mealy potato with muriate of potash, he makes the color of cabbage bright green with nitrate, he makes onions which live longer with phosphates, he makes the cauliflower head early by withholding nitrogen. His powers continue to grow.

Phosphoric acid, nitrogen fertilizers, ammonium sulfate, white phosphate, potash, iron sulfate, nitrate of soda, superphosphate, calcium cyanamide, calcium oxide, calcium magnesium, zinc sulfate, phenobarbital, amphetamine, magnesium, estrogen, copper sulfate, meprobamate, thalidomide, benzethonium chloride, Valium, hexachlorophene, diethylstilbestrol.

What device she can use to continue she does. She says that the pain is unbearable. *Give me something,* she says. What he gives her she takes into herself without asking why. She says now that the edges of what she sees are blurred. The edges of what she sees, and what she wants, and what she is saying, are blurred. *Give me something,* she says. What he gives her she takes without asking. She says that the first pain is gone, or that she cannot remember it, or that she cannot remember why this began, or what she was like before, or if she will survive without what he gives her to take, but that she does not know, or cannot remember, why she continues.

He says she cannot continue without him. He says she must have what he gives her. He says also that he protects her from predators. That he gives her dichlorodiphenyltrichloroethane, dieldrin, chlorinated naphthalenes, chlordan, parathion, Malathion, selenium, pentachlorophenol, arsenic, sodium arsenite, amitrole. That he has rid her of pests, he says.

And he has devised ways to separate himself from her. He sends machines to do his labor. His working has become as effortless as hers. He accomplishes days of labor with a small motion of his hand. His efforts are more astonishing than hers. No longer praying, no longer imploring, he pronounces words from a distance and his orders are carried out. Even with his back turned to her she yields to him. And in his mind, he imagines that he can conceive without her. In his mind he develops the means to supplant her miracles with his own. In his mind, he no longer relies on her. What he possesses, he says, is his to use and to abandon.

JANICE MIRIKITANI

LOVE CANAL

from *Shedding Silence* (1987)

Janice Mirikitani (1942–   ), like Susan Griffin and other writers in this section, draws parallels between the treatment of women and the treatment of the earth. Her outspoken poetry deliberately cuts through the silence that allows so many forms of tyranny and oppression to go unnoticed, from the treatment of Japanese-Americans during World War II to our daily tacit cooperation with systemic racism, sexism, and classism. Love Canal is the former toxic waste dump site in Niagara Falls, New York, on which a school and homes were built; when the deadly effects of the chemical contamination became apparent, the city and Hooker Chemical Company did not respond until twenty-six-year-old housewife Lois Gibbs began a neighborhood crusade.

And you will forget
even this
      the earth
      gray, its sickness
      bubbling
      through the cracked lips
      of packed dirt.
      Maria
      lies in her bed
      lined with mourners,
      suitors, priests, sons.
      In love,
      her eyes dropping

sorrow,
her pale gray hands
thinned to the bone
fingering the beads,
hope emaciated like starved
women.
Maria,
mother, lover,
opening for them
like a moist cave
promising tomorrow,
forever.

And you will forget
even this.
They wound
the heart,
burn, pierce,
bludgeon the breast
of Love Canal.
Her lips, lungs swell,
heave, spit
Maria dreams
between her pain,
her skin burning,
cells screaming
armpits glowing
with bright embers
of radiation treatments.
He brought sunshine
like marigolds
into her lap
made her heart pump full
with rhythms of a young colt.
And in the streams
surrounding Love Canal,
they would dip, sip,
deep into each other's skin.

JANICE MIRIKITANI

Her body
a canal for love
glistens with pain
sores like water
running to the edges of
her flesh.

And you will forget
even this

Hooker Chemical Company
pours the poison
dumps its waste
into vessels of earth
at Love Canal.
Mothers sip
from its wells,
children sleep
in the fragrant air
of buried waste,
fathers infertile
hum lullabies to unborn.
Maria awakens
from her toxic pillow
wet from the canal
of her polluted body,
flesh aflame,
bubbling pain,
like the angry earth
spewing sickness.

The priests and suitors
pray   fear no evil
              fear no evil
              fear evil
              evil . . .
over her body
once Love's Canal.

RACHEL CARSON

EARTH'S GREEN MANTLE

from *Silent Spring* (1962)

Rachel Carson (1907–1964) "created a tide of environmental consciousness that has not ebbed," according to the citation accompanying the Presidential Medal of Freedom she was posthumously awarded in 1980. Born in Springdale, Pennsylvania, she entered college with the intention of becoming a writer, but changed her career goal when she studied with a woman biology professor. She eventually earned a B.A. in science from Pennsylvania College for Women and an M.A. in zoology from Johns Hopkins University. She then worked for the U.S. government for seventeen years (1935–1952), eventually as editor-in-chief of publications for the Fish and Wildlife Service, before royalties from her first two books allowed her to retire and devote full time to writing. She bought a coastal retreat in Maine where she lived, studying nature and writing about it. (After her death the Department of the Interior bought her Maine retreat and transformed it into the 4,000-acre Rachel Carson National Wildlife Refuge, dedicated in 1970.)

Her training as an aquatic biologist led her to write about the sea in her first three books, *Under the Sea-Wind* (1941), *The Sea Around Us* (1950), and *The Edge of the Sea* (1955). *The Sea Around Us* won the National Book Award for nonfiction in 1951 and the John Burroughs Medal for nature writing in 1952. She was prompted to undertake the research for *Silent Spring* by a letter from Olga Owens Huckins, a friend in Massachusetts, complaining that antimosquito pesticide sprayed on her two-acre nature sanctuary had destroyed birds as well as mosquitos. For the next four and a half years, Carson collected evidence that indiscriminate use of pesticides was changing the very nature of life. Her solidly researched and carefully presented book warned that if pesticide use continued unabated, a silent spring would dawn, bereft of songbirds and other wildlife. At the book's publication, Carson was labeled a hysterical woman by the pesticide industry, but her work was vindicated by the 1963 report of the President's Science Advisory Committee. In spite of deteriorating health, Carson carried the fight into the state legislatures, where by the end of 1962, over forty-two bills had been introduced to curtail the use of pesticides.

Water, soil, and the earth's green mantle of plants make up the world that supports the animal life of the earth. Although modern man seldom remembers the fact, he could not exist without the plants that harness the sun's energy and manufacture the basic foodstuffs he depends upon for life. Our attitude toward plants is a singularly narrow one. If we see any immediate utility in a plant we foster it. If for any reason we find its presence undesirable or merely a matter of indifference, we may condemn it to destruction forthwith. Besides the various plants that are poisonous to man or his livestock, or crowd out food plants, many are marked for destruction merely because, according to our narrow view, they happen to be in the wrong place at the wrong time. Many others are destroyed merely because they happen to be associates of the unwanted plants.

The earth's vegetation is part of a web of life in which there are intimate and essential relations between plants and the earth, between plants and other plants, between plants and animals. Sometimes we have no choice but to disturb these relationships, but we should do so thoughtfully, with full awareness that what we do may have consequences remote in time and place. But no such humility marks the booming "weed killer" business of the present day, in which soaring sales and expanding uses mark the production of plant-killing chemicals.

One of the most tragic examples of our unthinking

bludgeoning of the landscape is to be seen in the sagebrush lands of the West, where a vast campaign is on to destroy the sage and to substitute grasslands. If ever an enterprise needed to be illuminated with a sense of the history and meaning of the landscape, it is this. For here the natural landscape is eloquent of the interplay of forces that have created it. It is spread before us like the pages of an open book in which we can read why the land is what it is, and why we should preserve its integrity. But the pages lie unread.

The land of the sage is the land of the high western plains and the lower slopes of the mountains that rise above them, a land born of the great uplift of the Rocky Mountain system many millions of years ago. It is a place of harsh extremes of climate: of long winters when blizzards drive down from the mountains and snow lies deep on the plains, of summers whose heat is relieved by only scanty rains, with drought biting deep into the soil, and drying winds stealing moisture from leaf and stem.

As the landscape evolved, there must have been a long period of trial and error in which plants attempted the colonization of this high and windswept land. One after another must have failed. At last one group of plants evolved which combined all the qualities needed to survive. The sage—low-growing and shrubby—could hold its place on the mountain slopes and on the plains, and within its small gray leaves it could hold moisture enough to defy the thieving winds. It was no accident, but rather the result of long ages of experimentation by nature, that the great plains of the West became the land of the sage.

Along with the plants, animal life, too, was evolving in harmony with the searching requirements of the land. In time there were two as perfectly adjusted to their habitat as the sage. One was a mammal, the fleet and graceful prong-horn antelope. The other was a bird, the sage grouse—the "cock of the plains" of Lewis and Clark.

The sage and the grouse seem made for each other. The original range of the bird coincided with the range of the sage, and as the sagelands have been reduced, so the populations of grouse have dwindled. The sage is all things to these birds of the plains. The low sage of the foothill ranges shelters their nests and their young; the denser growths are loafing and roosting areas; at all times the sage provides the staple food of the grouse. Yet it is a two-way relationship. The spectacular courtship displays of the cocks help loosen the soil beneath and around the sage, aiding invasion by grasses which grow in the shelter of sagebrush.

The antelope, too, have adjusted their lives to the sage. They are primarily animals of the plains, and in winter when the first snows come those that have summered in the mountains move down to the lower elevations. There the sage provides the food that tides them over the winter. Where all other plants have shed their leaves, the sage remains evergreen, the gray-green leaves—bitter, aromatic, rich in proteins, fats, and needed minerals—clinging to the stems of the dense and shrubby plants. Though the snows pile up, the tops of the sage remain exposed, or can be reached by the sharp, pawing hoofs of the antelope. Then grouse feed on them too, finding them on bare and windswept ledges or following the antelope to feed where they have scratched away the snow.

And other life looks to the sage. Mule deer often feed on it. Sage may mean survival for winter-grazing livestock. Sheep graze many winter ranges where the big sagebrush forms almost pure stands. For half the year it is their principal forage, a plant of higher energy value than even alfalfa hay.

The bitter upland plains, the purple wastes of sage, the wild, swift antelope, and the grouse are then a natural system in perfect balance. Are? The verb must be changed—at least in those already vast and growing areas where man is attempting to improve on nature's way. In the name of progress the land management agencies have set about to satisfy the insatiable demands of the cattlemen for more grazing land. By this they mean grassland—grass without sage. So in a land which nature found suited to grass growing mixed with and under the shelter of sage, it is now proposed to eliminate the sage and create unbroken grassland. Few seem to have asked whether grasslands are a stable and desirable goal in this region. Certainly nature's own answer was otherwise. The annual precipitation in this land where the rains seldom fall is not enough to support good sod-forming grass; it favors rather the perennial bunchgrass that grows in the shelter of the sage.

Yet the program of sage eradication has been under way for a number of years. Several government agencies are active in it; industry has joined with enthusiasm to promote and encourage an enterprise which creates expanded markets not only for grass seed but for a large assortment of machines for cutting and plowing and seeding. The newest addition to the weapons is the use of chemical sprays. Now millions of acres of sagebrush lands are sprayed each year.

What are the results? The eventual effects of eliminating sage and seeding with grass are largely conjectural. Men of long experience with the ways of the land say that in this country there is better growth of grass between and under the sage than can possibly be had in pure stands, once the moisture-holding sage is gone.

But even if the program succeeds in its immediate objective, it is clear that the whole closely knit fabric of life has been ripped apart. The antelope and the grouse will disappear along with the sage. The deer will suffer, too, and the land will be poorer for the destruction of the wild things that belong to it. Even the livestock which are the intended beneficiaries will suffer; no amount of lush green grass in summer can help the sheep starving in the winter storms for lack of the sage and bitterbrush and other wild vegetation of the plains.

These are the first and obvious effects. The second is of a kind that is always associated with the shotgun approach to nature: the spraying also eliminates a great many plants that were not its intended target. Justice William O. Douglas, in his recent book *My Wilderness: East to Katahdin,* has told of an appalling example of ecological destruction wrought by the United States Forest Service in the Bridger National Forest in Wyoming. Some 10,000 acres of sagelands were sprayed by the Service, yielding to pressure of cattlemen for more grasslands. The sage was killed, as intended. But so was the green, life-giving ribbon of willows that traced its way across these plains, following the meandering streams. Moose had lived in these willow thickets, for willow is to the moose what sage is to the antelope. Beaver had lived there, too, feeding on the willows, felling them, and making a strong dam across the tiny stream. Through the labor of the beavers, a lake backed up. Trout in the mountain streams seldom were more than six inches long; in the lake they thrived so prodigiously that many grew to five pounds. Waterfowl were attracted to the lake, also. Merely because of the presence of the willows and the beavers that depended on them, the region was an attractive recreational area with excellent fishing and hunting.

But with the "improvement" instituted by the Forest Service, the willows went the way of the sagebrush, killed by the same impartial spray. When Justice Douglas visited the area in 1959, the year of the spraying, he was shocked to see the shriveled and dying willows—the "vast, incredible damage." What would become of the moose? Of the beavers and the little world they had constructed? A year later he returned to read the answers in the devastated landscape. The moose were gone and so were the beaver. Their principal dam had gone out for want of attention by its skilled architects, and the lake had drained away. None of the large trout were left. None could live in the tiny creek that remained, threading its way through a bare, hot land where no shade remained. The living world was shattered.

BARBARA MOR

BITTER ROOT RITUALS, STANZAS I, II, AND III

from *Bitter Root Rituals* (1975)

Barbara Mor (1936–) is a poet whose main theme is the female spirit and body of earth, mother of us all. Born in San Diego and educated at San Diego State College (B.A.), she now lives in New Mexico and rides a bicycle through "blizzards and spring winds and summer lightning." She has published three volumes of poetry and coauthored *The Great Cosmic Mother: Rediscovering the Religion of the Earth* (1987) with Monica Sjöö. Her long poem *Bitter Root Rituals,* first printed in an early edition of *WomanSpirit* magazine and later performed as a dance piece in Taos and Washington, D.C., expresses the violence that has been done to earth and her creatures, and sees the seeds of healing in a unitary vision, female in character, of the connections among body, animals, and earth.

I

white woman enters
the councils of the rock

she is dressed in the skin
of her people

to the elders of the rock
she speaks   saying

our tree is white   with
dying roots

I have just eaten
                a bitter root

the young men of the rock
draw their knives

she gives them her body
                a dry tree

II

and in the dream   the tree
        grows white
        with death

and the year   opens
        to the silent knife

and the thighs   open
        to the ancient knife

and the earth
                dies
        in the hands
        of lovers

III

and they strip her
        the dead leaves
            fly to the wind

they say
        you are our mother
        our great eagle

they snap the dry branches
        bone by bone

BARBARA MOR   297

singing
    our cow
    our whore
    tree of life

and with the knives
they slice
    her skin   from her nerves
    her arms   from the sky
her voice   from the echo
and they say

        for us you fly

        we suck you dry

    sweet is the milk
    of the   mother tree

and they stand above her
             singing
their tongues are knives
    for us you die
    we die in you

and laughing they slit
the roots of her feet

and she laughs
    and cries
    screams
    dies

    BARBARA MOR

HAZEL HECKMAN

RAPE

from *Island Year* (1972)

> Hazel Heckman (1904–   ) lives on "a wooded oasis sur-
> rounded by water," six-by-three-mile Anderson Island in
> Puget Sound, Washington. Born in Kansas, Heckman had
> been a summer visitor and then a permanent resident of
> Anderson Island for twenty years when she wrote *Island
> Year,* her month-by-month record of the flora and fauna she
> had observed there. Her earlier book *Island in the Sound*
> (1967) dealt primarily with the island's human population.
> The unhappy changes she has seen the island undergoing,
> described in the final chapter of her book reprinted here, are
> the same kinds of changes we all see going on around us, no
> matter where we live.

So far as is known, the first permanent settler, Christian
Christensen, reached Anderson Island shores about the
year 1870.

During a century of slow settlement, man and nature
lived together here in symbiotic harmony, each taking ac-
cording to need and giving in turn. Trees were harvested,
clearing accomplished, to warm, feed, and shelter families.
The community expanded, as have thousands of communi-
ties, in a leisurely fashion, closely knit, isolated, self-reliant,
and content. Save for a brief interlude of brick-making from
local clay, a kind of folk art that engendered a small popula-
tion impetus, the Island remained essentially agricultural.

A few subdivisions occurred—Villa Beach, along the
east shore, Miller and Dunkel's and Thorlands, in the vicin-

ity of Amsterdam Bay, the waterfronts we call "Little Burien" and "Mailman's Point." But these were acreages. Our own plat in Villa Beach, purchased in 1950, comprises some seven acres. An occasional "second home" was built. Several buyers, as we did, settled into old houses no longer occupied. We were summer people, week-enders. We made little impact.

Although privately owned, the big lakes area on a high bluff in the eastern sector retained its wild character, as did most of the central portion—the swamp and its tributaries, the woods, the several gulches. Abandoned farms reverted, and were lost in growth. The lakes area was a haven for wild fowl and deer, a territory of bald eagles, great blue heron, great horned owl, pileated woodpecker, and all manner of smaller birds. Islanders took huckleberries and blackberries, greens, fuel, fish, an occasional venison, wild ducks in migration. The road in was an unimproved trail through brush and trees.

A few years ago, at one end of Lake Josephine, a small project began. A little clearing was made, lots were surveyed and staked. Three or four modest buildings materialized. But the long road in, past the Island cemetery, remained little more than a wide path choked with bracken and blackberry and alder seedlings, winding through woods and underbrush and turning aside for big trees, as had the first roads on the Island. Efforts to construct a year-around switchback from the high bluff to the beach failed because of springs and seeps in winter.

The first flurry of trepidation subsided. With the owner's consent and knowledge, Islanders continued to look upon most of the lakes area as more or less open range, as they had always done.

Only when change comes swiftly does one feel its full impact. During these past three years Island woods have undergone more "erosion" than any of us would have believed possible. Roads that were little more than lanes have been widened to accommodate heavy traffic and smoothed to allow for (and, incidentally, to encourage) speed. Acres upon acres of woods, comprising approximately one-fifth of the Island land mass, have been surveyed, mapped, platted into small lots, infiltrated by a latticed network of wide slashed roads that go nowhere. One broad section of beautiful trees has been replaced by a parklike, well-kept, privately owned golf course and a landscaped "country club."

In a recent effort to come at some kind of estimate of the mileage entailed, we drove over a few of these roads, checking and making notes. Linkages proved so frequent, "Drives," "Lanes," "Places," "Circles," and cul-de-sacs so numerous and so engineered, that we gave up long before we had exhausted the mileage on the first project. Even so, the sum of our notations was scarcely credible.

The Island remains, of course, as it has always been, a good place to live. Islanders are a hospitable as well as an adaptable people. Now that Lake Josephine and all of the surrounding acres are "project," they no longer trespass. The few buyers who have come to make their homes in the area are welcomed in community affairs. The Island is not bridged to the mainland. There are, as yet, no overnight facilities, no restaurants, no taverns, no movie houses. There is still a feeling of isolation, a strong sense of community. We have not yet reached the status of a suburban development with scattered interests. But we may well do so.

When half of Lake Florence, too, was taken over, an effort (as yet unsuccessful) was made to secure at least a small portion of the lake for public swimming. Prices that the developers have set on lake-front lots remain, so far, prohibitive.

Meanwhile, the creeping destruction continues. Hundreds of acres have been added. Woods have been bulldozed, chain-sawed, segmented into thousands of building lots. Miles upon miles of rocked roads have opened woods that were once a natural preserve for native fauna and flora. Marsh and swamp have been invaded, fills made and drain tiles laid to create more land for profitable segmentation.

Given half an opportunity in this temperate climate,

healing sets in at a rapid rate. As I have pointed out, some shoots, some roots, will penetrate asphalt to reach light, air, soil, if need be. Much wildlife, too, such as deer, raccoons, and chipmunks, adapts to man's poor ways. If they are fed, raccoons and chipmunks and sometimes deer become so cheeky as hardly to merit the name of wildlife.

The loss will be among the shy, the scarce, the timid— pileated and downy woodpeckers, band-tailed pigeons, cedar waxwings, the hermit thrush, the dusky horned owl, the bald eagle, the great blue heron. The loss of flora, of "little lives," cannot be estimated. Kinnikinnick and twin-flower are readily killed and do not replace themselves. The admission of light does away with such as coral root, mahonia, and rattlesnake plantain, to which shade is a necessity for survival. Many species of fauna—chickadee, owl, woodpecker, nuthatch, creeper, wren, flycatcher—cannot thrive without the stumps and snags that provide food and nesting sites, stumps and snags that have, with the help of truckloads of discarded tires, undergone cremation. The wilderness erodes.

To clear shore lines for swimming and boat-launching, an underwater mower is kept at work clipping wild iris, cattails, and pond lilies. Interlocking roads are widened still further by "frontage roads," kept clean of growth by busy scrapers—mile upon mile upon mile of parking strips. The building of one wide roadway, of a single golf course, may well result in the elimination of a species in an area with a natural barricade such as an island.

Although few houses have gone up around the lakes as yet, Lake Josephine is already altered to the point where many swimmers fear to enter. Whether because of fertilizer runoff from the small well-kept lawns and park sites that touch the shore line and the golf course that adjoins the water-side country club grounds, or from some other cause, a deep algal slime now carpets the lake floor. Only a few years ago water from either lake was sufficiently clean for house use. By the summer of 1971 Lake Josephine was murky and filled with stinking debris. In the vicinity of the diving raft, a floating rainbow of oil (some say from the busy underwater mower) coated the once-sparkling surface that Michael Luark described, aptly, as a mirror for trees and sky.

Should homes arise on lots already sold, hundreds of septic systems will surround the lakes. Although test-holes were required at intervals on all land platted in order to determine filtration, no sewer line nor treatment plant was provided for. One engineer experienced in development problems faced too late remarked sadly, "It will be a sea of sewage." How much pollution can the earth tolerate?

"Prospects in the hands of a well-briefed salesman are a queer lot," he mused. "They'll buy a little parcel on which to build a house, without seeming to notice the network of stakes that mark several hundred other parcels. By the time they've cleared sufficient space to build a house and carport, bury a septic tank, lay out a drainfield and a parking area, and their neighbors do likewise, there won't be any woods left."

"We only bought our lot as investment," some say. "I will argue," wrote Sylvia Porter, syndicated columnist of *Your Money's Worth*, "with touting these tiny parcels as a great 'investment.' There are millions of land parcels on the market today, so scarcity certainly won't be a factor driving up prices in the foreseeable future. In many cases all of the 'investment' value . . . and then some . . . is being reaped by the developers."

Regrettable as it seems to have opened the lakes area to these profitable bits, the invasion of the swamp, nurse-ground to a variety of life, is perhaps the more damaging. The swamp teems with life. Once unknown save to Islanders and to the occasional passerby in winter who may have caught a glimpse of seasonal water through defoliated trees, woods leading to the swamp have become a potential suburbia.

Rocked roads have been cut through as far as the terrain would allow and labeled with street names. Roads parallel each other or run in neat artistic curves. Mobile homes and trailers occupy a developed camping site. Wheels and blades have scraped away elder bushes, blackcap, hardhack, and huckleberry. One evening in early spring I trespassed past rows of numbered stakes and sleeping earth-movers. Crushed salamanders, caught in migration, lay in the roadway. The air was filled with the smell and the presence of wood smoke, pitch fragrance of conifers that smoldered in heaps in clearings from which stumps had been blasted, the slightly bitter smell of burning madroña.

Depressed by damp air, smoke hung trapped in the woods and stood in a blue-gray pall over the stagnant water. The swamp had lost the brooding mystery that gave it distinction. The entire character of the place was changed. Whatever the incalculable loss to wildlife, the *human* race has lost something, too.

Some predict, hopefully, that the urban density of building will be a long time in coming, citing building costs and Island inaccessibility. But, open and enticing as they are, these woods will be trampled by those who fail to notice the small, the seemingly insignificant forms of life, or by those who simply attach no value to such. Nor can a bulldozer stop for a clump of coral root which the operator in all probability cannot see. Who could expect a machine as big as a house to turn aside for a salamander?

I do not reject the fact that the time has come when we must share our space. The human population of the earth, this state, the county is on the increase. On the ferry one day I heard a salesman remark to a prospect, "The Islanders have had *their* way long enough." I assume he meant *human* Islanders. Perhaps he is right. How do you reply to accusations of selfishness, of wanting things *your* way, of a pigheaded reluctance to share?

Were we to parcel the Island (a hypothetical solution) into ten- or even five-acre tracts, served by county roads already in existence, many more inhabitants than we currently support could enjoy the wildness with a minimum of damage to other species. We would still be a community instead of a conglomerate.

It has been said that when roads open up the land it is permanently gone. Nature suffers defeat under tons of crushed rock. And then there are the "little roads" that wend their way picturesquely into the woods between each segment of lots—trails and paths that, given a bit of slope, become silt-carrying freshets.

Anderson Island is no Grand Canyon, no Everglades, no redwood forest, to arouse public indignation. It is only one of the "little wild places," one endangered island in Puget Sound. But great losses are made up of small losses. We can not shrug this off as *progress.* Nor is it just we who have lost. America has been deprived. Our children and our children's children have been cheated out of that wildness that should have been their heritage.

MARGE PIERCY

HOMESICK

from *Circles on the Water* (1982)

Marge Piercy (1936–   ) is a versatile writer whose fierce dedication to a vision of a culture respectful of all living beings has caused her to be harshly critical of the present state of affairs. In eleven volumes of poetry, ten novels, and *The Last White Class,* a play coauthored with her husband, Ira Wood, she has made strong statements for civil rights, peace, economic justice, feminism, and a way of life in harmony with nature. Born in Detroit, she was educated at the

University of Michigan (B.A.) and Northwestern University (M.A.), and now lives in Wellfleet, Massachusetts.

Finally I have a house
where I return.
House half into the hillside,
wood that will weather to the wind's gray,
house built on sand
drawing water like a tree from its roots
where my roots too are set
and I return.

Where the men rode crosscountry on their dirt bikes in
    October
the hog cranberry will not grow back.
This land is vulnerable like my own flesh.
In New York the land seems cast out by a rolling mill
except where ancient gneiss pokes through.
Plains and mountain dwarf the human, seeming
    permanent,
but Indians were chasing mammoth with Folsom points
before glacial debris piled up Cape Cod where I return.

The colonists found beech and oak trees high as steeples
and chopped them down.
When Thoreau hiked from Sandwich outward
he crossed a desert
for they had farmed the land until it blew away
and slaughtered the whales and seals extinct.

Here you must make the frail dirt where your food
    grows.
Fertility is created of human castings and the sea's.
In the intertidal beach around each sand grain
swims a minute world dense with life.
Each oil slick wipes out galaxies.

Here we all lie on the palm of the poisoned sea our
   mother
where life began and is now ending
and we return.

ANNE W. SIMON

SEA

from *The Thin Edge* (1978)

> Anne W. Simon (1914–) has picked up where Rachel
> Carson left off to warn us of the harm we are doing to the
> coast and the ocean. She was born in Greenwich, Connecti-
> cut, educated at Smith College (B.A.) and Columbia Uni-
> versity (M.S.), and lives in New York City and Martha's
> Vineyard, Massachusetts, the subject of her book *No Island
> Is an Island: The Ordeal of Martha's Vineyard* (1973). In both
> *The Thin Edge: Coast and Man in Crisis* and *Neptune's Revenge:
> The Ocean of Tomorrow* (1984), she brings together facts
> from a number of scientific disciplines and makes a poetic
> plea for more farsightedness in our dealings with the ocean
> than we have heretofore been able to muster.

There is an extraordinary mix where land meets sea, a
watery amalgam of civilization and the primordial ocean,
mother of us all. These coastal waters are the link between
man and the sea. The end product of what we terrestrial
beings do eventually goes into them, transported there by

the great rivers that pierce the coastline, by the water that washes the shore, or by man himself, deliberately or accidentally.

Until now we have depended on the vastness, the limitless ocean, the marvelous wild waters, believing the sea to be a resource without end, all-accepting, all-forgiving. "Roll on, thou deep and dark blue ocean, roll!" Lord Byron writes. "Ten thousand fleets sweep over thee in vain; / Man marks the earth with ruin,—his control / Stops with the shore." Ever since the ancient Greeks pictured Zeus in charge of whatever lay beyond the ocean rim, we have inched along in understanding it, tortuously charting its surface, measuring its depths. We learned that there were no Elysian fields beyond the horizon, but water, covering 70 percent of the globe, 330 million cubic miles of it as presently estimated, deep, continuous, salty. The more we measured, the more we trusted the enormous ever-rocking sea to be impervious to man. Our tampering has come about so fast that in 1950, just a second ago in ocean time, Rachel Carson didn't even suspect its effects. Her research led her to echo the same belief that inspired Byron. Man confronts his mother sea only on her own terms, Carson said. "He cannot control or change the ocean as, in his brief tenancy on earth, he has subdued and plundered the continents." By a curious twist, the very excellence of her work may have encouraged what she was sure could not happen.

We have discovered since then that we can and do control the ocean from the shore, change its capacity to support life on which our own lives depend. There is marine life in every part of the sea but it thins out in the dark depths where the sun cannot penetrate. Most of it teems in the surface layers, the top 2 or 3 percent of the ocean. Of these top waters, only a small part produce food and shelter for the rest, some where the tide runs over the land creating wetlands, some where the shallow sea surrounds the continents, a fraction of a percent of the ocean . . . the crucial fraction.

It is a terrible irony that at the precise moment of discovering that we are affecting the entire ocean from this crucial fraction, we are pressed to invade these waters in ways never possible before this era, and for urgent contemporary reasons.

There are 108 million submerged acres off the Atlantic coast, from shoreline to 200 meters of depth. Energy resources are buried there—oil and natural gas—that we want now as never before; there are . . . huge sand beds and fish and shellfish we are desperate to retrieve. There are also unprecedented crowds on the coast, producing proliferating tons of sewage emptied into this same fraction of the ocean. Corroding acids and hot industrial wastes are discharged into it, and barring an unlikely policy reversal, there soon will be some sort of supertanker ports—a string of man-made offshore islands is the favored proposal. "Whichever way the problem is solved," Noël Mostert says in *Supership,* "what cannot be solved is the damage any form of tanker unloading causes." The effect of oil on the waters is "the essential nightmare."

It is painful to absorb the fact that one generation, our generation, has not only poisoned the air to a degree which is causing us serious disabilities, and plundered the earth, but now is beyond any doubt corrupting the ocean. The mysterious human bond with the great seas that poets write about has a physiological base in our veins and in every living thing, where runs fluid of the same saline proportions as ocean water. It is no wonder that we are instinctively drawn to the sea and would avoid any sign that we are damaging it.

LINDA HOGAN

OIL

from *Eclipse* (1983)

Linda Hogan, introduced earlier in this anthology, writes
that "from Hiroshima to Three Mile Island there has been
a violation of the spirit of earth and of feminine energy." In
her work as a writer and an activist she has been concerned
with focusing attention on the destruction of the earth, and
with encouraging skills for survival. Her first novel, *Mean
Spirit* (1990), is about the exploitation of the Indian people
and the land during the oil boom of the 1920s in Oklahoma.

Men smile like they know everything
but walking in slant heel boots
their butts show they are tense.
Dark shirts.
Blue fire
puts out the sun. Rock bits
are clenched metal fists.

The earth is wounded
and bleeds.
Pray to Jesus.

An explosion could knock us all
to our knees

while the bosses stretch out,
white ridge of backbone
in the sun.

We're full of bread and gas,
getting fat on the outside
while inside we grow thin.

The earth is wounded
and will not heal.

Night comes down like a blackbird
with blue flame that never sleeps
and spreads its wings around us.

JANE HOLLISTER WHEELWRIGHT

THE ALEGRÍA CANYON *and* AFTERWORD

from *The Ranch Papers* (1988)

Jane Hollister Wheelwright (1905–   ) was born in Sacramento, California, and grew up "in a world of miracles": the Hollister Ranch, a 39,000-acre cattle ranch near Santa Barbara that had belonged to her family for generations and that, she writes, "in dreams and memory, became the central part of me." *The Ranch Papers: A California Memoir* is at once a personal farewell to the ranch, necessitated by her father's death and the decision to sell the land, and a protest against the toll civilization takes on the wilderness and on what is wild in us. A special sympathy with the Chumash Indians, the land's first residents, permeates her account. "What might have been if we had come to this coast with more humility and understanding!" she laments. "Civilized people no longer experience nature deeply enough for them to deal with crises adequately. They seem instead destined in the long run to destroy themselves." Apart from her life at the ranch, Wheelwright became a Jungian analyst, and with her husband, Joseph B. Wheelwright, founded the first Jungian training center in the world in San Francisco.

The Alegría Canyon

October and November, the year's nadir, is normally the dead time of year. The unexpected rain that had occurred a month too early was confusing things. In spite of the dominant gray, small fine green grass cropped up in spots like punctuation in a paragraph.

The Alegría, with its whispering secrecy and quiet, reminded me of a great sleeping animal that appears to be dead, though the slow, relaxed rise and fall of its breathing reveals otherwise. So it was with the canyon resting, waiting hopefully, if not apprehensively, for more rain. Should the rains come on time, there would be cause for exuberance; should they not, stolid acceptance. There was much to read in that one small glimpse into the lower reaches of the Alegría.

In a vast untouched area like ours, you can hear what you need to hear. You can see for your own good. Messages come through your touch. You are soaked, submerged, immersed; full to the brim with beauty. Each visit can be a final answer, but the next visit brings you something else. It never ends. It becomes an endless process: you and nature have become one and you borrow its infinitude. You then have to go back again and again, because each time you outgrow, in some way, the self you were before.

You struggle for the words to make nature finite, to capture her, to take her with you, and you are defeated, which is right.

The day before from Tepitates I had seen a thick layer of fog roll shoreward across the channel. It extended all the way to the island bases, making them appear to be resting on clouds. This did not relieve the worry about drought, nor did another sign of rain, a view of the islands so clear that their canyons and ridges were visible. From years of experience I knew that at the last moment the most favorable conditions could be a letdown. Promise is characteristic of drought. A number of brief signs of rain and their disappearance at the start of the season are sure signs of a punishing dry year. Nature's will to create is gone—or, from nature's perspective, a rest period for the land is indicated, and then a fresh start.

I felt the impersonal quality of the cold, which matched the graying mustard. Death of the year—any year—is so utterly impersonal. By contrast then, is life personal?

In the fall the land is a composition of earth colors—subtle, hardly noticeable browns, hennas and oranges. Ground colors, with so much vegetation gone, were having their brief day. Life had gone to earth, had gone underground. Energy and life were lost to view.

Sounds and scents, just as fleeting as the colors, were also faint; the scent was an essence, as the sounding wind was a presence. But it is the sound of silence that carries one away.

Will Big Coyote of the Chumash win the game of chance and bring us plenty, or will Sun and Eagle parch us?

Yet the uniqueness of the coast here directly relates to the lack of rainfall. Its overwhelming attraction is as much, if not more, the outcome of harsh conditions as of benevolent rains. Droughts have always been with us—three years out of ten, and at least one exaggeratedly dry. The twisted, gnarled oaks, the snarled shrubbery, the tough sage with its delicate tentative lavender and white flowers in perverse ways prove the beneficence of dry years. Life, desperately but surely hanging on until the next rain—no matter how slight—gives the place an overall sense of beauty in strength. The desert cactus, a miracle of even greater tenaciousness, helps to make the Southwest what it is.

Unfortunately, in the cattle business long dormant periods mean bankruptcy; and there is no comeback. But nature's life force returns. The hard seed lying in the ground, no matter how long, sprouts and sets into motion the food chain.

The essence of the land, as it has been since the beginning of time—its evolution—still needs to be translated for human understanding. Descriptions, impacts, impressions come from the human side; but what is nature's view of us humans? What would the message be if a tree spoke to us, or an animal, or an insect? What would come from "out there"? Would "the other" in nature reach into "the other" in ourselves? If only it would.

So many thoughts, and for whom? The world is drowned by thoughts, most of them watered-down to satisfy too many people. But there is the need to capture the real stuff of this coast, no matter how difficult and personal and elusive a task it is. My notes need no justification; they are a thing in themselves, just as the coast is. Besides, one needs to have a say in one's old age.

As I walked along the beach later that day, a motor fishing boat paralleled along the shore, with its powerful, encroaching, self-assured engine noises. It was barely outside the breakers. To shut it out of my consciousness I carefully noted in detail what was around me. So that was it. Even though often redundant, my notes were also my protection.

In the afternoon the ocean began to build for the incoming tide, and the gray overcast mounted heavily out of the west. It moved deliberately toward the south where storms gather for the final push. Dampness in the air gave off the sense of a storm already spent; yet, underfoot, it was still crisply dry. There was not a sign of life at the beach.

I wanted to hurry home. I was a little frightened, yet there was absolutely nothing to fear. I had an unaccountable feeling of crisis that comes with the uneasy dusk as it also does with the dawn. Since it is neither day nor night it is a strange time. And it never lasts long enough for one to become used to it.

Standing there, watching, color finally came to the clouds, promising a vivid sunset. I knew it would be a brief one; there would be a flash of color, then the dark.

In the foreground there was no differentiation between sand and sea. The light shafts, at first so faint, were becoming distinct. There had to be open skies somewhere, for the sea kicked up a very bright sparkle in places. Wide, soft light bands intensified and searched downward. Three islands—San Miguel, Santa Rosa, and Santa Cruz—displayed their ridge tops in the descending sun; they stood out above the general faintness around their island bases.

I had a driving need to prove the uniqueness of this country. My fate was deeply involved in it.

Abalone shades of pearl, gray and pink drifted into the distant clouds. The sun, descending more and more, suddenly lightened the sky to the west, forcing into the northeast a contrasting heaviness. Rays from the sun, now on the western horizon, pointed up a white swish of vapor above, cutting through the layers of gray. Minutes later sun rays shot up from below the horizon separating the real from the unreal. All too soon, large patches of deep blue were revealed. The storm had fallen back. My impulse was to turn away and start for home, but with no warning the pink of the sky turned the whole vast expanse of ocean to pink.

The last verse of the Night Chant of the Navajos, the *Yeibechai,* came to me:

    In beauty, I walk,
    With beauty before me, I walk,
    With beauty behind me, I walk,
    With beauty above me, I walk,
    With beauty all around me, I walk,
    With beauty within me, I walk,
    It is finished in beauty,
    It is finished in beauty,
    It is finished in beauty,
    It is finished in beauty.

Each moment made the preceding moment a lie, but I could no longer look into the sun, it had already left black moons in my eyes.

Afterword

June 27, 1986

Chevron authorities locked our gates yesterday.

Our appeal for a stay has not been decided by the judges in the California Supreme Court, yet Chevron has started operations. At least, they have brought their heavy equipment onto our property. They intend to lay huge pipes along the coastline—one for sour gas and one for oil.

Their detectives are already stationed at each end of the ranch. Their new uniforms and helmets are spanking and up to date compared to our general dishevelment from the dust, patched roads and mended fences. The legal fees we have had to pay have made it impossible to allow us more than a minimum standard of maintenance on the ranch.

The story of how they have managed to do this is a human, or merely political one, but it happened some time after our original sale to an enterprising but environment-minded Los Angeles man who—sad to report—has since died. The property ownership went through the proverbial revolving door, becoming almost unrecognizable in the process. But that is another story, for another day.

Part of it involved parcelling prime wild land in the coast ranch in one-hundred-acre lots for individual owners, and my husband, Joe, and I bought one of them back.

Am I suspect as well, since one hundred acres now belong to me? I hope not; I am respectful of it in its wild state and consider myself its steward. Chevron claims it will restore the land to its virginal state—but once raped, hardly twice a virgin. They could have laid the pipe at the bottom of the channel, disturbing only a narrow strip of underwater sea land. In that case, in the event of an explosion, the damage done to the wild coast, to the shifting, underwater life, and to those of us on land would be minimized.

But Chevron has chosen to tear into a fragile coastline. Their decision indicates that they feel this land is expendable and unimportant in the face of the public's need for oil, the army's insistence on preparedness, and an American need to go on being powerful—our "manifest destiny." I can only believe that their appearance on the ranch means just one thing: another expression of man's historical arrogance and hatred of nature. He cannot understand this vast land still uncluttered by civilization, so he condemns it. The land is unknowable: therefore, destructible.

A few of us deliberately chose to live as far away as possible from the playground beaches to find the sanity and health the wilderness would give us. The others, living between us and Chevron's pollution, are even more vulnerable. The one or two families on the mesas bordering the ocean who heroically refused to negotiate with Chevron, in spite of the huge monetary settlements offered, will suffer the most.

Tepitates—February 28, 1987

The "right to take" was judged in favor of Chevron by the Supreme Court in Sacramento. The pipeline for oil and its partner, the one for sour gas, lying parallel to it, are in the ground. I am wondering how they can be adequately monitored for leaks.

They called me "sentimental" to cling to a financially losing proposition.

Ranching was always a struggle; but struggle fit the original character of this place. There were floods and droughts—and always the midsummer heat and January cold. Dust and relentless winds, drying out the land after too little rain, blow to hurricane proportions, driving the sand from the beach. Shipwrecks off Point Conception and Point Arguello and offshore winds that have driven fishermen's rowboats out to sea, and to their deaths, are witness.

But when millions of dollars are poured into the place, the struggle will be over. The winds will be controlled by special planting in the canyons and by cabañas on the beach. The droughts will be relieved by water wells or water recovered from the ocean. The dust will be laid under cement. Only fire can wreak some havoc and revive some need for wariness—a last reminder that man is not all-powerful.

There will be about fifty signs along the stretch. There will be mileage markers and indications of bends and turnings of pipe. These will be installed before the pipelines go into operation and will be read by fixed-wing aircraft once a week to observe possible problems. The wording on the signs is a miracle of economy and precision. It is the Night Chant of the White Man:

NATURAL GAS LINE

CAUTION

HIGH PRESSURE

POISONOUS

OIL

POISONOUS

WARNING

PETROLEUM

PIPELINE

ADRIENNE RICH

CONTRADICTIONS: TRACKING POEMS, PART 18

from *Your Native Land, Your Life* (1986)

Adrienne Rich (1929–   ) is "in one woman the history of
women in our country; from careful and traditional obedi-
ence to cosmic awareness," as one critic remarked. Born in
Baltimore and educated at Radcliffe, she has evolved from
a faculty wife and mother to a civil rights and antiwar activist
to a lesbian feminist poet, an evolution traceable in her
dozen published volumes of poetry. In *Your Native Land,
Your Life,* she comments, "In these poems I have been try-
ing to speak from, and of, and to, my country . . . to speak
of the land itself."

The problem, unstated till now, is how
to live in a damaged body
in a world where pain is meant to be gagged
uncured   un-grieved-over   The problem is
to connect, without hysteria, the pain
of any one's body with the pain of the body's world
For it is the body's world
they are trying to destroy forever
The best world is the body's world
filled with creatures   filled with dread
misshapen so   yet the best we have
our raft among the abstract worlds
and how I longed to live on this earth
walking her boundaries   never counting the cost

Healing Her:
Walking in Balance
with Nature

My deepest longing is to live in a world that respects life in every form, a world whose people have a fierce love of and loyalty to the earth and their particular place thereon. The world we live in is not that world, but it could be. To get there from here, we need to recognize that our own well-being is intimately connected to the well-being of the land and of other creatures. All of us—men as well as women—need to bring to bear in our daily lives the qualities that women traditionally have been encouraged to develop: caring, concern for future generations, protectiveness and responsibility toward lives besides our own, gentleness, tenderness, patience, sensitivity, nurturance, reverence for life, aesthetic intuition, receptivity. These are the qualities that have been so lacking in our culture's relationship to nature.

The writing that follows explores ways of being that might allow us to walk once again in balance with nature.

These writers make one thing clear: the change we are required to make is radical, and it must happen both within our hearts and in our actions. We cling to our societal bad habits only at our very great peril. There is a different path; these women show us the way.

BARBARA DEMING

SPIRIT OF LOVE

from *We Are All Part of One Another* (1984)

Barbara Deming (1917–1984) described herself as a radical
pacifist lesbian feminist, and sought to embrace all life with
care and concern. Born in New York and educated at Ben-
nington College (B.A.) and Case Western Reserve Univer-
sity (M.A.), she was inspired by reading Gandhi to become
active in the civil rights and antiwar movements of the
1960s, and eventually published six books on issues of
women and peace, feminism and nonviolence. Her work
was about healing by acknowledging our anger at the
wounds inflicted by patriarchy. She saw an awakening into
feminist consciousness, the awakening she prays for in
"Spirit of Love," as an absolute necessity for the continu-
ance of life on earth.

> Spirit of love
> That flows against our flesh
> Sets it trembling
> Moves across it as across grass
> Erasing every boundary that we accept
> And swings the doors of our lives wide—
> This is a prayer I sing:
> Save our perishing earth!
>
> Spirit that cracks our single selves—
> Eyes fall down eyes,
> Hearts escape through the bars of our ribs
> To dart into other bodies—

Save this earth!
The earth is perishing.
This is a prayer I sing.

Spirit that hears each one of us,
Hears all that is—
Listens, listens, hears us out—
Inspire us now!
Our own pulse beats in every stranger's throat,
And also there within the flowered ground beneath our
    feet,
And—teach us to listen!—
We can hear it in water, in wood, and even in stone.
We are earth of this earth, and we are bone of its bone.
This is a prayer I sing, for we have forgotten this and so
The earth is perishing.

ELIZABETH DODSON GRAY

TURNING TO ANOTHER WAY

from *Green Paradise Lost* (1979)

Elizabeth Dodson Gray (1929–   ) would like to see women
"lead the way into a new kind of responsive dialogue that
enlarges the circle from the human family to include the *real*
other dancers in our dance of life on this planet." The
mother of two children, she is also codirector of the Bolton
Institute for a Sustainable Future, in Wellesley, Massachu-
setts, and coordinator of the Theological Opportunities Pro-

gram at Harvard Divinity School. Her works include *Green Paradise Lost, Patriarchy as a Conceptual Trap* (1982), and *Sacred Dimensions of Women's Experience* (1988).

In the ancient days a solemn council was called to consider the origin of death. Great men, movers of empires and corporations, assembled to debate the question. "Death came with our bodies," they said. "Our natural world, of which our bodies are a part, is full of death. Only our minds and spirits are immortal, akin to the gods. And that is why we sharpen our minds and toughen our spirits, and gird up the loins of our souls to be heroic, to project such a magnificent trajectory of a life-span that we conquer the ignominy of our beginnings in the blood and humanness of childbirth, and the dependence of childhood, as well as the humiliation of our endings in the weakness of old age and the blotting-out of death."

As the men talked, they paced the floor and filled the air with their dreams of glory. Great martial adventures, great philosophical and theological systems, great scientific and technological advances, achievements of epic proportions were planned and executed with courage and strength and daring which surely would conquer the beginnings and the endings of man. "We are like gods," the men rhapsodized as they erected. "We are a little lower than the angels, and all other creatures who do not erect as we do, are below us and subject to us. All of nature itself, like the ground we walk upon, will reverberate to the majesty of our footprints upon the sands of time."

But a funny thing happened as the men worked. Some of the vast heroic enterprises, instead of conquering death, began to cause it. Toxic substances, iron laws of economics, megaton killbacks, and blank-faced robot machines began to stalk the earth and "hunt for humans" like demented snipers of the rooftop. Benign Mother Nature turned on her children with murderous ferocity, slowly choking off the air and water which had flowed freely from her abused breasts. Men were cast back upon the despised dependence of their infantile memories.

"This is intolerable!" the men cried out. "We cannot live as we desire. We cannot control the world and all that in it lies. If we live like this, we die and the world dies with us. But not to live like this, not to control and subdue the world, is still worse for us than death! What shall we do? Who shall we kill to make it right?"

In the silence that followed, an old woman sitting in the corner knitting clothes for her grandchildren finally spoke. "You men live your lives in agonies of striving, you kill and take the world with you. And for what? You do not know who you are. Always you try to escape your bodies, to put down your flesh, to conquer nature, and where does it get you? He who cannot deal with his birth from a woman, cannot deal with his death. Life comes from death, and death is in life. They are all of a piece."

The men stared at her in disbelief. What could this woman, this other-than-man, know of life or death? Only men cast their cosmologies out upon reality; their metaphors of dualism and hierarchy had etched the ontological skies for so long that they seemed embedded in truth itself. Could it be that there was another way to perceive? Another standing point? Could it be that erection itself had betrayed them into thinking linearly about everything? Could it be that they had missed the basic metaphor of life?

"All right," the men taunted her, "you tell us a story. You tell us about the beginning and the ending, and about the meaning of the middle of life. You tell us."

"I am not like you," the old woman said slowly. "I do not tell stories. I see visions. I see that life is not a line but a circle. Why do men imagine for themselves the illusory freedom of a soaring mind, so that the body of nature becomes a cage? 'Tis not true. To be human is to be circled in the cycles of nature, rooted in the processes that nurture us in life, breathing in and breathing out human life just as plants breathe in and out their photosynthesis. Why do men see themselves as apart from this, or above this? Is it that the natural reproductive processes surge so little through their bodies that they cannot feel their unity with nature in their blood and tissue and bones, as women can? Or is it that they so envy and fear women for their more integral part in nature that they seek to escape from both women and nature into a fantasy world of culture which they themselves can control because they made it up?"

The men roared in anger. "How dare you question the world which we have made, woman, you who were not made by God but made from our rib! We have given birth to you! How could we possibly think that we were born of you, or envy you, or fear you? It is against all rational thought!"

But the old woman merely looked at them and said, "To be human is to be born, partake of life, and die. Life itself is the gift. It does not have to be wrenched out of shape, trying to deny both the borning and the dying. Women produce children, and they and the children die. But they know that it was good to have lived. Perhaps someday men too can rest upon the affirmation of being, and there find reassurance and an end to their ceaseless striving. Perhaps someday they shall come to know the circle which is the whole—that which validates being-without-achieving, that which allows one to rest and stop running, that which accepts one as a person and not a hero. The sweet nectar of that whole awaits you in the precious flower of the Now, not in your dreams of glory. Perhaps, someday, men will find their humanity, and give up their divinity."

The old woman had finished speaking and there was silence in the great council room. It was a time for silence.

NANCY NEWHALL

DYNAMICS

from *This Is the American Earth* (1960)

> Nancy Newhall (1908–1974) wrote that "to any beauty we must come as lovers, not destroyers, / come humbly, softly, to look, listen, learn, / to cherish and to shield." She was born and raised in New England, educated at Smith College, and married the eminent photohistorian Beaumont Newhall. In the course of a remarkable career as curator, critic, editor, designer, and historian, she was influenced by their friend the photographer Ansel Adams to develop a deep concern for the earth and the cause of conservation, and Adams became her most frequent collaborator in expressing these concerns. Their most important collaboration was *This Is the American Earth*, combining Newhall's writing with photos by Adams and others in a review of human civilization and a plea for conservation. To Adams, she wrote, "I think our job is to prepare the way for a new faith and a new world."

Shall we not learn from life its laws, dynamics, balances?
Learn to base our needs not on death, destruction,
    waste, but on renewal?
In wisdom and in gentleness learn to walk again with
    Eden's angels?
Learn at last to shape a civilization in harmony with the
    earth? . . .
What, to continue their renewal,
    do air, water, life require of Man?
—Only that below the snows and glaciers of peaks, the
    alpine meadows and trees at timberline on precarious

slopes face storms and meltings undisturbed and here
no mouse, nor eagle, no wolf nor antelope, snake nor
butterfly be hindered from his errand.

—Only that on lower spines and ridges forests stand
sentinel in the rains and Man take from them only
their abundance.

—Only that lakes lie cool and pure, and rivers brim
their banks yearlong running clear and stainless from
spring to estuary.

—Only that grasslands wave deep even under late
summer suns, and field and orchard be so cared for
that a thousand years shall but increase their richness.

—Only that Man use water wisely, to help life and be
helped by it.

—Only that in cities air and light be clear and enough
leaves remain to shadow a living land.

—Only that in each rise of land, each fall of water, each
form of life, Man sense its character, its function in
the whole, love it, and learn its ways, and when we
turn it to our use, plan with inspired skills to fit to it
our habitations and our needs to enhance—not to
obliterate—its beauty.

How little, from the resources unrenewable by Man,
    cost the things of greatest value—
        wild beauty, peace, health and love,
        music and all testaments of spirit!

How simple our basic needs—
        a little food, sun, air, water, shelter, warmth and
    sleep!

How lightly might this earth bear Man forever!

BROOKE MEDICINE EAGLE

THE RAINBOW BRIDGE

from *Shamanic Voices: A Survey of Visionary Narratives,*
edited by Joan Halifax (1979)

Brooke Medicine Eagle (1943–   ) combines training in the
Northern Plains Indian medicine path and in Western ways
of healing in her unique work as a poet and writer, vision-
ary, healer, singer, teacher, and ceremonial leader. Brought
up on the Crow reservation in Montana, Medicine Eagle
undertook ritual training with a Northern Cheyenne medi-
cine woman while in her twenties, and also studied at the
University of Denver (B.A. in psychology and mathematics)
and Mankato State University (M.A. in counseling psychol-
ogy). She writes, "Our generation has the opportunity and
challenge of making real on Earth a way of life which brings
the age of harmony, abundance, and peace foreseen by the
old ones: the Good Red Road where the Tree of Life blos-
soms again."

My initiatory vision quest was done with my teacher, Stands
Near the Fire, an eighty-year-old Cheyenne woman who
was the keeper of a sacred lodge whose sacred object repre-
sents the Renewing Power of the Feminine. She and a
younger medicine woman took me to the centuries-old fast-
ing, vision-questing place of the Sioux and Cheyenne, Bear
Butte, located in the plains country that goes up into the
Black Hills. The traditional way is to fast and cleanse one-
self bodily, emotionally, and psychically; then to go atop a
sacred mountain for four days and nights wearing only a
breechcloth and carrying a buffalo robe, staying there with-

out food or water, praying for vision. This is the kind of quest that I did.

The younger medicine woman took me up the butte. She prepared and blessed a bed of sagebrush on a very rocky hill halfway up the mountain. This was to be my bed. After we smoked a pipe and offered prayers, she painted me and left me. So I spent the time there fasting and praying for vision.

Several days and nights have passed and it is again just after twilight. Up here on the mountain, I can look down over the country. There's a lake down below me; in the far distance are the Black Hills, and I can see the lights of Rapid City. A few small clouds are drifting across the sky, but it is relatively warm, the late fall. I'm lying, comfortable and peaceful even on the sharp rocks, remembering the evening we arrived and the half rainbow that arched across the sky to my right, accenting the golden light on the prairie.

Suddenly there appears beside me a woman, older than me, but not really an old woman. She's dressed very simply in buckskin, and I'm surprised she doesn't have beading on her dress. She has raven black hair in long braids. As she stands there beside me, she begins to speak to me. Her message comes clearly through, but not in my ears. It's as though she's feeding something in at my navel, and it comes up through all of me; I can interpret part of it in words but not all of it. It just keeps flowing in and filling up my whole being. So the words that I have put to it are my own, and I have discovered more and more of what she told me as time has gone on.

The little clouds that are over the moon move off, and as they move away, the moonlight shining on her dress creates a flurry of rainbows, and I see that her dress is beaded with crystal beads, hundreds of tiny crystal beads; the slightest movement she makes sends those flurries of soft rainbows all over.

About this time, something else starts to happen. Down off the high part of the mountain, lights begin to come, and

I hear soft drumbeats begin, very soft. Descending in a slow, gentle dance step are the old women spirits of that mountain, ancient gray-haired women, Indian women, dancing down. They either are light or carry light as they wind down the trail and circle the hill I am on. As they dance around in a circle, very quickly into that circle comes another circle, this one of young women of my age and time, young women that I know, and they, too, are dancing. Those two rings are dancing and moving, and then they begin to weave in and out of each other, sway in and out of each other, blending. Then inside that circle comes another circle of seven old grandmothers, white-haired women, women who are significant to me, powerful and nurturing old women. Again inside comes a circle of seven young women, friends and sisters to me, weaving and swaying, blending with the grandmothers.

In the Indian tradition, there is a wonderful amount of humor. And the humor comes when all this very solemn, very slow and beautiful ceremony is taking place. Running off the mountain, with her hair flying, is a special friend of mine. She's typically late, a very high person and quite unpredictable. Into the circle, stopping breathless beside the Rainbow Woman, trying to appear nonchalant, comes Diane, carrying on her left hand a dove. The Rainbow Woman looks down on me and says, "Her name is Moon Dove," and smiles. Diane then lets the dove fly, swirling high into the sky, and all around me disappears except the Rainbow Woman, standing radiant beside me.

She reminds me that the Mother Earth is in trouble, her renewing powers threatened, and that here on this land, this Turtle Island, this North American land, what needs to happen is a balancing. The thrusting, aggressive, analytic, building, making-it-happen energy has seriously over-balanced the feminine, receptive, allowing, harmonizing, intuitive energy. She says that what must happen is an uplifting and a balancing—more emphasis on surrendering, being receptive, nurturing all the people, using the inexhaustible resources within us rather than raping and tearing the Mother Earth. She speaks to me as a woman, and I am to carry this message to women specifically, to reawaken their profound intuitive, protective, nurturing natures. But not only do women need to become strong in this way; we all need to do this, men and women alike.

Women are born more naturally receptive and nurturing; that's what being a woman in this body is about. But even the women in our society don't do that very well. None of us have ever been taught that way. We know how to *do* something; we know how to *make* something, how to exert effort; but we need to allow, to be receptive, listen to the Earth, find the Universal knowledge and ancient truths within ourselves, to surrender and serve. Each of us must find that balance, heal ourselves, become whole.

Another thing she relates is that we on this North American continent are all children of the rainbow, all of us; we are primarily mixed-bloods. And especially to me she is speaking, saying that she feels I will be a carrier of the message between the two cultures, across the rainbow bridge, from the old culture to the new, from the Indian to the dominant society, bridging any and all gaps. And in a sense, all of us in this generation can be that. We can help construct, using the full potential of ourselves, that bridge into the new age, creating a beautiful abundant life for all.

These are the kinds of things she reminds me of, and asks me to remind others of—about clearing ourselves to allow love and light to come through us, through our hearts. And when she finishes her message, she stands quietly for a moment. Then, her feet staying where they are, she shoots out across the sky in a rainbow arc that covers the heavens. Slowly the lights that formed the rainbow begin to die out, fall like fireworks from the sky, die out from her feet and die out and fade. She is gone and I am looking into the moon-lighted sky.

When I awoke the next morning, in the left-hand portion of the sky was the completion of the half rainbow that I had seen as I arrived here. For days and days after that, rainbows kept appearing in my life, one a magnificent triple rainbow the likes of which I had never before witnessed.

I know few women who are on the path of the shaman, and yet, this is my way. I was raised on the Crow Reservation in Montana. My blood is primarily Sioux and Nez Percé. The Indian tradition was very much hidden when I was growing up; however, I have gotten back more and more to the ancient ways. This happened as I began to have visions; I was drawn back to the old ways by them. I did not choose it outwardly; it came as I released old ways of being, its irresistible call bringing me home.

About the quest for vision, the traditional Indians prayed always thus: "Not only for myself do I ask this, Grandfather, Great Spirit, but that the people may live, the people may live." Any of us can dream, but seeking vision is always done not only to heal and fulfill one's own potential, but also to learn to use that potential to serve all our relations: the two-leggeds, the four-leggeds, the wingeds, those that crawl upon the Earth, and the Mother Earth herself. I feel my purpose is to help in any way I can to heal the Earth; we are in a time when Our Mother is in dire need of healing. We see it everywhere: the droughts, earthquakes, storms, and pollution. Yes, Mother Earth needs our nurturance. My mission is to heal, to make whole, to pay attention to that wholeness not only in ourselves but in all that is.

The Indian people are the people of the heart. The finest of my elders remind me that being Indian is an attitude, a state of mind, a way of being in harmony with all things and all beings. It is allowing the heart to be the distributor of energy on this planet: to allow feelings and sensitivities to determine where energy goes; bringing aliveness up from the Earth and down from the Sky, pulling it in and giving it out from the heart, the very center of one's being. That is the Indian way.

When the white man came to this land he brought the intellect, the analytic way of being, which has become dominant. The prophecies say that when those two come together and balance, the new age will begin. It has only been a couple hundred years since that coming together and we are all becoming natives here.

Our dominant society and education give us the way of the Mind; the way of the Heart is being born from the very land itself into our cells and genes. We are that blend; we are those children of whom Rainbow Woman spoke. We are the ones who will make the vision real.

And the time is now. Many different traditions tell us of four or five worlds that have been, and say that the Creator made all these worlds with one simple law: That we shall be in harmony and balance with all things and all beings. Time and time again people have destroyed that harmony; we have destroyed that harmony, and have done it needlessly. This is the last world, our last chance to prove that we can live peaceably upon the Earth.

We must achieve a clarity and lack of resistance as we seek vision—a surrendering, a relinquishing. If we are unwilling to be in our experience now, then vision will not open for us. We need to get on that circle where there is no resistance, no up, no down, where there are no square corners to hide in or stumble on. Then, someday, we become that circle.

This is dedicated to Stands Near the Fire, the Woman Who Knows Everything, who went to "the beyond-country" a few hours after I was with her on January 3, 1980. With her passing, an era ended. May she find clear water and buffalo there, and live with them forever in perpetual summer.

PAULA GUNN ALLEN

KOPIS'TAYA (A GATHERING OF SPIRITS)

from *Songs from This Earth on Turtle's Back: An Anthology of Poetry by American Indian Writers,* edited by Joseph Bruchac (1984)

Paula Gunn Allen (1939–   ), a scholar who has specialized in American Indian literature, comments that "the sense of the connectedness of all things, of the spiritness of all things, of the intelligent consciousness of all things, is the identifying characteristic of American Indian tribal poetry." Born of Laguna Pueblo/Scots-Irish/Lebanese-American ancestry and raised near the Laguna reservation in New Mexico on the Cubero Land Grant, she earned a doctorate at the University of New Mexico and is now a full professor at UCLA. She has written seven books of poetry, many short stories, a novel, and a work of nonfiction, and has edited volumes of Native American literature.

Because we live in the browning season
the heavy air blocking our breath,
and in this time when living
is only survival, we doubt the voices
that come shadowed on the air,
that weave within our brains
certain thoughts, a motion that is soft,
imperceptible, a twilight rain,
   soft feather's fall, a small body
dropping into its nest, rustling, murmuring,
settling in for the night.

Because we live in the hardedged season,
where plastic brittle and gleaming shines
and in this space that is cornered and angled,
we do not notice wet, moist, the significant
drops falling in perfect spheres
that are the certain measures of our minds;
almost invisible, those tears,
soft as dew, fragile, that cling to leaves,
petals, roots, gentle and sure,
every morning.

We are the women of daylight; of clocks and steel
foundries, of drugstores and streetlights,
of superhighways that slice our days in two.
Wrapped around in glass and steel we ride
our lives; behind dark glasses we hide our eyes,
our thoughts, shaded, seem obscure, smoke
fills our minds, whisky husks our songs,
polyester cuts our bodies from our breath,
our feet from the welcoming stones of earth.
Our dreams are pale memories of themselves,
and nagging doubt is the false measure of our days.

Even so, the spirit voices are singing,
their thoughts are dancing in the dirty air.
Their feet touch the cement, the asphalt
delighting, still they weave dreams upon our
shadowed skulls, if we could listen.
If we could hear.
Let's go then. Let's find them. Let's
listen for the water, the careful gleaming drops
that glisten on the leaves, the flowers. Let's
ride the midnight, the early dawn. Feel the wind
striding through our hair. Let's dance
the dance of feathers, the dance of birds.

TERRY TEMPEST WILLIAMS

A WOMAN'S DANCE

from *Coyote's Canyon* (1989)

> Terry Tempest Williams, whose story "The Bowl" is in-
> cluded earlier in this anthology, conveys in her writing a
> sense of how we might reinvest the earth and our relation
> to it with sacred meaning, how we might attune once more
> to the spirit voices Paula Gunn Allen refers to. Williams
> wrote in *Pieces of White Shell*, "Each of us bears a unique
> relationship with landscape if we allow ourselves to let go—
> let go of cultural biases and societal constraints, taking the
> time to experience earth as it is, raw and self-defined. We
> need to imagine ourselves flying on the backs of owls, for
> a people without natural vision is a people without insight.
> We have the power to rethink our existence, our time in
> earth's embrace, and step forward with compassionate intel-
> ligence. If we align ourselves with the spirit of place we will
> find humility infused with joy."

She came to the desert to dance. The woman gathered a
variety of plants: mullen, sage, chamisa, mint, Oregon
grape, aster, equisetum, and yarrow. She carried them in
the folds of her long, red skirt to a clearing. It was a
meadow defined by juniper. She placed the plants in the
center and returned to the trees. She took off her paisley
bandana wrapped around her forehead and knelt on the red
soil.

"Good death," she said, as her hands sifted the wood
dust of a decaying tree. She opened her scarf and placed the

henna wood chips on the silk square. After she had gathered enough for the task, she brought the four corners together, tied them, and walked back to the clearing. She was not alone. Flickers, robins, magpies, and jays accompanied her. The woman carefully untied one of the corners and let the wood dust sprinkle to the ground as she walked in a circle. Next, she retrieved the plants from the center and arranged them end to end on top of the wood dust to define her circle more clearly. She liked what she saw.

Movement surrounded her. The wind, clouds, grasses, and birds—all reminded her that nothing stands still. She held up the hem of her skirt in both hands and began walking briskly around the circle. Deep breaths took the aroma of mint and sage down to her toes. Her long, spirited stride broke into short leaps with extended arms as she entered the circle dancing, without guile, without notice, without any thought of herself. She danced from the joy of all she was a part.

Pronghorn Antelope entered the circle through her body. She danced Eagle, Raven, and Bear. The Four Seasons sent her swirling as she danced to ignite the Moon. She danced until gravity pulled her down, and then she rested, her eyes closed, with nothing moving but her heart and lungs, beating, breathing, against the hot, dry desert.

With her ear against the earth, the woman listened. A chant began to rise. Slowly, she raised her body like a lizard. An audience had gathered. Each individual sat cross-legged around the plant circle with a found instrument: rocks, bones, sticks, stumps, whistles, and voices. For hours, they played music, organic and whole, as she danced. Her hands, like serpents, encouraged primal sounds as she arched forward and back with the grasses. She was the wind that inspired change. They were a tribe creating a landscape where lines between the real and imagined were thinly drawn.

The light deepened, shadows lengthened, and the woman began to turn. Her turns widened with each rotation until she stopped, perfectly balanced. The woman stepped outside the circle and kissed the palms of her hands and placed them on the earth. The dance was over.

The audience rose, refreshed. Each picked up one of the plants that held the circle and took a handful of wood dust to scatter, leaving no clues in the clearing of ever having been there. They disappeared as mysteriously as they had arrived.

And the woman who came to the desert to dance simply ran her fingers through her long, black hair and smiled.

MARGE PIERCY

THE COMMON LIVING DIRT

from *Stone, Paper, Knife* (1983)

Marge Piercy, introduced earlier, has a profound sense of the interconnectedness of all life and our utter dependence on the earth's abundance. Among the powerful realizations she articulates is that we must come to a radical new relationship with elements as basic as the soil.

> The small ears prick on the bushes,
> furry buds, shoots tender and pale.
> The swamp maples blow scarlet.
> Color teases the corner of the eye,
> delicate gold, chartreuse, crimson,
> mauve speckled, just dashed on.

The soil stretches naked. All winter
hidden under the down comforter of snow,
delicious now, rich in the hand
as chocolate cake: the fragrant busy
soil the worm passes through her gut
and the beetle swims in like a lake.

As I kneel to put the seeds in
careful as stitching, I am in love.
You are the bed we all sleep on.
You are the food we eat, the food
we ate, the food we will become.
We are walking trees rooted in you.

You can live thousands of years
undressing in the spring your black
body, your red body, your brown body
penetrated by the rain. Here
is the goddess unveiled,
the earth opening her strong thighs.

Yet you grow exhausted with bearing
too much, too soon, too often, just
as a woman wears through like an old rug.
We have contempt for what we spring
from. Dirt, we say, you're dirt
as if we were not all your children.

We have lost the simplest gratitude.
We lack the knowledge we showed ten
thousand years past, that you live
a goddess but mortal, that what we take
must be returned; that the poison we drop
in you will stunt our children's growth.

Tending a plot of your flesh binds
me as nothing ever could, to the seasons,
to the will of the plants, clamorous

in their green tenderness. What
calls louder than the cry of a field
of corn ready, or trees of ripe peaches?

I worship on my knees, laying
the seeds in you, that worship rooted
in need, in hunger, in kinship,
flesh of the planet with my own flesh,
a ritual of compost, a litany of manure.
My garden's a chapel, but a meadow

gone wild in grass and flower
is a cathedral. How you seethe
with little quick ones, vole, field
mouse, shrew and mole in their thousands,
rabbit and woodchuck. In you rest
the jewels of the genes wrapped in seed.

Power warps because it involves joy
in domination; also because it means
forgetting how we too starve, break
like a corn stalk in the wind, how we
die like the spinach of drought,
how what slays the vole slays us.

Because you can die of overwork, because
you can die of the fire that melts
rock, because you can die of the poison
that kills the beetle and the slug,
we must come again to worship you
on our knees, the common living dirt.

BETH BRANT

NATIVE ORIGIN

from *Mohawk Trail* (1985)

Beth Brant (1941–), a Mohawk of the Turtle Clan, makes her home in Detroit, where she was born. Her articles and poems have appeared in magazines and anthologies of Native American literature; she edited *A Gathering of Spirit* (1984), a collection of writing by North American Indian women, and is a cofounder of Turtle Grandmother, an archive and library of information about North American Indian women. What is striking about her description of a traditional Indian women's ritual in "Native Origin" is how comfortable and right seems the deep, unhurried, celebratory honoring of natural artifacts, culminating with a fistful of black earth, tangible signs of the many strands binding us to the web of life.

The old women are gathered in the Longhouse. First, the ritual kissing on the cheeks, the eyes, the lips, the top of the head; that spot where the hair parts in the middle like a wild river through a canyon. On either side, white hair flows unchecked, unbinded.

One Grandmother sets the pot over the fire that has never gone out. To let the flames die is a taboo, a breaking of trust. The acorn shells have been roasted the night before. Grandmother pours the boiling water over the shells. An aroma rises and combines with the smell of wood smoke, sweat, and the sharp, sweet odor of blood.

The acorn coffee steeps and grows dark and strong. The old women sit patiently in a circle, not speaking. Each set of eyes stares sharply into the air, or into the fire. Occasionally, a sigh escapes from an open mouth. A Grandmother has a twitch in the corner of her eye. She rubs her nose, then smooths her hair.

The coffee is ready. Cups are brought out of a wooden cupboard. Each woman is given the steaming brew. They blow on the swirling liquid, then slurp the drink into their hungry mouths. It tastes good. Hot, strong, dark. A little bitter, but that is all to the good.

The women begin talking among themselves. They are together to perform a ceremony. Rituals of women take time. There is no hurry.

The magic things are brought out from pockets and pouches.

A turtle rattle made from a she-turtle who was a companion of the woman's mother. It died the night she died, both of them ancient and tough. Now, the daughter shakes the rattle, and mother and she-turtle live again. Another Grandmother pulls out a bundle that contains a feather from a hermit thrush. This is a holy feather. Of all the birds in the sky, hermit thrush is the only one who flew to the Spirit World. It was there she learned her beautiful song. She is clever and hides from sight. To have her feather is great magic. The women pass around the feather. They tickle each other's chins and ears. Giggles and laughs erupt in the dwelling.

From that same bundle of the hermit thrush, come kernels of corn, yellow, red, black. They rest in her wrinkled, dry palm. These are also passed around. Each woman holds the corn in her hand for a while before giving it to her sister. Next come the leaves of Witch Hazel and Jewelweed. Dandelion roots for chewing, Pearly Everlasting for smoking. These things are given careful consideration, and much talk is generated over the old ways of preparing the concoctions.

A woman gives a smile and brings out a cradleboard from behind her back. There is nodding of heads and smiling and long drawn-out ahhhhs. The cradleboard has a beaded back that a mother made in her ninth month. An old woman starts a song; the rest join in:

Little baby
Little baby
Ride on Mother's back
Laugh, laugh
Life is good
Mother shields you

A Grandmother wipes her eyes, another holds her hands and kisses the lifelines. Inside the cradleboard are bunches of moss taken from a menstrual house. This moss has staunched rivers of blood that generations of young girls have squeezed from their wombs.

The acorn drink is reheated and passed around again. A woman adds wood to the fire. She holds her hands out to the flames. It takes a lot of heat to warm her creaky body. Another woman comes behind her with a warm blanket. She wraps it around her friend and hugs her shoulders. They stand quietly before the fire.

A pelt of fur is brought forth. It once belonged to a beaver. She was found one morning, frozen in the ice, her lodge unfinished. The beaver was thawed and skinned. The women worked the hide until it was soft and pliant. It was the right size to wrap a new born baby in, or to comfort old women on cold nights.

A piece of flint, an eagle bone whistle, a hank of black hair, cut in mourning; these are examined with reverent vibrations.

The oldest Grandmother removes her pouch from around her neck. She opens it with rusty fingers. She spreads the contents in her lap. A fistful of black earth. It smells clean, fecund. The women inhale the odor, the metallic taste of iron is on their tongues, like sting.

The oldest Grandmother scoops the earth back into her

pouch. She tugs at the strings, it closes. The pouch lies between her breasts, warming her skin. Her breasts are supple and soft for one so old. Not long ago, she nursed a sister back to health. A child drank from her breast and was healed of evil spirits that entered her while she lay innocent and dreaming.

The ceremony is over. The magic things are put in their places. The old women kiss and touch each other's faces. They go out in the night. The moon and stars are parts of the body of Sky Woman. She glows on, never dimming. Never receding.

The Grandmothers go inside the Longhouse. They tend the fire, and wait.

LINDA HOGAN

WAKING UP THE RAKE

from *Parabola* magazine (Summer 1988)

> Linda Hogan, whose writing is included earlier ("Walking" and "Oil") works as a volunteer at the Birds of Prey Rehabilitation Foundation, seeing it as a way for her to begin healing "the severed trust we humans hold with earth." She believes that "earth consciousness is the foundation of women's growing, and it is an honor for us to give back to the earth, to care for the animals, plants, people, minerals." She points out that in the process of becoming whole, we need to pay homage to the earth as well as to our lives and works, a theme she explores in the following essay.

In the still dark mornings, my grandmother would rise up from her bed and put wood in the stove. When the fire began to burn, she would sit in front of its warmth and let down her hair. It had never been cut and it knotted down in two long braids. When I was fortunate enough to be there, in those red Oklahoma mornings, I would wake up with her, stand behind her chair, and pull the brush through the long strands of her hair. It cascaded down her back, down over the chair, and touched the floor.

We were the old and the new, bound together in front of the snapping fire, woven like a lifetime's tangled growth of hair. I saw my future in her body and face, and her past was alive in me. We were morning people, and in all of earth's mornings the new intertwines with the old. Even new, a day itself is ancient, old with earth's habit of turning over and over again.

Years later, I was sick, and I went to a traditional healer. The healer was dark and thin and radiant. The first night I was there, she also lit a fire. We sat before it, smelling the juniper smoke. She asked me to tell her everything, my life spoken in words, a case history of living, with its dreams and losses, the scars and wounds we all bear from being in the world. She smoked me with cedar smoke, wrapped a sheet around me, and put me to bed, gently, like a mother caring for her child.

The next morning she nudged me awake and took me outside to pray. We faced east where the sun was beginning its journey on our side of earth.

The following morning in red dawn, we went outside and prayed. The sun was a full orange eye rising up the air. The morning after that we did the same, and on Sunday we did likewise.

The next time I visited her it was a year later, and again we went through the same prayers, standing outside facing the early sun. On the last morning I was there, she left for her job in town. Before leaving, she said, "Our work is our altar."

Those words have remained with me.

Now I am a disciple of birds. The birds that I mean are eagles, owls, and hawks. I clean cages at the Birds of Prey Rehabilitation Foundation. It is the work I wanted to do, in order to spend time inside the gentle presence of the birds.

There is a Sufi saying that goes something like this: "Yes, worship God, go to church, sing praises, but first tie your camel to the post." This cleaning is the work of tying the camel to a post.

I pick up the carcasses and skin of rats, mice, and of rabbits. Some of them have been turned inside out by the sharp-beaked eaters, so that the leathery flesh becomes a delicately veined coat for the inner fur. It is a boneyard. I rake the smooth fragments of bones. Sometimes there is a leg or shank of deer to be picked up.

In this boneyard, the still-red vertebrae lie on the ground beside an open rib cage. The remains of a rabbit, a small intestinal casing, holds excrement like beads in a necklace. And there are the clean, oval pellets the birds spit out, filled with fur, bone fragments and now and then, a delicate sharp claw that looks as if it were woven inside. A feather, light and soft, floats down a current of air, and it is also picked up.

Over time, the narrow human perspective from which we view things expands. A deer carcass begins to look beautiful and rich in its torn redness, the muscle and bone exposed in the shape life took on for a while as it walked through meadows and drank at creeks.

And the bone fragments have their own stark beauty, the clean white jaw bones with ivory teeth small as the head of a pin still in them. I think of medieval physicians trying to learn about our private, hidden bodies by cutting open the stolen dead and finding the splendor inside, the grace of every red organ, and the smooth, gleaming bone.

This work is an apprenticeship, and the birds are the teachers. Sweet-eyed barn owls, such taskmasters, asking us to be still and slow and to move in time with their rhythms, not our own. The short-eared owls with their startling yellow eyes require the full presence of a human. The marsh hawks, behind their branches, watch our every move.

There is a silence needed here before a person enters the bordered world the birds inhabit, so we stop and compose ourselves before entering their doors, and we listen to the musical calls of the eagles, the sound of wings in air, the way their feet with sharp claws, many larger than our own hands, grab hold of a perch. Then we know we are ready to enter, and they are ready for us.

The most difficult task the birds demand is that we learn to be equal to them, to feel our way into an intelligence that is different from our own. A friend, awed at the thought of working with eagles, said, "Imagine knowing an eagle." I answered her honestly, "It isn't so much that we know the eagles. It's that they know us."

And they know that we are apart from them, that as humans we have somehow fallen from our animal grace, and because of that we maintain a distance from them, though it is not always a distance of heart. The places we inhabit, even sharing a common earth, must remain distinct and separate. It was our presence that brought most of them here in the first place, nearly all of them injured in a clash with the human world. They have been shot, or hit by cars, trapped in leg hold traps, poisoned, ensnared in wire fences. To ensure their survival, they must remember us as the enemies that we are. We are the embodiment of a paradox; we are the wounders and we are the healers.

There are human lessons to be learned here, in the work. Fritjof Capra wrote: "Doing work that has to be done over and over again helps us to recognize the natural cycles of growth and decay, of birth and death, and thus become aware of the dynamic order of the universe." And it is true, in whatever we do, the brushing of hair, the cleaning of cages, we begin to see the larger order of things. In this place, there is a constant coming to terms with both the sacred place life occupies, and with death. Like one of those early physicians who discovered the strange, inner secrets of our human bodies, I'm filled with awe at the very presence of life, not just the birds, but a horse contained in its living fur, a dog alive and running. What a marvel it is, the fine shape life takes in all of us. It is equally marvelous that life is quickly turned back to the earth-colored ants and the soft white maggots that are time's best and closest companions. To sit with the eagles and their flute-like songs, listening to the longer flute of wind sweep through the lush grasslands, is to begin to know the natural laws that exist apart from our own written ones.

One of those laws, that we carry deep inside us, is intuition. It is lodged in a place even the grave-robbing doctors could not discover. It's a blood-written code that directs us through life. The founder of this healing center, Sigrid Ueblacker, depends on this inner knowing. She watches, listens, and feels her way to an understanding of each eagle and owl. This vision, as I call it, directs her own daily work at healing the injured birds and returning them to the wild.

"Sweep the snow away," she tells me. "The Swainson's hawks should be in Argentina this time of year and should not have to stand in the snow."

I sweep.

And that is in the winter when the hands ache from the cold, and the water freezes solid and has to be broken out for the birds, fresh buckets carried over icy earth from the well. In summer, it's another story. After only a few hours the food begins to move again, as if resurrected to life. A rabbit shifts a bit. A mouse turns. You could say that they have been resurrected, only with a life other than the one that left them. The moving skin swarms with flies and their offspring, ants, and a few wasps, busy at their own daily labor.

Even aside from the expected rewards for this work, such as seeing an eagle healed and winging across the sky it fell from, there are others. An occasional snake, beautiful and sleek, finds its way into the cage one day, eats a mouse and is too fat to leave, so we watch its long muscular life stretched out in the tall grasses. Or, another summer day, taking branches to be burned with a pile of wood near the little creek, a large turtle with a dark and shining shell slips soundlessly into the water, its presence a reminder of all the lives beyond these that occupy us.

One green morning, an orphaned owl perches nervously above me while I clean. Its downy feathers are roughed out. It appears to be twice its size as it clacks its beak at me, warning me: stay back. Then, fearing me the way we want it to, it bolts off the perch and flies, landing by accident onto the wooden end of my rake, before it sees that a human is an extension of the tool, and it flies again to a safer place, while I return to raking.

The word "rake" means to gather or heap up, to smooth the broken ground. And that's what this work is, all of it, the smoothing over of broken ground, the healing of the severed trust we humans hold with earth. We gather it back together again with great care, take the broken pieces and fragments and return them to the sky. It is work at the borderland between species, at the boundary between injury and healing.

There is an art to raking, a very fine art, one with rhythm in it, and life. On the days I do it well, the rake wakes up. Wood that came from dark dense forests seems to return to life. The water that rose up through the rings of that wood, the minerals of earth mined upward by the burrowing tree roots, all come alive. My own fragile hand touches the wood, a hand full of my own life, including that which rose each morning early to watch the sun return from the other side of the planet. Over time, these hands will smooth the rake's wooden handle down to a sheen.

Raking. It is a labor round and complete, smooth and new as an egg, and the rounding seasons of the world revolving in time and space. All things, even our own heartbeats and sweat, are in it, part of it. And that work, that watching the turning over of life, becomes a road into what is essential. Work is the country of hands, and they want to live there in the dailiness of it, the repetition that is time's language of prayer, a common tongue. Everything is there, in that language, in the humblest of labor. The rake wakes up and the healing is in it. The shadows of leaves that once fell beneath the tree the handle came from are in that labor, and the rabbits that passed this way, on the altar of our work. And when the rake wakes up, all earth's gods are reborn and they dance and sing in the dusty air around us.

DOROTHY RICHARDS *with* HOPE SAWYER BUYUKMIHCI

END OF THE BEGINNING

from *Beaversprite* (1977)

Dorothy Richards (1894–1985) grew up in the once beaver-rich Mohawk Valley of New York, but she had never seen a beaver until the day a van from the state's Department of Environmental Conservation delivered a pair to the falling-down farmhouse near Little Falls, New York, that she and her husband, Al, had recently purchased. The beavers that arrived that day, part of a program to reestablish the creature after its near-extinction by trapping, captured Dorothy's interest and then her heart. Thus began her nearly fifty years of devotion to beavers, during which she acquired several hundred acres of surrounding land and established Beaversprite Sanctuary while she and Al supported themselves by running a small stationery supply business. *Beaversprite: My Years Building an Animal Sanctuary* is her story, and the story of the beavers that became as children to her, some even living in her home.

Hope Sawyer Buyukmihci (1913–), born in Lorraine, New York, also founded a beaver sanctuary with her husband, Cavit, where she writes, draws, and works for animal rights. Her books *Unexpected Treasure* (1968) and *Hour of the Beaver* (1971) tell the story of the Unexpected Wildlife Refuge, and the newsletter of her organization, the Beaver Defenders (Unexpected Wildlife Refuge, Newfield, NJ 08344), gathers news of threats to and efforts in behalf of beavers. "When it came to beavers, Dorothy's feelings and mine were identical," she writes, so it was fitting that she should coauthor Dorothy's story. *Beaversprite* is finally a lesson in ecological thinking, both a model and an eloquent plea for change in human-animal relationships.

Spring is wonderful here in the foothills of the Adirondacks. There is a special vigor in the air that I have found nowhere else. The birds return and the shadbush brightens the woods. If it were not for one persistent sadness Beaversprite would be heaven. A beaver trapping season is opened each year, and as soon as it is over I have to say goodbye to those who have been with me for two years. Those in the wild also will leave home and I will never see them again. I have tried hard not to make pets of the captive beavers, never handling them nor allowing anyone else to do so. If they could stay within the boundaries of the sanctuary they might have a chance to live normal and long lives. But their avoidance of incest makes them go in search of mates and of distant locations in which to establish homes.

As I write, the current trapping season is still open, and ads in local papers offer thirty-four dollars for a beaver pelt, for the life of a beautiful intelligent creature who benefits the world and could teach human beings a great deal about gentleness, thrift, and morals in general. Beavers' enemies now consist almost entirely of two species—man and dogs. They are in more danger than ever before, for though the number of species preying on them has decreased, the force and numbers of the two species left has become overwhelming.

Only now, after half a lifetime of observation, do I feel confident of what I have learned about beavers, and keenly aware of how much there is yet to be learned. Having no scientific training I have had to rely on common sense and perception and faithful daily observation. These have led me to disagree with those who believe that the intelligence of animals is proportional to the size of the brain, and to distrust much else of what I have read. The new science of ethology—"scientific study of animal behavior and formation of characteristics"—offers hope for the future. But only if it is pursued with love for the subjects of study. There can be no understanding without love.

Each person born into this world has a right to everything he needs. His right, however, is bound up with that of every other creature and gives him no license to grab everything he can without allowing a share for others. Beavers give more than they take. They are an asset no matter where they live. Somehow we must make room for them, and come to appreciate them as a lively, integral part of wild beauty—as keepers of the streams, for which role they were born.

To accommodate ourselves to beavers and a variety of other creatures, we must learn to *think small* in the realm of human population. Even before Beaversprite was created I could see that the human population needed to be curbed. The mandate, "Be fruitful and replenish the earth," had changed to an ominous, "Be fruitful and *destroy* the earth." Our species had taken to ravishing the land to feed billions of people and poisoning the earth and the animals to make room for overcrowded humans and their insatiable desires. Al and I, much as we loved children—in fact, *because* we loved them—decided early not to add to the burden.

After becoming addicted to beavers for a few months I began to read the works of great naturalists and humanists such as Henry David Thoreau, John Muir, Albert

Schweitzer, Joseph Wood Krutch, and Konrad Lorenz. Their philosophy never contradicted what I saw around me, but added insight and inspiration. Meanwhile the beavers welcomed me into their lives, invited me to swim with them, and actually showed patience while I slowly realized the meaning of their actions.

I am convinced that biology should be taught as a course in human-animal relationships—not as a study of dead bodies or caged victims. Reams of paper have been wasted on the natural history of beavers, and their population statistics and commercial value. But it is the individual beaver, trying to make a living while beset with natural hazards that keep him inventive and strong, who deserves our study. To know fellow creatures we must establish mutual trust, communication, and empathy. That's what children need to learn. We need to appeal to their natural love for animals and their sense of fair play, not to selfish or materialistic motives.

What we need most is positive humane education that will overcome negative attitudes long established. The youth who sets traps does not realize the agony he causes. The people who wear fur on their clothing are not aware of their crime. Those who "manage" wildlife have allowed themselves to be blindfolded. Humane education can show youth that animals have feelings and rights like their own, fashion-conscious people that wearing of fur is a barbaric hangover, and well-meaning wildlife managers that they, like the animals, are victims of monied interests.

My heart goes out to children. Unless their minds have already been warped by adults, they love animals and want to share life with them. It is not their fault that they have been deprived of friendly contact with wildlife in all its bewitching variety.

Mere curiosity motivates many of the visitors to our sanctuary, but those with open minds expand visibly as they watch the beavers' actions. Although timid at first when finding themselves surrounded by these humped, ambulating creatures whose teeth, so they've heard, can take your arm off, most of our guests soon express surprised delight. "How could anybody hurt one of those animals!" they say, when a beaver kit lifts his small hands in an appealing gesture. I am pretty sure those who visit Beaversprite will never be tempted to wear beaver fur. (Once a woman did ask, though, how many of "those things" it took to make a fur coat.)

One neighbor was a frequent visitor when she first came to our vicinity. She had bought a place on another road for the purpose of enjoying exclusive hunting rights. For her a few contacts with the beavers was enough. "To me animals have always been moving targets and I took pride in a 'good shot,' " she declared. "You've spoiled it for me—they don't look like targets anymore. Now I'm spoiling it for everyone else. Already I've converted a few of my friends. And God pity the man I find on my land with a gun!"

Letters come to me, and most of them express appreciation of my work and sympathy with the beavers. One man wrote, "I like beavers, too, but they should be left alone in the wild." I agree with him. This is my aim, too, and thousands of visitors over the years have left my house with at least a little knowledge of beavers and their important place in the ecosystem. I make sure to tell them that floods are prevented wherever beavers are allowed to inhabit the headwaters of streams. Also that beaver ponds conserve water by forcing it to seep into the surrounding land rather than running off in torrents, thereby benefiting the land in times of drought. Most of all I make them aware of the abundance of fish, birds, and other animals who profit by a source of water in which to drink, swim, live, feed—or do all four. Visitors see this for themselves as they look from my windows to a beaver dam only a hundred feet away.

Once I got a letter from a professional trapper, who offered me money if I would divulge beaver secrets that would help him ply his grisly trade. His request made me ponder. Was I forging a two-edged sword that would be turned against the beavers? The thought of children, who should not be deprived of beaver knowledge as I had been, set me straight. I would trust a new generation to put my information to good use. As for making our free beavers more vulnerable by befriending them, I knew that they had as much chance as completely wild ones—and as little—of escaping traps set at hidden entrances, or on dams they must maintain in order to survive.

To me protecting wildlife is the most worthwhile cause on earth, because it is a fundamental good as well as a personally rewarding experience. Since the whole human race is dependent on the balance of nature and our neglect and abuse can go only so far before we cause a fatal debacle, what else is as worthwhile? If man does not reverse the trend of overpopulation, destroying and upsetting the balance of nature, interdependent species will become extinct one by one, and man himself will perish—the victim of his own reckless way of life. . . .

People ask me, "What about the future of Beaversprite? What will happen to your beavers and to the land?"

My friend Adam had one answer. As he lay dying his last words were, "When you're gone, Dot, there won't be any more beavers here. They'll go, too." I don't believe that. My work has been only a beginning. Young hands are growing up and taking hold and they'll go on when I leave. I hope that the rolling, wooded acres of Beaversprite will always be a sanctuary, that they will never be cut up into building lots, and that hunting and trapping will never be allowed. I trust that some dedicated person will continue to study beavers here for a long time to come—until the day when beavers are protected in the wild and anyone who wishes may find a colony where he may sit down, call his beaver friends to him, and commune with them.

Acquisition of land has meant nothing to me except a reaching out of arms to protect more wild animals, at a time when ownership of land is the only way to save them. Our sanctuary consists of old farms along winding country roads. Giant sugar maples arch across and cast shade over mossy stone walls, along which chipmunks scamper. On hills around the five beaver ponds of the resident colony grow a riot of evergreens and deciduous trees, sprung up to reforest pasture and cropland long since given over by man. Along the edges of ponds and streams willow, alder, and a variety of aquatic plants flourish which nourish the beavers.

Every part of the sanctuary has its special beauty, enhanced by the songs of the Littlesprite and Middlesprite as they make their way through leafy haunts to join the Bigsprite and East Canada Creek. These in turn blend with the Mohawk River on its way to the mighty Hudson. Listening to these infant streams, born as springs or melt water in the Adirondacks above, I envision their entire course inhabited by and cared for by generations of beavers in a world where people unafraid of emotion will share life with fellow animals.

My dream is not an impossible one. Man can fit himself in. Like a beaver, he can build the structure of a new life. One stick at a time, he can stem the flood of materialism that is threatening to sweep him off the face of the earth. When he goes back to a simple life in harmony with nature he will find a happiness no other generation has known.

JOAN MCINTYRE

MIND IN THE WATERS

from *Mind in the Waters* (1974)

Joan McIntyre (1931–) founded Project Jonah in the early seventies to stop the slaughter of whales. In her introduction to *Mind in the Waters: A Book to Celebrate the Consciousness of Whales and Dolphins,* she writes, "We have for too long accepted a traditional way of looking at nature, at nature's creatures, which has blinded us to their incredible essence, and which has made us incomparably lonely. It is our loneliness as much as our greed which can destroy us." She suggests that in returning to an older way of relating to animals we might begin to heal the alienation and desolation in ourselves. She has sought to live that older way of relating, first moving from California to Lanai, to live the life chronicled in *The Delicate Art of Whale Watching* (1982), and then to Fiji, after marrying a native Fijian (making her Joana McIntyre Varawa), as she recounts in *Changes in Latitude: An Uncommon Anthropology* (1989).

There was a time in our culture, not long ago, when the essential role of men and women was to nurture and protect each other, to be the caretakers of life and earth. At that time, when the sun sparkled on the sea of our imagination as freshly as it sparkled on the sea herself, we thought of our world and each other in ways which were life-venerating and death-respecting. The porpoise school that weaves its history protectively around its common existence, the whales that tune body and mind in a continuous awareness of life, are not symbols of an alien mythology—they are evocative of what was once the core of human relationships.

Animals were once, for all of us, teachers. They instructed us in ways of being and perceiving that extended our imaginations, that were models for additional possibilities. We watched them make their way through the intricacies of their lives with wonder and with awe. Seeing the wolf pick his delicate way across the snowy forest floor, the eyes of the owl hold the image of the mouse, the dark shape of the whale break the surface of the sea—reminded us of the grand sweep and diversity of life, of its infinite possibilities. The connection of humans with totemic animals was an essential need to ally ourselves with the power and intelligence of non-human life, to absorb some of the qualities bestowed by the evolutionary process on other creatures.

Whales and dolphins—all Cetaceans—are intensely interesting to us now. They seem to speak for a form of consciousness we are beginning to re-explore in our own inner natures. They help us chart our interior wilderness. We can hear whales singing. If we pay attention and let them live, perhaps we will hear them speak, in their own accents, their own language. It would be an extravagant reward to experience, by empathy, a different band of reality.

We are animals of the land. They are animals of the oceans. We have hands to move and mold the things of the earth. They do not. But with an intelligence imagined as grand as ours—what do they do? What can they do, with mind imprisoned in all that flesh and no fingers for releasing it?

I have stroked, and swum with, and looked at, these creatures, and felt their essence rise to meet me like perfume on a spring day. Touched by it, I felt gentler myself, more open to the possibilities that existed around me. There may be only one way to begin to learn from them— and that is to begin. We would not be harmed by returning to the roots which once nourished us, which still, unseen, link together all life that lives, and feels, and thinks, and dies, on this, our common planet.

URSULA LE GUIN

MAY'S LION

from *Buffalo Gals and Other Animal Presences* (1987)

Ursula Le Guin (1929–) has been classified as a science fiction writer, but her work really defies categorization. What her novels, short stories, poems, and essays have in common is a questioning of the way we normally perceive the world. In her later work, starting with the imaginative novel *Always Coming Home* (1985), Le Guin has begun to explore the power of writing like a woman, from the viewpoint of one who, with animals and children, has been considered Other by a phallocentric culture. In the introduction to *Buffalo Gals,* LeGuin writes that "by climbing up into his head and shutting out every voice but his own, 'Civilized Man' has gone deaf. He can't hear the wolf calling him brother—not Master, but brother. He can't hear the earth calling him child—not Father, but son."

She was born in Berkeley, California, the daughter of anthropologist Alfred L. Kroeber and writer-folklorist Theodora Kroeber (author of the classic *Ishi in Two Worlds*), educated at Radcliffe (B.A.) and Columbia (M.A.), and married a historian whom she met while in Paris studying on a Fulbright scholarship. They settled in Portland and raised three children. Le Guin explains that she wrote "May's Lion" as a warm-up exercise for *Always Coming Home,* trying to imagine how a familiar scene might play itself out differently in the fictional Na Valley of the novel, in a culture more respectful of and receptive toward earth's creatures and the mythic meanings we might invest them with. Her thinking seems to parallel Joan McIntyre's in this, and indeed, in *Mind in the Waters* McIntyre suggests sitting

with and singing to a dying whale, presenting ourselves in
empathy rather than objectivizing.

Jim remembers it as a bobcat, and he was May's nephew,
and ought to know. It probably was a bobcat. I don't think
May would have changed her story, though you can't trust
a good story-teller not to make the story suit herself, or get
the facts to fit the story better. Anyhow she told it to us
more than once, because my mother and I would ask for it;
and the way I remember it, it was a mountain lion. And the
way I remember May telling it is sitting on the edge of the
irrigation tank we used to swim in, cement rough as a lava
flow and hot in the sun, the long cracks tarred over. She was
an old lady then with a long Irish upper lip, kind and wary
and balky. She liked to come sit and talk with my mother
while I swam; she didn't have all that many people to talk
to. She always had chickens, in the chickenhouse very near
the back door of the farmhouse, so the whole place smelled
pretty strong of chickens, and as long as she could she kept
a cow or two down in the old barn by the creek. The first
of May's cows I remember was Pearl, a big handsome Hol-
stein who gave fourteen or twenty-four or forty gallons or
quarts of milk at a milking, whichever is right for a prize
milker. Pearl was beautiful in my eyes when I was four or
five years old; I loved and admired her. I remember how
excited I was, how I reached upward to them, when Pearl
or the workhorse Prince, for whom my love amounted to
worship, would put an immense and sensitive muzzle
through the three-strand fence to whisk a cornhusk from my
fearful hand; and then the munching and the sweet breath
and the big nose would be at the barbed wire again: the
offering is acceptable. . . . After Pearl there was Rosie, a
purebred Jersey. May got her either cheap or free because
she was a runt calf, so tiny that May brought her home on
her lap in the back of the car, like a fawn. And Rosie always
looked like she had some deer in her. She was a lovely,
clever little cow and even more willful than old May. She
often chose not to come in to be milked. We would hear

May calling and then see her trudging across our lower pasture with the bucket, going to find Rosie wherever Rosie had decided to be milked today on the wild hills she had to roam in, a hundred acres of our and Old Jim's land. Then May had a fox terrier named Pinky, who yipped and nipped and turned me against fox terriers for life, but he was long gone when the mountain lion came; and the black cats who lived in the barn kept discreetly out of the story. As a matter of fact now I think of it the chickens weren't in it either. It might have been quite different if they had been. May had quit keeping chickens after old Mrs. Walter died. It was just her all alone there, and Rosie and the cats down in the barn, and nobody else within sight or sound of the old farm. We were in our house up the hill only in the summer, and Jim lived in town, those years. What time of year it was I don't know, but I imagine the grass still green or just turning gold. And May was in the house, in the kitchen, where she lived entirely unless she was asleep or outdoors, when she heard this noise.

Now you need May herself, sitting skinny on the edge of the irrigation tank, seventy or eighty or ninety years old, nobody knew how old May was and she had made sure they couldn't find out, opening her pleated lips and letting out this noise—a huge, awful yowl, starting soft with a nasal hum and rising slowly into a snarling gargle that sank away into a sobbing purr. . . . It got better every time she told the story.

"It was some meow," she said.

So she went to the kitchen door, opened it, and looked out. Then she shut the kitchen door and went to the kitchen window to look out, because there was a mountain lion under the fig tree.

Puma, cougar, catamount; *Felis concolor,* the shy, secret, shadowy lion of the New World, four or five feet long plus a yard of black-tipped tail, weighs about what a woman weighs, lives where the deer live from Canada to Chile, but always shyer, always fewer, the color of dry leaves, dry grass.

There were plenty of deer in the Valley in the forties, but no mountain lion had been seen for decades anywhere near where people lived. Maybe way back up in the canyons; but Jim, who hunted, and knew every deer-trail in the hills, had never seen a lion. Nobody had, except May, now, alone in her kitchen.

"I thought maybe it was sick," she told us. "It wasn't acting right. I don't think a lion would walk right into the yard like that if it was feeling well. If I'd still had the chickens it'd be a different story maybe! But it just walked around some, and then it lay down there," and she points between the fig tree and the decrepit garage. "And then after a while it kind of meowed again, and got up and come into the shade right there." The fig tree, planted when the house was built, about the time May was born, makes a great, green, sweet-smelling shade. "It just laid there looking around. It wasn't well," says May.

She had lived with and looked after animals all her life; she had also earned her living for years as a nurse.

"Well, I didn't know exactly what to do for it. So I put out some water for it. It didn't even get up when I come out the door. I put the water down there, not so close to it that we'd scare each other, see, and it kept watching me, but it didn't move. After I went back in it did get up and tried to drink some water. Then it made that kind of meowowow. I do believe it come here because it was looking for help. Or just for company, maybe."

The afternoon went on, May in the kitchen, the lion under the fig tree.

But down in the barnyard by the creek was Rosie the cow. Fortunately the gate was shut, so she could not come wandering up to the house and meet the lion; but she would be needing to be milked, come six or seven o'clock, and that got to worrying May. She also worried how long a sick mountain lion might hang around, keeping her shut in the house. May didn't like being shut in.

"I went out a time or two, and went shoo!"

Eyes shining amidst fine wrinkles, she flaps her thin arms at the lion. "Shoo! Go on home now!"

But the silent wild creature watches her with yellow eyes and does not stir.

"So when I was talking to Miss Macy on the telephone, she said it might have rabies, and I ought to call the sheriff. I was uneasy then. So finally I did that, and they come out, those county police, you know. Two carloads."

Her voice is dry and quiet.

"I guess there was nothing else they knew how to do. So they shot it."

She looks off across the field Old Jim, her brother, used to plow with Prince the horse and irrigate with the water from this tank. Now wild oats and blackberry grow there. In another thirty years it will be a rich man's vineyard, a tax write-off.

"He was seven feet long, all stretched out, before they took him off. And so thin! They all said, 'Well, Aunt May, I guess you were scared there! I guess you were some scared!' But I wasn't. I didn't want him shot. But I didn't know what to do for him. And I did need to get to Rosie."

I have told this true story which May gave to us as truly as I could, and now I want to tell it as fiction, yet without taking it from her: rather to give it back to her, if I can do so. It is a tiny part of the history of the Valley, and I want to make it part of the Valley outside history. Now the field that the poor man plowed and the rich man harvested lies on the edge of a little town, houses and workshops of timber and fieldstone standing among almond, oak, and eucalyptus trees; and now May is an old woman with a name that means the month of May: Rains End. An old woman with a long, wrinkled-pleated upper lip, she is living alone for the summer in her summer place, a meadow a mile or so up in the hills above the little town. Sinshan. She took her cow Rose with her, and since Rose tends to wander she keeps her on a long tether down by the tiny creek, and moves her into fresh grass now and then. The summerhouse is what they call a nine-pole house, a mere frame of poles stuck in the ground—one of them is a live digger-pine sapling—with stick and matting walls, and mat roof and floors. It doesn't rain in the dry season, and the roof is just for shade. But the house and its little front yard where Rains End has her camp stove and clay oven and matting loom are well shaded by a fig tree that was planted there a hundred years or so ago by her grandmother.

Rains End herself has no grandchildren; she never bore a child, and her one or two marriages were brief and very long ago. She has a nephew and two grandnieces, and feels herself an aunt to all children, even when they are afraid of her and rude to her because she has got so ugly with old age, smelling as musty as a chickenhouse. She considers it natural for children to shrink away from somebody part way dead, and knows that when they're a little older and have got used to her they'll ask her for stories. She was for sixty years a member of the Doctors Lodge, and though she doesn't do curing any more people still ask her to help with nursing sick children, and the children come to long for the kind, authoritative touch of her hands when she bathes them to bring a fever down, or changes a dressing, or combs out bed-tangled hair with witch hazel and great patience.

So Rains End was just waking up from an early afternoon nap in the heat of the day, under the matting roof, when she heard a noise, a huge, awful yowl that started soft with a nasal hum and rose slowly into a snarling gargle that sank away into a sobbing purr. . . . And she got up and looked out from the open side of the house of sticks and matting, and saw a mountain lion under the fig tree. She looked at him from her house; he looked at her from his.

And this part of the story is much the same: the old woman; the lion; and, down by the creek, the cow.

It was hot. Crickets sang shrill in the yellow grass on all the hills and canyons, in all the chaparral. Rains End filled a bowl with water from an unglazed jug and came slowly out of the house. Halfway between the house and the lion she set the bowl down on the dirt. She turned and went back to the house.

The lion got up after a while and came and sniffed at the water. He lay down again with a soft, querulous groan, almost like a sick child, and looked at Rains End with the yellow eyes that saw her in a different way than she had ever been seen before.

She sat on the matting in the shade of the open part of her house and did some mending. When she looked up at the lion she sang under her breath, tunelessly; she wanted to remember the Puma Dance Song but could only remember bits of it, so she made a song for the occasion:

> You are there, lion.
> You are there, lion. . . .

As the afternoon wore on she began to worry about going down to milk Rose. Unmilked, the cow would start tugging at her tether and making a commotion. That was likely to upset the lion. He lay so close to the house now that if she came out that too might upset him, and she did not want to frighten him or to become frightened of him. He had evidently come for some reason, and it behoved her to find out what the reason was. Probably he was sick; his coming so close to a human person was strange, and people who behave strangely are usually sick or in some kind of pain. Sometimes, though, they are spiritually moved to act strangely. The lion might be a messenger, or might have some message of his own for her or her townspeople. She was more used to seeing birds as messengers; the four-footed people go about their own business. But the lion, dweller in the Seventh House, comes from the place dreams come from. Maybe she did not understand. Maybe someone else would understand. She could go over and tell Valiant and her family, whose summerhouse was in Gah-heya meadow, farther up the creek; or she could go over to Buck's, on Baldy Knoll. But there were four or five adolescents there, and one of them might come and shoot the lion, to boast that he'd saved old Rains End from getting clawed to bits and eaten.

Mooooooo! said Rose, down by the creek, reproachfully.

The sun was still above the southwest ridge, but the branches of pines were across it and the heavy heat was out of it, and shadows were welling up in the low fields of wild oats and blackberry.

Moooooo! said Rose again, louder.

The lion lifted up his square, heavy head, the color of dry wild oats, and gazed down across the pastures. Rains End knew from that weary movement that he was very ill. He had come for company in dying, that was all.

"I'll come back, lion," Rains End sang tunelessly. "Lie still. Be quiet. I'll come back soon." Moving softly and easily, as she would move in a room with a sick child, she got her milking pail and stool, slung the stool on her back with a woven strap so as to leave a hand free, and came out of the house. The lion watched her at first very tense, the yellow eyes firing up for a moment, but then put his head down again with that little grudging, groaning sound. "I'll come back, lion," Rains End said. She went down to the creekside and milked a nervous and indignant cow. Rose could smell lion, and demanded in several ways, all eloquent, just what Rains End intended to *do?* Rains End ignored her questions and sang milking songs to her: "Su bonny, su bonny, be still my grand cow . . ." Once she had to slap her hard on the hip. "Quit that, you old fool! Get over! I am *not* going to untie you and have you walking into trouble! I won't let him come down this way."

She did not say how she planned to stop him.

She retethered Rose where she could stand down in the creek if she liked. When she came back up the rise with the pail of milk in hand, the lion had not moved. The sun was down, the air above the ridges turning clear gold. The yellow eyes watched her, no light in them. She came to pour milk into the lion's bowl. As she did so, he all at once half rose up. Rains End started, and spilled some of the milk she was pouring. "Shoo! Stop that!" she whispered fiercely, waving her skinny arm at the lion. "Lie down now! I'm afraid of you when you get up, can't you see that, stupid? Lie down now, lion. There you are. Here I am. It's all right. You know what you're doing." Talking softly as she went, she returned to her house of stick and matting. There she sat down as before, in the open porch, on the grass mats.

The mountain lion made the grumbling sound, ending with a long sigh, and let his head sink back down on his paws.

Rains End got some cornbread and a tomato from the pantry box while there was still daylight left to see by, and ate slowly and neatly. She did not offer the lion food. He had not touched the milk, and she thought he would eat no more in the House of Earth.

From time to time as the quiet evening darkened and stars gathered thicker overhead she sang to the lion. She sang the five songs of *Going Westward to the Sunrise,* which are sung to human beings dying. She did not know if it was proper and appropriate to sing these songs to a dying mountain lion, but she did not know his songs.

Twice he also sang: once a quavering moan, like a house cat challenging another tom to battle, and once a long, sighing purr.

Before the Scorpion had swung clear of Sinshan Mountain, Rains End had pulled her heavy shawl around herself in case the fog came in, and had gone sound asleep in the porch of her house.

She woke with the grey light before sunrise. The lion was a motionless shadow, a little farther from the trunk of the fig tree than he had been the night before. As the light grew, she saw that he had stretched himself out full length. She knew he had finished his dying, and sang the fifth song, the last song, in a whisper, for him:

The doors of the Four Houses
are open.
Surely they are open.

Near sunrise she went to milk Rose, and to wash in the
creek. When she came back up to the house she went closer
to the lion, though not so close as to crowd him, and stood
for a long time looking at him stretched out in the long,
tawny, delicate light. "As thin as I am!" she said to Valiant,
when she went up to Gahheya later in the morning to tell
the story and to ask help carrying the body of the lion off
where the buzzards and coyotes could clean it.

It's still your story, Aunt May; it was your lion. He
came to you. He brought his death to you, a gift; but the
men with the guns won't take gifts, they think they own
death already. And so they took from you the honor he
did you, and you felt that loss. I wanted to restore it. But
you don't need it. You followed the lion where he went,
years ago now.

GENEVIEVE TAGGARD

DEMETER

from *Slow Music* (1946)

Genevieve Taggard (1894–1948), born in a small town in eastern Washington, began to write at thirteen when she lived with her parents, schoolteacher-missionaries, in Hawaii. She eventually graduated from the University of California at Berkeley, lived and traveled in a number of different parts of the United States and the world, taught at several colleges, and published eleven volumes of poetry, as well as book reviews, articles, short stories, and a biography of Emily Dickinson. She was married twice and had one daughter, for whom she wrote the following poem. Demeter was the Goddess of the Corn, one of the two major Greek deities of the earth (Dionysus was the other). Demeter brought forth the grain, but also withheld her gifts from the earth in grief during the third of the year when her daughter Persephone dwelt in the underworld with Hades. Demeter's advice in Taggard's poem seems to apply to us in this time when to walk in balance with nature requires us to find a new way of being.

In your dream you met Demeter
Splendid and severe, who said: Endure.
Study the art of seeds,
The nativity of caves.
Dance your gay body to the poise of waves;
Die out of the world to bring forth the obscure
Into blisses, into needs.
In all resources

Belong to love. Bless,
Join, fashion the deep forces.
Asserting your nature, priceless and feminine.
Peace, daughter. Find your true kin.
                    —then you felt her kiss.

Bibliography and Further Reading

The following pages list sources of selections reprinted in this anthology, as well as selected other works by women about nature. Although many of the books listed here are out of print, most are available in libraries and through interlibrary loan.

Ackerman, Diane. *A Natural History of the Senses.* New York: Random House, 1990. Exploration by a self-confessed sensuist (one who rejoices in sensory experience) of the origins and evolution of the senses, their range and reputation, folklore and science.

Allen, Paula Gunn. *Shadow Country.* Los Angeles: American Indian Studies Center, University of California, 1982. Poems grounded in the rhythms of nature and a spirit-informed view of the universe.

————. "Kopis 'taya" ("A Gathering of Spirits"). In *Songs from This Earth On Turtle's Back: An Anthology of Poetry by American Indian Writers,* Joseph Bruchac, ed. Greenfield Center, NY: Greenfield Review Press, 1984.

————, ed. *Spider Woman's Granddaughters: Traditional Tales and Contemporary Writing by Native American Women.* Boston: Beacon Press, 1989. Collection of literature by Native American women that reflects the spiritual basis of native people's aesthetics and the principle of kinship extending beyond human kin to encompass supernaturals, animals, fire, rain, rocks, rivers, and plants.

Atwood, Margaret. *Surfacing.* New York: Simon & Schuster, 1972; Ballantine Books, 1987. Remarkable novel by a Canadian author about a woman's journey into wilderness and the insight she carries back with her to civilized life.

Austin, Mary. *The Land of Little Rain.* Boston: Houghton Mifflin, 1903. Albuquerque: University of New Mexico Press, 1974. New York: Penguin Books, 1988. Austin's first published book, a collection of essays on the desert and foothill lands between Death Valley and the High Sierra.

————. *The Flock.* Boston: Houghton Mifflin, 1906. Sketches about sheep and sheepherders in the Southwest that show Austin's ecological concern and her sympathy with the land.

————. *Lost Borders.* New York: Harper & Bros., 1909. Reprinted in its entirety, along with *The Land of Little Rain,* in *Stories from the Country of Lost Borders,* Marjorie Pryse, ed. (New Brunswick, NJ: Rutgers University Press, 1987). Short stories that rank among Austin's best work, exploring souls that have been marked by the land the Indians called Lost Borders—the high California desert east of the Sierra. The women in these stories are particularly noteworthy, liberated as they are from societal norms of femininity by the vastness and harshness of the landscape they inhabit.

————. *California, Land of the Sun.* London: A. & C. Black, and New York: Macmillan, 1914. Later published as *The Lands of the Sun* (Boston: Houghton Mifflin, 1927). Hymn to the geography of California, written while Austin was living briefly in London, and commissioned to accompany Sutton Palmer's watercolor paintings of California.

————. *The Land of Journeys' Ending.* New York: Appleton-Century, 1924. Tucson: University of Arizona Press, 1983. Description of the Southwest based on reading and a six-week-long tour of Arizona and New Mexico undertaken while Austin was living in New York and longing for the desert.

———. *Earth Horizon.* Boston: Houghton Mifflin, 1932. Austin's autobiography, a work with a strong feminist bias that also conveys her love for and mystical rapport with the Southwest and its native peoples.

———. *Western Trails: A Collection of Short Stories by Mary Austin,* Melody Graulich, ed. Reno: University of Nevada Press, 1987. A selection of Mary Austin's stories, some previously unpublished, in which she effectively merged her interests in culture, art, nature, and women. Graulich's sensitive and perceptive commentary is invaluable.

Back, Mary. *Seven Half Miles from Home.* Boulder, CO: Johnson Books, 1985. Record of an artist transplanted from Illinois to Wyoming who began walking a mile every day before breakfast on the advice of her doctor. The stated purpose of her book is "to get numbers of people like me into a state of frantic curiosity about the walkable country around their own homes . . . to get them as excited as I am by the discovery that all life is one thing, and that each of us is part of it."

Baylor, Byrd. *The Way to Start a Day.* New York: Scribner's, 1978. Children's book full of wisdom about how we might begin to relate more reverently to the natural world.

Bird, Isabella. *A Lady's Life in the Rocky Mountains.* Norman: University of Oklahoma Press, 1960. London: Virago, 1982. Collection of letters written by a Victorian woman who traveled from England to visit the Rocky Mountains in the fall and winter of 1873. Bird journeyed on horseback, seeking a religious, meditative experience of nature, and deploring the development by miners and entrepreneurs that she saw.

Bishop, Elizabeth. *The Complete Poems, 1927–1979.* New York: Farrar, Straus & Giroux, 1983. The entire poetic output of one of America's great writers. Many of Bishop's poems convey a delightful intimacy with the natural world, her response to which is fresh and imaginative, especially in such poems as "To a Tree," "The Fish," and "The Moose."

Blanchan, Neltje. *Nature's Garden.* Garden City, NY: Doubleday, Page & Co., 1900. Catalog of wildflowers, written in a personal vein by the wife of publisher Frank Nelson Doubleday; later adapted with drawings by Asa Don Dickinson as *Wild Flowers Worth Knowing* (Garden City, NY: Doubleday, Page & Co., 1917). Blanchan, a friend of Gene Stratton-Porter's, also wrote four books about birds that tended to be chatty and moralistic, although her 1917 book, *Birds Worth Knowing,* (also published by Doubleday, Page & Co.) contains an excellent introductory essay on the value of wild birds to human beings.

Brant, Beth. *Mohawk Trail.* Ithaca, NY: Firebrand Books, 1985. Collection of poems and stories by a Mohawk woman.

———, ed. *A Gathering of Spirit.* Rockland, ME: Sinister Wisdom Books, 1984. Anthology of writing by North American Indian women.

Bryant, Dorothy. *The Kin of Ata Are Waiting for You.* Berkeley, CA: Moon Books, 1976. Visionary novel depicting a society that lives respectfully with nature.

Buyukmihci, Hope Sawyer. *Hour of the Beaver.* Chicago: Rand McNally, 1971. Story of beaver and other animal life the author observed when she slept in the woods by a stream in the New Jersey wildlife sanctuary she and her husband created.

———, with Hans Fantel. *Unexpected Treasure.* New York: M. Evans & Co., 1968. Account of the founding of Unexpected Wildlife Refuge and experiences with wildlife there. A convincing argument for animal preservation in natural surroundings.

Carrighar, Sally. *One Day on Beetle Rock.* New York: Knopf, 1944. Lincoln: University of Nebraska Press, 1978. The result of seven years of study, a detailed and widely acclaimed narrative of the events in the lives of nine animals on a June day on Beetle Rock in Sequoia National Park, told from inside the animals' skins.

—. *One Day at Teton Marsh.* New York: Knopf, 1947. Lincoln: University of Nebraska Press, 1979. Stories of a September day in the lives of a variety of animals at Teton Marsh in Jackson Hole, Wyoming, later adapted for a 1966 Disney movie.

—. *Icebound Summer.* New York: Knopf, 1953. Saga of the summer courtship and mating of several animals in the Arctic, where Carrighar spent nine years, thanks in part to a Guggenheim fellowship.

—. *Moonlight at Midday.* New York: Knopf, 1958. Personal account of Carrighar's adventures researching *Icebound Summer* in the tiny village of Unalakleet, describing traditional Eskimo life and the changes brought by the white man.

—. *Wild Voice of the North.* Garden City, NY: Doubleday, 1959. Portrait of the Siberian husky Carrighar rescued and cared for while she was living in Nome, and with whom she developed a unique friendship.

—. *Wild Heritage.* Boston: Houghton Mifflin, 1965. Ambitious synthesis of pioneering work in the field of ethology (animal behavior), including Carrighar's personal observations from years of wilderness living.

—. *Home to the Wilderness.* Boston: Houghton Mifflin, 1973. Carrighar's autobiography, a deeply felt tale of her difficult childhood, her discovery of a special rapport with animals, and her joyful sense of having found healing in nature and her vocation of writing about wild creatures.

————. *The Twilight Seas.* New York: Weybright & Talley, 1975. Narrative account of the life and death of a blue whale, including a strong critique of the whaling industry.

Carson, Rachel. *Under the Sea-Wind: A Naturalist's Picture of Ocean Life.* New York: Oxford University Press, 1941, 1952. Vignettes of shore and ocean life dramatizing the ecological relationships there. When this book was first published, just before Pearl Harbor, reviews were excellent but sales poor. When it was reissued in 1952, it joined *The Sea Around Us* on the best-seller list.

————. *The Sea Around Us.* New York: Oxford University Press, 1950; Simon & Schuster, 1958. Rev. ed., Oxford University Press, 1961. Clear presentation of the sea's origins, dynamics, and relationship to humankind, meticulously researched and couched in poetic prose. This book, which remained on the best-seller list for eighty-six weeks and was translated into thirty-two languages, won the National Book Award for nonfiction in 1951 and the John Burroughs Medal in 1952, and was made into an Academy Award–winning documentary.

————. *The Edge of the Sea.* Boston: Houghton Mifflin, 1955. Portrait of shore life and guide to identification of flora and fauna on rock shores, sand beaches, and coral reefs.

————. *Silent Spring.* Boston: Houghton Mifflin, 1962, 1988. New York: Fawcett Crest, 1964; Ballantine, 1982. The book that sparked international controversy with its exposure of the harm that results from thoughtless and uncontrolled use of pesticides. More than 300,000 copies were sold within the first three months of publication.

————. *The Sense of Wonder.* New York: Harper & Row, 1965, 1987. Beautiful essay on how parents can instill in children a sense of wonder about nature "so indestructible that it [will] last throughout life, as an unfailing antidote against the boredom and disenchantments of later years, the sterile preoccupation with things that are artificial, the alienation from the sources of our strength."

Cather, Willa. *O Pioneers!* Boston: Houghton Mifflin, 1913. Cather's second novel, drawn directly from her childhood memories of life on the Nebraska prairie and dedicated to Sarah Orne Jewett, contrasting pioneer woman Alexandra Bergson's love for the land, which "seemed beautiful to her, rich and strong, and glorious," with her brothers' attitude of farming only for profit.

————. *The Song of the Lark.* Boston: Houghton Mifflin, 1915. Story of the artistic awakening and struggle of young opera singer Thea Kronborg, and of her escape from the smug, self-satisfied, provincial world of her upbringing in frontier Colorado.

————. *My Ántonia.* Boston: Houghton Mifflin, 1918. Cather's most widely read novel, recounting the youthful friendship of Ántonia Shimerda and Jim Burden as they grew up on the Nebraska prairie and as their lives took separate paths, he building a career in the East and she a great family in Nebraska.

————. *The Professor's House.* New York: Knopf, 1925; Vintage Books, 1990. Novel contrasting the contemporary materialistic world with a more ideal world in harmonious relation with nature. The center of the novel is an account of the discovery of the ruins of cliff dwellings in the Southwest.

————. *Death Comes for the Archbishop.* New York: Knopf, 1927; Vintage Books, 1990. Chronicle of two nineteenth-century French priests setting up a vicarage in New Mexico Territory.

Caufield, Catherine. *In the Rainforest.* New York: Knopf, 1985. American journalist's highly readable account of the ecology, natural and human history, and current exploitation of the world's rainforests.

Church, Peggy Pond. *The House at Otowi Bridge: The Story of Edith Warner and Los Alamos.* Albuquerque: University of New Mexico Press, 1959, 1960. Stirring story of the legendary woman who lived at the river crossing between two worlds: that of the Indians of San Ildefonso Pueblo and that of the scientists who developed the atomic bomb at Los Alamos. Church was herself a native New Mexican and an accomplished poet who understood the sustenance Edith Warner drew from the energy of earth and sky.

Clark, A. Carman. *From the Orange Mailbox: Notes from a Few Country Acres.* Gardiner, ME: Harpswell Press, 1985. Observations of country life in and around the writer's home in Union, Maine, collected from her weekly column for the Camden, Maine, *Herald.*

Clifton, Lucille. *An Ordinary Woman.* New York: Random House, 1974. Poetry reflecting this daring and exuberant black writer's sense of rootedness in the generations of her family, in a religious and cultural milieu, and in her own experience.

Coatsworth, Elizabeth. *Atlas and Beyond.* New York: Harper & Row, 1924.

———. *Down Half the World.* New York: Macmillan, 1968. Poems saturated with Coatsworth's love of nature, both in the rural New England settings of her children's books and on her extensive travels around the world.

Comstock, Anna Botsford. *Ways of the Six-Footed.* Boston: Ginn & Co., 1903. Ithaca: Cornell University Press, 1977. Ten stories illustrating the social organization of insects, their methods of communication and defense, and the ways they have adapted to surmount problems.

———. *Handbook of Nature Study.* Ithaca: Comstock Publishing Company, 1911. Compendium of Comstock's earlier work, consolidated into a teaching guide dealing with animal and plant life and the earth and sky. This key text of the nature study movement became known as the nature

Bible because of the sensitive advice it gave on such topics as children's attitudes toward death from predation and returning creatures to their natural habitat after study.

Conkling, Hilda. *Poems by a Little Girl.* New York: Frederick A. Stokes Co., 1920. Fresh poems by a nine-year-old in which imagery of the hills and woods of central Massachusetts—Emily Dickinson's country—crops up often.

Coolbrith, Ina. *Songs from the Golden Gate.* Boston: Houghton Mifflin, 1896. Poems whose main theme is unhappiness abated in the simple pleasures of nature. With their strong imagery, they manage to transcend the sentimentalism of the day.

Cooper, Susan Fenimore. *Rural Hours.* New York: G. P. Putnam, 1850, 1868, 1876. Rev. ed., Boston: Houghton Mifflin, 1887. Syracuse, NY: Syracuse University Press, 1968. Record of natural events in the environs of Otsego Lake in New York, arranged around the seasons of the year. Condensed and tightened in the 1987 edition.

Crisler, Lois. *Arctic Wild.* New York: Harper & Row, 1958. Narrative of the experiences of Crisler and her husband in Alaska's Brooks Range, where they spent a year and a half filming caribou and wolves for a major Hollywood studio.

Cruickshank, Helen Gere. *Flight into Sunshine.* New York: Macmillan, 1948. Account of Florida birding that gently educates the reader, illustrated by photographs by the author's husband, official photographer of the National Audubon Society. Winner of the John Burroughs Medal in 1948.

Davidson, Laura Lee. *A Winter of Content.* Nashville, TN: Abingdon-Cokesbury Press, 1922. A Baltimore schoolteacher's account of passing a winter alone on a Canadian lake.

————. *Isles of Eden.* New York: Minton, Balch, & Co., 1924. Story of camp life in Frontenac County, Ontario.

Dean, Barbara. *Wellspring: A Story from the Deep Country.* Covelo, CA: Island Press, 1979. Account of a young woman's life on a square mile of wilderness land in northern California, focusing on her relationship with nature and the adjustments she had to make after twenty-five years of city life.

de Santis, Marie. *California Currents: An Exploration of the Ocean's Pleasures, Mysteries, and Dilemmas.* Palo Alto, CA: Tioga, 1985. Volume of personal essays on the Pacific Ocean by a chemist, former commercial fisherwoman, and storyteller.

Deming, Barbara. *We Are All Part of One Another: A Barbara Deming Reader,* Jane Meyerding, ed. Philadelphia: New Society Publishers, 1984. Essays, speeches, stories, letters, and poems spanning four decades by a self-described radical pacifist lesbian feminist whose life was a pilgrimage toward wholeness.

Dickinson, Emily. *Poems by Emily Dickinson,* Mabel Loomis Todd and Thomas Wentworth Higginson, eds. Boston: Roberts Bros., 1890. First edition of the poems on love, nature, death, and God left by one of the greatest poets of our language.

Dillard, Annie. *Pilgrim at Tinker Creek.* New York: Harper & Row, 1974. Theological inquiry conducted on the banks of Tinker Creek in Virginia's Blue Ridge Mountains, where the author lived for a solitary stretch. Won the Pulitzer Prize for nonfiction in 1975.

———. *Teaching a Stone to Talk.* New York: Harper & Row, 1982. Essays prompted by various of Dillard's travels.

Donahoe, Mary. *You Are Mountain.* Austin, TX: Plain View Press, 1984. Slim volume of poetry honoring this Oregon mountain woman's deep roots in earth and native tradition.

Douglas, Marjory Stoneman. *Everglades: River of Grass.* New York: Rinehart & Co., 1947. Rev. ed., Englewood, FL:

Pineapple Press, 1987. Natural history of the Everglades, written for the Rivers of America series (edited by Constance Lindsay Skinner), that affected Floridians the way Rachel Carson's *Silent Spring* later sparked the nation.

————, with John Rothchild. *Voice of the River: Memoirs of a Friend of the Everglades.* Englewood, FL: Pineapple Press, 1987. Life history of an early conservationist and pioneer feminist who has for most of her life stubbornly defended Florida's swampy middle against developers and engineers.

Ehrlich, Gretel. *The Solace of Open Spaces.* New York: Viking, 1985. Appreciation of the vast landscape of Wyoming and the people who live in daily contact with its elemental rigors.

————. "River History." In *Montana Spaces,* William Kittredge, ed. New York: Nick Lyons Books, 1988.

Eifert, Virginia S. *River World.* New York: Dodd, Mead, 1959. Stories of the flora and fauna of the Mississippi River by a popular and articulate Illinois naturalist, writer, and artist who traveled its length on riverboats.

————. *Land of the Snowshoe Hare.* New York: Dodd, Mead, 1960. Stories based on Eifert's experiences as a guide and nature teacher in the Canadian border country.

Endrezze-Danielson, Anita. *Burning the Fields.* Lewiston, ID: Confluence Press, 1983. Chapbook of poems rich in nature imagery by a woman with Yaqui Indian roots.

Engel, Marian. *Bear.* Toronto: McClelland & Stewart, Ltd., 1976. Controversial novel by a Canadian author about the close relationship a woman develops with a bear, and the way it changes her life.

Evans, Abbie Huston. *Outcrop.* New York: Harper & Bros., 1928.

————. *The Bright North.* New York: Macmillan, 1938.

————. *Fact of Crystal.* New York: Harcourt, Brace & World, 1961.

————. *Collected Poems.* Pittsburgh: University of Pittsburgh Press, 1970. Volumes of poetry rooted in the rocky soil of Maine, celebrating craggy hills, storms, the seasons, rocks, and trees, and permeated with a deep sense of the umbilical tie to earth.

Fiske, Erma J. *The Peacocks of Baboquivari.* New York: Norton, 1983. Sprightly story of the five months the author (age seventy-three) spent living alone in a cabin at the foot of the Baboquivari Mountains in Arizona, banding birds for the Nature Conservancy.

Flanner, Hildegarde. *Brief Cherishing: A Napa Valley Harvest.* Santa Barbara: John Daniel, 1985. Essays conveying Flanner's loving attachment to the Napa Valley of California, where she and her husband spent their later years.

————. *At the Gentle Mercy of Plants: Essays and Poems.* Santa Barbara: John Daniel, 1986. Informative pieces about the California landscape and reminiscenses of a long life's devotion to plants and the natural world.

Free, Ann Cottrell. *No Room, Save in the Heart: Poetry and Prose on Reverence for Life—Animals, Nature, and Humankind.* Washington, DC: Flying Fox Press, 1987. Poems and fragments of prose bearing witness to Albert Schweitzer's philosophy of reverence for life by celebrating the natural world and grieving over the threats against its integrity. The author is a seasoned journalist, a crusader for animal protective legislation, and initiator of the Rachel Carson National Wildlife Refuge.

Fuller, Margaret. *Summer on the Lakes.* In *The Writings of Margaret Fuller,* Mason Wade, ed. New York: Viking Press, 1941. Record of a trip Fuller, transcendentalist peer of Emerson and Thoreau, took on the Great Lakes in the summer of 1843, describing the beauty of that then mostly unspoiled country and commenting on the blight that would inevitably come with settlement "where 'go ahead' is the only motto." Fuller also comments at length on her observations of Native Americans and the white man's treatment of them.

Galland, China. *Women in the Wilderness.* San Francisco: Harper & Row, 1980. Accounts of several contemporary all-women adventures in the wilderness, along with portraits of women adventurers of the past, discussions of the history and politics of women's relationship to the wilderness, an interview with Susan Griffin, and a directory of resources.

Gawain, Elizabeth. *The Dolphins' Gift.* Mill Valley, CA: Whatever Publishing, 1981. Description of encounters with dolphins on a beach in western Australia and a meditation on what we might learn from them.

Gearhart, Sally Miller. *The Wanderground: Stories of the Hill Women.* Watertown, MA: Persephone Press, 1978. Radical lesbian-feminist novel of a time when Mother Earth has revolted, men's machines no longer function outside the highly technological, computerized cities, and women have fled to the hills, where they struggle to live in harmony with nature and each other.

Gilborn, Alice Wolf. *What Do You Do with a Kinkajou?* New York: Lippincott, 1976. Story of growing up on a Colorado ranch with a menagerie of domestic and exotic animals kept by the author's mother.

Gonzales, Rebecca. *Slow Work to the Rhythm of Cicadas.* Fort Worth, TX: Prickly Pear Press, 1985. Poems reflecting a Hispanic woman's close identification with the desert landscape.

Grahn, Judy. *Mundane's World.* Freedom, CA: Crossing Press, 1988. Woman-centered novel about a prehistoric world where plants, animals, and humans all have a voice and what matters most is their interrelationships.

Gray, Elizabeth Dodson. *Green Paradise Lost.* Wellesley, MA: Roundtable Press, 1979. A feminist's answer to the question, Why did we ever think it was OK to do what we've done to the earth?

Griffin, Susan. *Woman and Nature: The Roaring Inside Her.* New York: Harper & Row, 1978. An electrifying prose poem contrasting the voice of patriarchal science—controlling, reducing, objectifying—with the voice of woman-as-nature and nature-as-woman.

Hall, Sharlot Mabridth. *Cactus and Pine.* Boston: Sherman, French & Co., 1911. Rev. ed., Phoenix: Arizona Republican Print Shop, 1924. First volume of poems, expressing her Western loyalties, by a woman who westered to Arizona from Kansas in the early 1880s, managed two ranches, wrote for and edited the magazine *Land of Sunshine* (later retitled *Out West*), served as Arizona's territorial historian, and undertook various historical projects and expeditions, including a trip by wagon across the Arizona Strip.

Hamerstrom, Frances. *An Eagle to the Sky.* New York: Nick Lyons Books, 1988. Account of a conservationist's experience with two golden eagles, caring for them, trying to get them to mate, and finally setting one free. The author, who lives in Plainfield, Wisconsin, started a raptor rehabilitation center when she was eleven years old, and has devoted much of her life to their study.

Harjo, Joy. *The Last Song.* Las Cruces, NM: Puerto del Sol, 1975.

———. *What Moon Drove Me to This?* Berkeley, CA: I. Reed Books, 1978.

———. *She Had Some Horses.* New York: Thunder's Mouth Press, 1983.

———. *In Mad Love and War.* Middletown, CT: Wesleyan University Press, 1990. Volumes of poetry reflecting the feminist and spirit-centered consciousness of a Creek Indian woman.

————, with Stephen Strom. *Secrets from the Center of the World.* Tucson: University of Arizona Press, 1990. Gemlike book of lyrical prose accompanied by landscape photographs of the Southwest.

Hasse, Margaret. *Stars Above, Stars Below.* St. Paul, MN: New Rivers Press, 1984. Poems with a midwestern flavor.

Hasselstrom, Linda. *Windbreak: A Woman Rancher on the Northern Plains.* Berkeley, CA: Barn Owl Books, 1987. Account of a year in the life of a woman who works as a writer and runs a cattle ranch in southwestern South Dakota with her parents and her husband.

————. *Going Over East.* Golden, CO: Fulcrum, Inc., 1987. Further adventures of a woman rancher.

Heckman, Hazel. *Island Year.* Seattle: University of Washington Press, 1972. Month-by-month observations of the flora and fauna of Anderson Island, a six-by-three-mile island in Puget Sound that the author had wandered for twenty years, first as a summer visitor and then as a permanent resident.

Henderson, Alice Corbin. *Red Earth: Poems of New Mexico.* Chicago: R. F. Seymour, 1920. This poet's finest volume of poetry. Already an established poet, she found her authentic voice when she moved to Santa Fe in 1916 for her tuberculosis. The poems were inspired by Spanish-American and Indian motifs and by Henderson's responses to the land.

Higginson, Ella. *When the Birds Go North Again.* New York: Macmillan, 1902. One of six published collections of verse by a woman who was a popular lyricist in her day.

Hinchman, Hannah. *A Life in Hand.* Salt Lake City: Gibbs Smith, 1991. Beautifully illustrated guide to keeping a natural history journal, by an artist and writer whose own ongoing journal numbers more than forty volumes.

Hogan, Linda. *Calling Myself Home.* Greenfield Center, NY: Greenfield Review Press, 1979.

————. *Eclipse.* Los Angeles: American Indian Studies Center, University of California, 1983.

————. *Seeing Through the Sun.* Amherst, MA: University of Massachusetts Press, 1985.

————. *Savings.* Minneapolis: Coffee House Press, 1988. Poems by a Chickasaw Indian whose vision is spirit-centered in the Indian tradition, and feminist.

————. *Mean Spirit.* New York: Atheneum, 1990. Novel about the exploitation of Indian people and land during the Oklahoma oil boom of the 1920s.

Hoover, Helen. *The Long-Shadowed Forest.* New York: Crowell, 1963. Account of plant and animal life encountered by the author and her husband around their cabin in the North Woods of Minnesota.

————. *The Gift of the Deer.* New York: Knopf, 1966. Story of the relationship the Hoovers developed with a family of white-tailed deer.

————. *A Place in the Woods.* New York: Knopf, 1969.

————. *The Years of the Forest.* New York: Knopf, 1973. Further adventures and insights of a pioneering couple.

Hubbell, Sue. *A Country Year: Living the Questions.* New York: Random House, 1986; Harper & Row, 1987. Account of a year's life in the Ozarks by a keeper of bees, a self-sufficient woman who, in the wake of divorce, looks closely at nature and herself and sometimes comes up with more questions than answers.

————. *A Book of Bees.* New York: Random House, 1988. More about the bee-keeping side of Hubbell's life in the Ozarks.

Jaques, Florence Page. *Birds Across the Sky.* New York: Harper & Bros., 1942. Chronicle of the author's struggles to become a bird lover as she accompanied her illustrator husband, Francis Lee Jaques, on birding trips to practically every state and several foreign countries.

————. *Snowshoe Country.* Minneapolis: University of Minnesota Press, 1944, 1979. Journal of one October through January spent in the border country of Minnesota and Canada, with wonderful pen-and-ink illustrations by the author's husband. Winner of the John Burroughs Medal for nature writing in 1946.

Jewett, Sarah Orne. *A White Heron and Other Stories.* Boston: Houghton Mifflin, 1886. Collection whose lead story is a plea for bird conservation that was ahead of its time.

————. *The Country of the Pointed Firs.* Boston: Houghton Mifflin, 1896. Enlarged ed., *The Country of the Pointed Firs and Other Stories.* New York: Norton, 1968. Loosely connected sketches about the lives of people in a declining Maine seacoast community, a masterpiece of regional literature.

Johnson, Cathy. *The Local Wilderness.* New York: Prentice Hall Press, 1987. Beautifully illustrated invitation to find a special place in nature and capture it on paper.

————. *The Nocturnal Naturalist: Exploring the Outdoors at Night.* Chester, CT: Globe Pequot Press, 1989. Ongoing night journal of an insomniac artist-naturalist living in Excelsior Springs, Missouri.

Johnson, Josephine. *Now in November.* New York: Simon & Schuster, 1934; Carroll & Graf, 1985. Powerful story of life on a family farm during the Depression. Only a deeply felt love of the land enables the narrator—middle daughter on a small Missouri farm—to endure a decade of uncertainty and calamity. Winner of the Pulitzer Prize in 1935.

————. *The Inland Island.* New York: Simon & Schuster, 1969. Columbus: Ohio State University Press, 1987. Nature journal by a realist crying out for the end of the Vietnam War while appreciating the beauty and essential sanity of life on the land in rural Ohio.

————. *The Circle of Seasons.* New York: Viking, 1974. Essay to accompany a book of photographs, both an ode and an elegy that questions whether our children will inherit "any feeling of the great circular flow of living things."

Kappel-Smith, Diana. *Wintering.* Boston: Little, Brown, 1984. New York: McGraw-Hill, 1986. A personal journey into winter on a Vermont farm and out again, by a biologist and artist.

————. *Night Life: Nature from Dusk to Dawn.* Boston: Little, Brown, 1990. Exploration of the night world of nature.

Kenyon, Jane. *The Boat of Quiet Hours.* Saint Paul, MN: Graywolf Press, 1986. Poems permeated with the steadying influence of nature by a New Hampshire poet.

Kumin, Maxine. *Up Country: Poems of New England.* New York: Harper & Row, 1972. Collection of unsentimental pastoral poems celebrating New England. Winner of the Pulitzer Prize for poetry in 1973.

————. *In Deep: Country Essays.* New York: Viking, 1987. Cycle of meditations on the chores and delights of farm living in rural New Hampshire.

————. *Nurture.* New York: Viking Penguin, 1989. More poems on Kumin's favorite themes of loss, survival, and our ties with animals.

LaBastille, Anne. *Woodswoman.* New York: Dutton, 1976, 1978. Story of how the author built a log cabin and a life in Adirondack Park, weathered the seasons of ten years, and developed the attitudes necessary for survival as a woman alone in the wilderness.

————. *Assignment: Wildlife.* New York: Dutton, 1980. Description of the author's efforts on behalf of the giant grebe in Guatemala, for which she received the World Wildlife Fund Gold Medal in 1974.

————. *Women and Wilderness.* San Francisco: Sierra Club Books, 1980. Profiles of fifteen contemporary women who work in wilderness areas and descriptions of several historical wilderness women.

————. *Beyond Black Bear Lake.* New York: Norton, 1987. Sequel to *Woodswoman,* in which LaBastille retreats farther into the Adirondack wilderness, builds a smaller cabin, and becomes more concerned and vocal about environmental problems.

LaChapelle, Dolores. *Earth Wisdom.* Silverton, CO: Finn Hill Arts, 1978. Background and practical steps to begin reinhabiting our place on earth.

————. *Sacred Land Sacred Sex: Rapture of the Deep.* Silverton, CO: Finn Hill Arts, 1987. Inquiry into the relationship between human sexuality and the natural world.

Lawrence, Louise de Kiriline. *The Lovely and the Wild.* New York: McGraw-Hill, 1968. Account of the author's awakening sensitivity to birds and nature while living with her husband on a lake in southeast Ontario. Winner of the John Burroughs Medal for nature writing in 1968.

Le Guin, Ursula. *Always Coming Home.* New York: Harper & Row, 1985. Imaginative novel that interweaves story, fable, poem, artwork, and music to create a total picture of the culture of the Kesh, a people who live peacefully and in harmony with nature in a valley on the northern Pacific coast.

————. *Buffalo Gals and Other Animal Presences.* Santa Barbara: Capra Press, 1987. Collection of stories and poems giving voice to the animals, minerals, and vegetables we have so long been deaf to.

Le Sueur, Meridel. *Salute to Spring.* New York: International Publishers, 1940. Collection that includes "Annunciation," a short story celebrating the unrestrainable fecundity of earth and woman.

————. *Rites of Ancient Ripening.* Minneapolis: Midwest Villages & Voices, 1975. Poems dedicated to "all the women of the dark earth rising into light and freedom," mourning the slaying of native peoples, celebrating the forces of procreation, and giving thanks to "grandmother of the center of the earth."

Leighton, Clare. *Southern Harvest.* New York: Macmillan, 1942. Personal impressions of the landscape and people of the American South, illustrated with woodcuts by the author, a transplant from England.

————. *Where Land Meets Sea: The Tide Line of Cape Cod.* New York: Rinehart & Co., 1954. Republished as *Where Land Meets Sea: The Enduring Cape Cod.* Greenwich, CT: Chatham Press, 1973. Boston: David R. Godine, 1984. A hymn of praise to the changing seasons and moods of the author's Cape Cod home.

Leimbach, Patricia Penton. *A Thread of Blue Denim.* Englewood Cliffs, NJ: Prentice Hall, 1974. Collection of newspaper columns by the wife of an Ohio farmer.

Leister, Mary. *Wildlings.* Owings Mills, MD: Stemmer House, 1976.

————. *Seasons of Heron Pond: Wildlings of Air, Earth and Water.* Owings Mills, MD: Stemmer House, 1981. Collections of columns originally written for the *Baltimore Sun* about "animals, and plants, and weather, and water, and earth" encountered by the author on her half-mile of land in Maryland.

Lembke, Janet. *Looking for Eagles: Reflections of a Classical Naturalist.* New York: Lyons & Burford, 1990. Collection of nature essays by a distinguished translator of Greek and Latin poetry who finds that much of what fascinates her in nature has classical origins.

Levertov, Denise. *Poems, 1960–1967.* New York: New Directions, 1983. Poems by a woman who often writes of the values of nature and nurture from a distinctly feminine perspective.

Lewis, Janet. *Poems Old and New, 1918–1978.* Athens, OH: Ohio University Press/Swallow Press, 1981. Poems by a wise woman attuned to the earth.

Liedloff, Jean. *The Continuum Concept: Allowing Human Nature to Work Successfully.* Reading, MA: Addison-Wesley, 1977. Chronicle of the author's journeys into the South American jungle and her attempt to understand the roots of human well-being.

Lindbergh, Anne Morrow. *Gift from the Sea.* New York: Pantheon, 1955; Vintage Books, 1991. An enduring favorite, wise and gentle meditations on how women can carry the lessons found in a life close to nature (in this case, the author's seashore retreat) back into the crucible of everyday modern life.

Luhan, Mabel Dodge. *Winter in Taos.* New York: Harcourt, Brace, 1935. Taos, NM: Las Palomas, 1982, 1987. A lyrical celebration of Luhan's adopted land, structured around the seasonal cycle of death and rebirth and richly integrating her emotional life with the physical landscape.

————. *Edge of Taos Desert: An Escape to Reality.* New York: Harcourt, Brace, 1937. Volume 4 of Luhan's memoirs, in which she dramatically proclaims her regeneration in the Southwest: "I had a complete realization of the fullness of Nature here and how everything was intensified for one—sight, sound, and taste—and I felt that perhaps I was more awake and more aware than I had ever been before."

Martinson, Sue Ann. *Changing Woman.* Austin, TX: Plain View Press, 1985. Poems by a midwestern poet conveying images of the world restored in beauty and peace.

McCombs, Judith. *Against Nature: Wilderness Poems.* Paradise, CA: Dustbooks, 1979. Poems from the Bruce Trail, the Boundary Waters, and the Rocky Mountains, exploring our relationship with nature and the extent to which we hold ourselves apart from wilderness for fear it might engulf us.

McIntyre, Joan. *The Delicate Art of Whale Watching*. San Francisco: Sierra Club Books, 1982. Journal of the author's life in Hawaii, where she moved to live more closely with the animals she had devoted years to crusading for.

———, ed. *Mind in the Waters: A Book to Celebrate the Consciousness of Whales and Dolphins*. New York: Scribner's, and San Francisco: Sierra Club Books, 1974. Collection of writings presenting the theory that whales and dolphins are aware, can think, have consciousness; and inviting us to respect and respond to them as a step toward healing our culturally created spiritual isolation and loneliness.

McNulty, Faith. *Must They Die? The Strange Case of the Prairie Dog and the Black-Footed Ferret*. Garden City, NY: Doubleday, 1971. Plea for the preservation of species, focusing on the story of how poisoning of prairie dogs has brought ferrets near extinction because they share a symbiotic relationship.

———. *The Great Whales*. Garden City, NY: Doubleday, 1974. Celebration of the great whales, originally published in a slightly different version in *The New Yorker*.

———. *The Wildlife Stories of Faith McNulty*. Garden City, NY: Doubleday, 1980. Essays about wild animals the author has encountered, studied, or lived with, overlaid with a sense of the danger humankind poses for these creatures.

Medicine Eagle, Brooke. "The Rainbow Bridge." In *Shamanic Voices*, Joan Halifax, ed. New York: Dutton, 1979.

Merriam, Florence A. *A-Birding on a Bronco*. Boston: Houghton Mifflin, 1896. High-spirited bird-watching narratives drawn from the few months the author passed on a ranch north of San Diego, California, while recovering from tuberculosis. She later married naturalist Vernon Bailey, accompanied him on numerous arduous field expeditions, and produced a highly respected body of work on bird life, culminating in *The Birds of New Mexico* (Santa Fe, NM: New Mexico Department of Game and Fish, 1928), which won the Brewster Medal for original scientific work in ornithology.

Meyn, Barbara. *The Abalone Heart.* Boise, ID: Ahsahta Press, 1988. Poems by an environmentalist with a strong sense of place derived from her life on the coast of northern California.

Millay, Edna St. Vincent. *Collected Poems.* New York: Harper & Row, 1956. Melodious poems of contemporary relevance about feminism, injustice, the beauty of nature, and the idiocy of environmental pollution and war, by an ardent feminist and antiwar activist.

————, with Ivan Massar. *Take Up the Song.* New York: Harper & Row, 1986. Poems by Edna St. Vincent Millay sensitively juxtaposed with black-and-white photographs by Ivan Massar to make a compelling statement about the earth's beauty.

Miller, Debbie S. *Midnight Wilderness: Journeys in Alaska's Arctic National Wildlife Refuge.* San Francisco: Sierra Club Books, 1990. Experiences and observations from thirteen years spent hiking, climbing, and kayaking in this northernmost wilderness sanctuary, and a plea for its preservation in its whole and natural state.

Miller, Olive Thorne (Harriet Mann). *A Bird-Lover in the West.* Boston: Houghton Mifflin, 1894. Highly readable nature and travel book by a prolific writer who discovered bird-watching relatively late in life and became a crusader against the slaughter of birds for women's hats and the despoiling of nature by careless human visitors.

Mills, Stephanie. *Whatever Happened to Ecology?* San Francisco: Sierra Club Books, 1989. Account of a woman who worked in the vanguard of the ecology movement in the seventies and more recently has been struggling to live her bioregional ideals in rural Michigan.

Minty, Judith. *Lake Songs and Other Fears.* Pittsburgh: University of Pittsburgh Press, 1974.

————. *In the Presence of Mothers.* Pittsburgh: University of Pittsburgh Press, 1981. Poems growing out of the Great Lakes region, by a woman who needs to be near water and woods and feels that "I've belonged to these places for longer than my lifetime."

Mirikitani, Janice. *Shedding Silence.* Berkeley, CA: Celestial Arts, 1987. Poems by a Japanese-American street poet breaking through the silence that has enabled many forms of oppression and injustice to occur, from Hiroshima to Love Canal.

Mor, Barbara. *Bitter Root Rituals.* Wolf Creek, OR: WomanSpirit, 1975. Powerful poetic lament about the rape of earth and woman, and affirmation of the undeniable force of life, woman wisdom, truth.

————. *Winter Ditch and Other Poems.* Santa Fe, NM: Second Porcupine Press, 1982. Poems of a transplanted southern California woman "riding through northern New Mexico blizzards and spring winds and summer lightning on a bicycle for ten years," getting "strong in a strong place," feeling "beautiful in a place of profound beauty."

Mora, Pat. *Chants.* Houston: Arte Publico Press, 1984.

————. *Borders.* Houston: Arte Publico Press, 1986. Poems by a Hispanic woman personifying the desert as a female ally of mostly female protagonists and building a new mythology of the integration of woman, land, and man.

Mueller, Ruth. *The Eye of the Child.* Philadelphia: New Society, 1985. Fantasy novel narrated by a six-year-old gypsy girl who can "speak bird" and who comes to understand the price our world is paying for our exploitation of the ecological order.

Murie, Margaret. *Two in the Far North.* New York: Knopf, 1962. 2nd ed., Anchorage, AK: Alaska Northwest, 1978. Reminiscence of the author's early life in Alaska, her marriage to biologist Olaus Murie (later director of the Wilderness Society), and several of their trips into the Alaska wilderness together.

————, with Olaus Murie. *Wapiti Wilderness.* New York: Knopf, 1966. Record of the authors' lives together in Jackson Hole, Wyoming, conveying a strong sense of place and a deep response to wild country.

Newhall, Nancy, with Ansel Adams and others. *This Is the American Earth.* San Francisco: Sierra Club Books, 1960. Begun as a modest conservation exhibit at Le Conte Lodge in Yosemite, this pairing of Newhall's words with nature photos by Adams and others was eventually built into a huge exhibit that was circulated throughout the United States by the Smithsonian Institution and throughout the world by the United States Information Service, and that was published as an Exhibit Format book by the Sierra Club.

Nice, Margaret Morse. *The Watcher at the Nest.* New York: Macmillan, 1939. Popular account of this leading ornithologist's revolutionary research into the life history of the song sparrow around her home on the Olentangy River in Ohio. This was the first book illustrated by Roger Tory Peterson.

Nicholson, Eliza Jane Poitevent (Pearl Rivers). *Lyrics.* Philadelphia: J. B. Lippincott, 1873. Poetry whose theme is nature and seasonal change. The only volume of poetry published by a woman who often wrote under the name Pearl Rivers, after the river near the Louisiana-Mississippi border where she grew up. She was New Orleans's first female journalist and at twenty-seven became the first woman to own and operate a metropolitan daily paper, when her husband died and left her ownership and management of the *New Orleans Daily Picayune.*

Oliver, Mary. *The River Styx, Ohio, and Other Poems.* New York: Harcourt Brace Jovanovich, 1972.

————. *Twelve Moons.* Boston: Little, Brown, 1979.

————. *American Primitive.* Boston: Little, Brown, 1983.

————. *Dream Work.* New York: Atlantic Monthly Press, 1986. Luminous poems that express a clear-eyed wonder at the facts of nature and at our place in it all. *American Primitive* won the Pulitzer Prize for poetry in 1984. Oliver declined to have her poem "Wild Geese" included in this anthology, stating that she feels "gender distinction (separation) dulls things, in a book as in the world."

Peden, Rachel. *Speak to the Earth: Pages from a Farmwife's Journal.* New York: Knopf, 1974. An account of the richness of life on an Indiana farm by a farmwife and newspaper columnist. The book consists largely of columns that originally appeared in the *Indianapolis Star* and the *Muncie Evening Press.*

Pepin, Yvonne. *Three Summers: A Journal.* Berkeley, CA: Shameless Hussy Press, 1987. Searchingly honest account of three summers the author spent by herself (at the time aged twenty-two to twenty-four) in a cabin she built in the Oregon mountains, coming to terms with her identity, limitations, and fears, and with nature's real dangers.

Perkins, Edna Brush. *The White Heart of Mojave: An Adventure with the Outdoors of the Desert.* New York: Boni & Liveright, 1922. Spirited account of the pilgrimage of two middle-aged suffragettes to Death Valley in an era when almost no one, let alone women, went there on purpose.

————. *A Red Carpet on the Sahara.* Boston: Marshall Jones, 1925. Further desert adventures and ruminations, this time in the Sahara, as the author and her friend Charlotte cross Algeria by camel in the company of an Arab guide.

Piercy, Marge. *Woman on the Edge of Time.* New York: Knopf, 1976. Utopian novel notable for the model it presents of a culture attuned to nature, which is also necessarily a deeply egalitarian culture. A personal favorite of Piercy's—"the best I've done so far."

————. *Living in the Open.* New York: Knopf, 1976.

————. *The Twelve-Spoked Wheel Flashing.* New York: Knopf, 1978.

————. *The Moon Is Always Female.* New York: Knopf, 1980.

————. *Circles on the Water.* New York: Knopf, 1982.

————. *Stone, Paper, Knife.* New York: Knopf, 1983.

————. *My Mother's Body.* New York: Knopf, 1985. Volumes of poetry grounded in a deep honoring of earth's fecundity, acknowledging our interrelatedness with all beings, celebrating nature's simple pleasures, and criticizing our current destructive ways.

Rawlings, Marjorie Kinnan. *The Yearling.* New York: Scribner's, 1938. The story of Jody Baxter and his pet fawn, conveying the feel of life in Florida's backcountry. Winner of the Pulitzer Prize in 1939.

————. *Cross Creek.* New York: Scribner's, 1942; Collier Books, 1987. Autobiographical account of Rawlings's life managing an orange grove in Cross Creek, Florida, her animal and human neighbors, jaunts and expeditions, and her philosophy of land ownership and use.

Reben, Martha. *The Healing Woods.* New York: Crowell, 1952. Highly readable account of the first two summers Reben spent in the Adirondack wilderness with her guide, Fred Rice, recovering from tuberculosis. "The wilderness did more than heal my lungs. . . . It taught me fortitude and self-reliance, and with its tranquility it bestowed upon me something which would sustain me as long as I lived: a sense

of the freshness and the wonder which life in natural sur-
roundings daily brings and a joy in the freedom and beauty
and peace that exist in a world apart from human beings."

———. *The Way of the Wilderness.* New York: Crowell,
1955. Further adventures, plus insights gleaned about live-
lihood, freedom, and human relationships as Reben worked
out in practical terms her determination to spend her life in
the woods.

———. *A Sharing of Joy.* New York: Harcourt, Brace &
World, 1963. Culling of the best wildlife stories from
Reben's two previous books.

Rich, Adrienne. *Your Native Land, Your Life.* New York:
Norton, 1986. Poems by a lesbian feminist "trying to speak
from, and of, and to, my country . . . to speak of the land
itself."

Rich, Louise Dickinson. *We Took to the Woods.* Philadelphia:
Lippincott, 1942. A chatty account of family living in a
cabin in Maine's wilderness, telling of woods lore, various
pets, and the birth of Rich's first child without the aid of a
midwife. Updated in her later books *Happy the Land* (1946)
and *My Neck of the Woods* (1950).

———. *The Peninsula.* Philadelphia: Lippincott, 1958. An
informal guide to the area around Maine's Gouldsboro
Peninsula, full of anecdotes and humor.

———. *The Natural World of Louise Dickinson Rich.* New
York: Dodd, Mead, 1962. Essays about the flora, fauna,
climate, and geological history of three geographical areas:
southeastern Massachusetts, northwestern Maine, and the
coast of Maine.

Richards, Dorothy, with Hope Sawyer Buyukmihci. *Bea-
versprite: My Years Building an Animal Sanctuary.* San Fran-
cisco: Chronicle Books, 1977. Story of Richards's
association with beavers as she and her husband established
a sanctuary in the foothills of New York's Adirondacks.

"For more than forty years beavers have been the source of my most rewarding insights and cherished memories."

Rinehart, Mary Roberts. *Through Glacier Park in 1915.* New York: Collier, 1916. Boulder, CO: Roberts Rinehart, 1983. Account of a trip by horseback across the Continental Divide, by a prolific writer of mysteries and serious novels who was America's most successful popular writer from 1910 to 1940. Her response to wild country seems stereotypically masculine in emphasis—what she values is "a sense of achievement; of conquering the unconquerable; of pitting human wits against giants and winning."

Rogers, Pattiann. *The Tattooed Lady in the Garden.* Middletown, CT: Wesleyan University Press, 1986.

———. *Splitting and Binding.* Middletown, CT: Wesleyan University Press, 1989. Lush, extravagant poems celebrating nature's abundance and diversity, yet discerning a unity behind it all.

Rudner, Ruth. *Forgotten Pleasures: A Guide for the Seasonal Adventurer.* New York: Viking, 1978. More than just a guidebook, this is a record of the author's delight in nature's seasons.

Ryden, Hope. *America's Last Wild Horses.* New York: Dutton, 1970. Rev. ed., 1978. History of wild horses in America and summary of the present-day controversy about them, written with a subjective involvement in the animals and their fate.

———. *God's Dog: A Celebration of the North American Coyote.* New York: Viking, 1979. Sympathetic natural history of the coyote based largely on field observation.

———. *Lily Pond: Four Years with a Family of Beavers.* New York: William Morrow, 1989. Chronicle of the lives of a beaver clan and of the author's coming to terms with her proper relationship to these wild lives.

———. *Bobcat Year.* New York: Nick Lyons Books, 1990. The fictional story of a family of bobcats as they progress through the cycle of their year, based on the author's three-year study.

Sanger, Marjorie Bartlett. *World of the Great White Heron: A Saga of the Florida Keys.* New York: Devin-Adair, 1967. Portrait of the ways and habitat of the largest white heron and associated other wildlife of the Florida Keys by a woman active in ornithology and bird preservation, author of the two earlier books *Mangrove Island* (1963) and *Cypress Country* (1965).

Sarton, May. *Plant Dreaming Deep.* New York: Norton, 1968. Prolific and revered writer's account of her renovation of an old house in Nelson, New Hampshire, conveying a sense of the nourishment she draws from nature.

Scherman, Katharine. *Spring on an Arctic Island.* Boston: Little, Brown, 1956. Account of a six-week scientific and bird-watching expedition to Bylot Island undertaken by the author, her husband, and a half dozen others.

Short, Clarice. *The Old One and the Wind.* Salt Lake City: University of Utah Press, 1973. A collection of poems showing a fine sensitivity to the natural world developed during a life as a farmer, rancher, and poet.

Silko, Leslie Marmon. "Love Poem." In *Voices of the Rainbow: Contemporary Poetry by American Indians,* Kenneth Rosen, ed. New York: Viking, 1975.

———. *Ceremony.* New York: Viking, 1977. Powerful novel of a Native American man's—and by extension, the Native American society's—illness and eventual healing through living a ceremony that returns him to harmony with the land, its creatures, and fellow humans.

Simon, Anne W. *No Island Is an Island: The Ordeal of Martha's Vineyard.* Garden City, NY: Doubleday, 1973. Plea for the preservation of Martha's Vineyard.

————. *The Thin Edge: Coast and Man in Crisis.* New York: Harper & Row, 1978. Appeal for protection of the world's coastlines.

————. *Neptune's Revenge: The Ocean of Tomorrow.* New York: Franklin Watts, 1984. Investigation of the changes humankind is making in the ocean and a strong call to change our ways and "put the ocean first."

Stanwell-Fletcher, Theodora. *Driftwood Valley.* Boston: Little, Brown, 1946. New York: Penguin Books, 1989. Journal of three years in the Driftwood River Valley of north-central British Columbia, where the author and her husband went to collect specimens and take photographs for the British Columbia Provincial Museum at Victoria. Winner of the John Burroughs Medal, 1947.

————. *The Tundra World.* Boston: Little, Brown, 1952. Description of the flora and fauna of western Hudson Bay.

————. *Clear Lands and Icy Seas.* New York: Dodd, Mead, 1958. Story of the first of the author's two voyages with the Hudson's Bay Company's supply ship to the eastern Arctic.

Steele, Mary Q. *The Living Year: An Almanac for My Survivors.* New York: Viking, 1972. Personal testament to nature written by a well-known author of children's books while she lived with her husband and three children in a "mildly rural suburb of a manufacturing town" in Tennessee.

Stratton-Porter, Gene. *What I Have Done with Birds.* Indianapolis: Bobbs-Merrill, 1907. Collection of articles that first appeared in *Ladies' Home Journal, Outing,* and *Metropolitan,* and whose gist is summarized by the book's subtitle: *Character Studies of Native American Birds Which Through Friendly Advances I Induced to Pose for Me, or Succeeded in Photographing by Good Fortune, with the Story of My Experiences in Obtaining the Pictures.* Revised, enlarged, and published by Doubleday, Page, & Co. in 1917 as *Friends in Feathers.*

————. *A Girl of the Limberlost.* New York: Grosset & Dunlap, 1909. Bloomington: Indiana University Press, 1984. New York: New American Library, 1988. Sentimental story of an impoverished girl who lives on the edge of the Limberlost Swamp and pays for her high school education by collecting and selling moths.

————. *Music of the Wild.* Cincinatti: Jennings & Graham, 1910. Delightful ode to the creatures of marsh, forest, and field, with photographs of rural Indiana by the author and with samples of her nature philosophy.

————. *Moths of the Limberlost.* Garden City, NY: Doubleday, Page, & Co., 1912. Readable and reliable introduction to moths and moth collecting, notable for its magnificent illustrations painstakingly watercolored by the author.

————. *Homing with the Birds.* Garden City, NY: Doubleday, Page, & Co., 1919. Best of the author's nature books, a collection of bird essays that contains autobiographical material as well as descriptions of unusual experiences in the field and a strong plea for the preservation of bird life.

————. *Tales You Won't Believe.* Garden City, NY: Doubleday, Page, & Co., 1925. Collection of magazine articles that first appeared in *Good Housekeeping,* recounting the author's further experiences in nature and showing a stronger conservation orientation than any of her other books.

Strobridge, Idah Meacham. *In Miners' Mirage-Land.* Los Angeles: self-published (printed by Baumgardt Press and bound by Strobridge at her Artemesia Bindery), 1904. Reprinted in 1986 by Falcon Hill Press, Box 1431, Sparks, NV 89432-1431.

————. *The Loom of the Desert.* Los Angeles: self-published, 1907.

————. *The Land of Purple Shadows.* Los Angeles: self-published, 1909. Tales of lost mines, desert wildlife, and prospectors, infused with the mystical sense of communion with the desert developed by the author during her girlhood in northwestern Nevada.

Sutherland, Audrey. *Paddling My Own Canoe.* Honolulu: University of Hawaii Press, 1978. Account of an adventurous woman's solo amphibious expeditions around the wild and lonely northeast coast of Molokai. "Some inner wildness, there since childhood, surged up and answered that wild country," she writes.

Swenson, May. *To Mix with Time: New and Selected Poems.* New York: Scribner's, 1963.

————. *Half Sun, Half Sleep.* New York: Scribner's, 1967.

————. *New and Selected Things Taking Place.* Boston: Little, Brown, 1978. Volumes of poetry by a keen observer of natural phenomena whose themes were "the organic, the inorganic, and the psychological world."

Taggard, Genevieve. *Slow Music.* New York: Harper & Bros., 1946. Poems by one attuned to the music and poetry of place.

————. *To the Natural World.* Boise, ID: Ahsahta Press, 1980. Collection of poems conveying Taggard's intense sense of place and of the natural world, selected by her daughter, Marcia D. Liles.

Tapahonso, Luci. *One More Shiprock Night.* San Antonio: Tejas Arts Press, 1981.

————. *Seasonal Woman.* Santa Fe: Tooth of Time Press, 1982.

————. *A Breeze Swept Through.* Albuquerque, NM: West End Press, 1987. Volumes of poetry by a Navajo woman to whom the land is an integral part of existence.

Thaxter, Celia Laighton. *Among the Isles of Shoals.* New York: James R. Osgood & Co., 1873. Boston: Houghton Mifflin, 1892. Collection of essays describing the geography, natural history, and inhabitants of the author's home, a group of rocky islands off the New Hampshire coast.

————. *An Island Garden.* Boston: Houghton Mifflin, 1894, 1988. A classic of garden writing, describing the author's small but colorful and imaginative garden outside her cottage on the island of Appledore, and her rich enjoyment of this microcosm of nature.

Thomson, Betty Flanders. *The Changing Face of New England.* New York: Macmillan, 1958. Boston: Houghton Mifflin, 1977. A compendium of intimate knowledge about and personal responses to New England's geography, geology, and ecology, by a botanist who was born and grew up in Ohio but was educated at Mount Holyoke in Massachusetts and remained in New England to become a professor of botany at Connecticut College.

Varawa, Joana McIntyre. *Changes in Latitude: An Uncommon Anthropology.* New York: Atlantic Monthly Press, 1989; Harper & Row, 1990. Captivating tale of how Joan McIntyre's quest for "something bushy and wild," something primitive, leads her to Fiji, into marriage to a Fijian, and into a new way of life.

Walker, Alice. *Living by the Word: Selected Writings 1973–1987.* San Diego: Harcourt Brace Jovanovich, 1988. Essays by a distinguished black writer whose more recent work shows a transcendent sense of connection with nature and earth's creatures. See especially "Am I Blue?" and "Everything Is a Human Being."

Warner, Edith. *See* Church, Peggy Pond.

Wayburn, Peggy. *Edge of Life: The World of the Estuary.* San Francisco: Sierra Club Books, 1972. Exploration of the life of the estuary by a Sierra Club activist and conservation writer.

West, Jessamyn. *Hide and Seek: A Continuing Journey.* San Diego: Harcourt Brace Jovanovich, 1973. Record of this noted writer's experiences and observations during a three-month stay in a travel trailer on the banks of the Colorado River.

Wheelright, Jane Hollister. *The Ranch Papers: A California Memoir*. Venice, CA: Lapis Press, 1988. Account of the author's memory-laden farewell to the 39,000-acre ranch near Santa Barbara where she grew up, one of the last wild tracts of land that size between Oregon and Baja California.

White, Katharine S. *Onward and Upward in the Garden*. New York: Farrar, Straus & Giroux, 1979. Series of fourteen opinionated and intensely personal pieces this devoted lover of flowers and vegetables wrote for *The New Yorker* after her retirement as editor, reviewing nursery stock and seed catalogs and gardening and flower arranging books.

Whiteley, Opal. *Opal: The Journal of an Understanding Heart*, adapted by Jane Boulton. New York: Macmillan, 1976. Palo Alto, CA: Tioga, 1984. Adaptation of Opal's diary—first published in 1920 as *The Story of Opal: The Journal of an Understanding Heart*—arranged in free verse form, with an afterword giving a brief history of Opal's life and the controversy surrounding the diary.

————. *The Singing Creek Where the Willows Grow: The Rediscovered Diary of Opal Whiteley*, Benjamin Hoff, ed. New York: Ticknor & Fields, 1986. Version of Opal's diary with punctuation, paragraph division, and chapter titles devised by Benjamin Hoff, and with a lengthy introduction telling the story of Opal's life.

Whiteman, Roberta Hill. *Star Quilt*. Minneapolis: Holy Cow! Press, 1984. Poems by an Oneida woman who notices the rich details of nature and also understands the meanings behind them.

Wilder, Laura Ingalls, and Rose Wilder Lane. *A Little House Sampler*, William T. Anderson, ed. Lincoln: University of Nebraska Press, 1988. Reminiscences; articles on pioneer living; short stories, essays, and poems about Laura's childhood in the Big Woods; and observations on how the midwestern frontier was transformed.

Williams, Terry Tempest. *Pieces of White Shell: A Journey to Navajoland.* New York: Scribner's, 1984. Retellings of Navajo stories by a museum curator seeking to find her own stories in the landscape of the Four Corners area (Utah, Arizona, New Mexico, Colorado).

———. *Refuge.* New York: Pantheon, 1991. Exploration of a Utah waterfowl refuge and a woman's soul.

———, with John Telford. *Coyote's Canyon.* Salt Lake City: Gibbs Smith, 1989. Stories evoking the beauty and mystery of southern Utah's desert canyons, illustrated with photographs by John Telford.

Wood, Nancy. *Hollering Sun.* New York: Simon & Schuster, 1972.

———. *Many Winters.* Garden City, NY: Doubleday, 1974. Poetic interpretations of the Taos Pueblo Indian way of seeing and understanding.

Woodin, Ann. *Home Is the Desert.* New York: Collier Books, 1964. Tucson: University of Arizona Press, 1984. Description of family living in close contact with nature. The author and her husband, director of the Arizona-Sonora Desert Museum, raised their four sons and an assortment of animals in the Tucson area.

Wright, Billie. *Four Seasons North: A Journal of Life in the Alaskan Wilderness.* New York: Harper & Row, 1973. Account of the experiences of the author and her husband living in a miner's cabin in the Brooks Range of Alaska.

Wright, Mabel Osgood. *The Friendship of Nature: A New England Chronicle of Birds and Flowers.* New York: Macmillan, 1894. Lyrical description of a year lived close to nature at the author's home in Connecticut. Wright was the first president of the Audubon Society of Connecticut and an important figure in popular nature writing, and this was the first of her twenty-four published books.

Young, Louise B. *The Blue Planet: A Celebration of the Earth.* Boston: Little, Brown, 1983. Exploration of the frontiers of geology and earth science, celebrating the beauties of the earth and emphasizing the earth's dynamic nature, by a woman trained as a physicist.

Zwinger, Ann. *Beyond the Aspen Grove.* New York: Random House, 1970; Harper & Row, 1981. Tucson: University of Arizona Press, 1988. Quiet ruminations on the natural communities the author encountered during her first years on the forty acres of Colorado mountain land where she spent part of each year with her husband and three daughters.

————. *Run, River, Run: A Naturalist's Journey Down One of the Great Rivers of the West.* New York: Harper & Row, 1975. Tucson: University of Arizona Press, 1984. Narrative of the author's journey by foot, by canoe, by river raft, and by air, tracing the entire course of the Green River from its source in Wyoming to its confluence with the Colorado River in Utah. Won the John Burroughs Medal for nature writing in 1976.

————. *Wind in the Rock: The Canyonlands of Southeastern Utah.* New York: Harper & Row, 1978. Tucson: University of Arizona Press, 1986. Appreciation of the solitude and natural history of a series of canyons leading into Utah's San Juan River, with attention to the impact of humankind on the area.

————. *A Desert Country near the Sea: A Natural History of the Cape Region of Baja California.* New York: Harper & Row, 1983. Tucson: University of Arizona Press, 1987. Leisurely ramble up into the mountains, through farmyards, into villages, along beaches, and snorkeling in the Gulf of California, with the author deriving both scientific and aesthetic pleasure from what she discovers.

————. *The Mysterious Lands: A Naturalist Explores the Four Great Deserts of the Southwest.* New York: E. P. Dutton, 1989. Journeys into the Chihuahuan, Sonoran, Mojave, and Great Basin deserts.

————, with Beatrice Willard. *Land Above the Trees: A Guide to American Alpine Tundra.* New York: Harper & Row, 1971, 1986. Description of the plants of the alpine zone, along with Zwinger's responses to the geography and climate.

————, with Edwin Way Teale. *A Conscious Stillness: Two Naturalists on Thoreau's Rivers.* New York: Harper & Row, 1982. Amherst, MA: University of Massachusetts Press, 1984. Account of the changes since Thoreau's time noted by the authors on canoe trips down the Assabet and Sudbury rivers.

Index of Authors and Titles

421

ABOUT THE EDITOR

Lorraine Anderson is a freelance editor and writer with a special interest in women's experience. A native Californian, she was educated at the University of Utah and Stanford and in the West's wild places. She now lives in a solar home in Davis, California, with her domestic partner and their cat.